The Satiric Eye ∾

The Satiric Eye

Forms of Satire in the Romantic Period

Edited by Steven E. Jones

First published 2003 by
PALGRAVE MACMILLAN™
175 Fifth Avenue, New York, N.Y. 10010 and
Houndmills, Basingstoke, Hampshire, England RG21 6XS.
Companies and representatives throughout the world.

PALGRAVE MACMILLAN IS THE GLOBAL ACADEMIC IMPRINT OF THE
PALGRAVE MACMILLAN division of St. Martin's Press, LLC and of Palgrave
Macmillan Ltd. Macmillan® is a registered trademark in the United States,
United Kingdom and other countries. Palgrave is a registered trademark in
the European Union and other countries.

ISBN 0-312-29496-4

Library of Congress Cataloging-in-Publication Data

The satiric eye : forms of satire in the romantic period / edited by
Steven E. Jones.
    p. cm.
  Includes bibliographical references and index.
  ISBN 0-312-29496-4
  1. Satire, English—History and criticism.   2. Verse satire, English—
History and criticism.   3. English literature—19th century—History and
criticism.   4. English literature—18th century—History and criticism.
5. Romanticism—Great Britain.   I. Jones, Steven E. (Steven Edward)

PR936.S37   2003
827'.709—dc21

                                                              2002072828

A catalogue record for this book is available from the British Library.

Design by Letra Libre, Inc.

First edition: January 2003
10   9   8   7   6   5   4   3   2   1

Printed in the United States of America

Contents

Introduction ∼

Forms of Satire in the Romantic Period

Steven E. Jones

The Satiric Eye is a collection of essays on satiric writing, images, and theatrical performances from 1780 to 1832. The title—from Wordsworth's famous "inward eye / Which is the bliss of solitude"[1]—alludes to significant critical questions about inwardness, solitude, sincerity, and authenticity in the period, questions that each of the essays address in one way or another. These diverse contributions on everything from advertising to Jane Austen, graphic prints to the pantomime, highlight and question many presuppositions about early-nineteenth-century literature. Taken together, they challenge critical conventions about what matters in the Romantic period, the preoccupations with nature, the Gothic, revolution, sentiment, the sublime, and the aesthetic. They also raise new questions concerning self-representation and self-criticism—how Romantic-period writers saw themselves and their world. Casting a satiric eye on the period, these essays both decenter Romanticism and reorient its canonical works and authors, along with the critical constructs that have defined them, situating them in a larger context of high and low verse and prose, literary and commercial writing, keenly critical or bitingly malicious texts and images.

Historically minded Romanticists have always been aware of satire during the period, and the present collection owes a great deal to this precedent. Critics such as Carl Woodring, David Erdman, Jerome McGann, and Marilyn Butler, for example, have read individual satiric works and voices within canonical Romanticism or, more often, as part of Romanticism's larger sociohistorical contexts.[2] As Butler once wryly observed, "the so-called Romantics did not know at the time that they were supposed to do without satire" (1984, p. 209), and historicist critics have repeatedly demonstrated that the Romantics did *not* do without it. To point to just one example: historicist criticism has tended for methodological reasons to "read" key political prints and graphic satires, those highly allusive verbal and visual texts by popular artists such as Rowlandson, Gillray, and Isaac or George Cruikshank, sometimes produced in collaboration with radical or populist writers and publishers such as William Hone, sometimes produced in support of the government. (George Cruikshank, for example, worked—and satirized—both sides of the struggle for parliamentary reform.) Historicist literary critics often read such graphic works alongside poems, plays, and novels, either as important evidence for cultural contexts or as visual analogs. In so doing they often implied that the satiric perspective itself offered something valuable to the complex "thick descriptions" they wished to produce.

Carl Woodring's 1970 *Politics in English Romantic Poetry,* for example, incorporates a number of popular prints among its illustrations, including a Cruikshank satire (on the Peterloo Massacre) on its cover. In Woodring's hands these prints are more than mere illustrations; they serve as visual representations of a shared satiric language, a popular semiotic discourse potentially available to poets as well as printmakers, and to diverse audiences at the time. Woodring suggestively remarks at one point that Shelley's radical satire *Swellfoot the Tyrant* in effect "verbalizes caricatures" by Gillray, Cruikshank, and others (p. 270). In a similar mode, Marilyn Butler's *Romantics, Rebels and Reactionaries* (1981; 1982), reads graphic satires as part of the "background" of English Romantic literature. The chapter entitled "Art for the People in a Revolutionary Decade" juxtaposes Blake, Wordsworth, and Gillray, under the assumption that the print-satirist provides "a parallel to Blake's career, which is also a commentary upon it" (p. 53). As the parallel unfolds, however, it becomes clear that Gillray also offers an example of a popular form of composite art, with an audience and effects to which Blake's also aspired.

> Gillray was capable of the sophisticated cross-reference, the allusiveness or intertextuality which was the by-product of the Neoclassical period's belief in imitation. He could construct large allegorical prints in the grandest Renaissance manner . . . [or] mimic an actual painting by Fuseli. But these effects, though enhanced by his public's familiarity with established art, did not absolutely depend on it. The aim was not burlesque but redeployment, the harnessing of the older work, with many of its characteristic effects intact, to a new purpose. (p. 54)

Butler's focus is primarily on canonical poets, but she repeatedly shifts our attention to the wider context—"the Arts in the Age of Revolution," as her introduction puts it. Once criticism moves outside the artificial enclosure of literary Romanticism, satiric works loom large. In recent historicism and cultural studies, satire has necessarily figured prominently, especially when it comes to nineteenth-century radical culture. Michael Scrivener, Jon Klancher, Kevin Gilmartin, Iain McCalman, and Marcus Wood have explored the works of important satiric writers, publishers, and cultural performers such as T. J. Wooler, William Cobbett, William Hone, Thomas Spence, and Samuel Waddington.[3] Marcus Wood in particular focuses on the protean forms in which radical satire expressed itself, from shop signs and advertisements, to commemorative coinage, to etchings, engravings, and prose and verse in print. In this context Wood aptly refers to Thomas Spence as a "multi-media satirist" (p. 76), one who was

> prepared to look at any available means of reproduction as a vehicle for his ideas. Conventional aesthetic notions involving hierarchy and quality, or distinctions between beauty and ugliness or literature and pulp, are difficult to apply to his works. His work showed that in popular political satire anything might be joined with anything else. (Wood, p. 67)

This promiscuous opportunism regarding medium and form is especially characteristic of radical political satire. But it is also evident in the satire of the marketplace, the kind of parodic puffery analyzed in this volume by John Strachan, whose unlikely subject is the entrepreneurial barber and gifted satirist J. R. D. Huggins, a tradesman and writer who existed within a sophisticated matrix of verbal and visual satiric activities reaching from New York to London and touching upon high politics and poetry as well as broad advertisements.

London at the end of the eighteenth century (and into the beginning of the nineteenth century) was awash in heteroglossic media, what Tim Fulford refers to below as "the dazzling tide of commerce" (p. 11). Often this culture of consumption and excess was understood in figural relation to the developing idea of the "Orient," with London as the new Babylon. This was appropriate enough, as Fulford says, "since its new wealth stemmed in great measure from the Oriental colonies that had, since Lord Clive's conquests in India, been pouring money into the coffers of the East India Company" (p. 11). Fulford's chapter traces the circulating energies of satiric representations of sexuality, Orientalism, and the marketplace.

In this same London (though mostly after Waterloo), William Hone produced his famous satires for the marketplace and the political arena, as Kyle Grimes' essay below demonstrates. Grimes reads Hone's parodic bank note as an example of a recognizable form of subversive, tactical satire, a scrappy kind of textual "jujitsu" he dubs "hacker satire" (in a rich double allusion connecting Hone to both hack writing of the eighteenth century and computer subcultures of our own time). Hone and other radical satirists habitually worked in hybrid visual and verbal forms—or for that matter in public speeches (as at his famous trial for blasphemous and seditious libel in 1817)—employing a kind of rough and ready bricolage of found and original texts, mixed media, and shifting venues.

Traditionally the word satire derives from *satura* or "mixed feast," as in certain kinds of Roman verse or Menippean satires, and mixed forms and generic medleys have characterized a wide spectrum of satiric works from the *Satyricon* to *Don Juan*. In fact, something of the mixed-media popular tradition and the *saturae* of the literary tradition meet in Byron's worldly "epic satire." One of his key sources, the English pantomime,[4] comprised a kind of theatrical microcosm of broader nineteenth-century cultural transformations, as Marilyn Gaull so clearly demonstrates in this volume's final chapter. Combining romance plots, fairy stories, historical narratives, and topical allusions with the traditional masks of the commedia dell'arte, the pantomime was ubiquitous, as much a ritual of the holiday calendar as a dramatic spectacle. "Every body 'pooh-poohs' the pantomime," said the *Times* in December 1823, "but every body goes to see it."

While the pantomime contained topical and political satire, it was usually muted of necessity. In part because the censorship of the times (especially under John Larpent) kept a keen surveillance and control on its political content, Regency pantomime became a recognizably *Romantic* form of satire, displacing direct attack in various idealizations and imaginative allegories. It can be seen as a popular dramatic expression of Friedrich Schlegel's much-discussed "romantic irony"—not surprising, given that Schlegel's favorite source and example for the mode was the commedia dell'arte itself and its tradition of "transcendental buffoonery."[5] This affinity with certain modes of emergent Romanticism—its own transcendence and preferred kinds of irony—may help to explain why Leigh Hunt referred to the popular English pantomime as "the best medium of dramatic satire" of the age.[6]

Carnival, charivari, mock processions, burning effigies, and public pageantry, the "rough music" and symbolic language of popular culture in general has always included a substantial admixture of the satiric. But in another way, in the realm of official culture, in the public sphere where taste was made and standards were arbitrated, satire often played the role of acknowledged legislator. That is to say, what was acknowledged at the time as satire's power has often been ignored or underestimated in modern criticism, which has privileged the Romantic sincerity of satiric victims over the authority of satire. This is clearly the case with the famous satiric attacks published in the *Anti-Jacobin,* for example, whose parodies of fashionable and sentimental works sometimes read as apt criticisms of emergent Romanticism's implicit assumptions.

Nicola Trott shows how the newly dominant nineteenth-century critical reviews as a genre used parody to underwrite their own authority vis-à-vis the (negative) example of Wordsworthian simplicity, thus setting up a "new school of criticism" in the (mirror) image of the new school of poetry. In this way, Trott undermines the received "opposition between satirical review and Romantic bard" (p. 72). Gary Dyer's chapter on Tom Moore's extremely popular *Intercepted Letters* and *Fudge Family* satires shows how the culture of surveillance could be turned against itself, turned into a figurative device at once topical and critical. In an era when real letters were routinely intercepted and everyone was potentially being spied upon by someone else, Moore's topical satires offer a winning satiric "critique of government information-gathering" (p. 152). Ultimately, they do this by playing upon and exploiting the general paranoia for comic and political effect, constructing a kind of counter-authority to satirize the authority of the government and of society at large.

Nowhere is the once-central, presumptive authority of satire clearer than in the case of William Gifford, his targets, and his authority, as Michael Gamer demonstrates in detail below. Gifford was the well-known translator of Juvenal and influential Tory critic whose attacks on the sentimental Della Cruscan poets taught the critical establishment to satirize the effeminate, ephemeral, sentimental, and improvisational in modern poetry—especially when it threatened to usurp literary authority. Gifford's own authority helped shape public taste not only against the tinsel school of Robert Merry but, in some cases, against emergent Romantics such as Hunt, Shelley, and Keats, all of whom were attacked, by at least one critic, as "modern Della Cruscans."

The overdetermined feminization of satiric targets like the Della Cruscans complicated matters for Romantic-period women authors who would be satirists. It is worth remembering that Mary Robinson, who was foremost among the second-wave Della Cruscans in England, also wrote satires—often under the name of "Horace Juvenal" (as if in proof that there is no easy critical taxonomy based on the two terms in the nineteenth century). And Jane Austen of course, as Karl Kroeber reminds us below, was always a satirist. But as Stuart Curran eloquently demonstrates, through the important example of Jane Taylor, many women writers of the Romantic period often stood in an awkward relation to the traditional power and aims of much literary satire. In Taylor's case the only solution was to turn the weapons of satire against the foundational authority of satire itself.

In a different way, children—emerging in the Romantic period as a kind of audience and new category of reader—stood in an ambivalent relation to the tools and tones of satire. Donelle Ruwe's chapter traces the circulation of satiric energy from chapbooks ostensibly for children (but actually "cross-written" for a dual audience) to political parodies to critical constructions of the Romantic ideology of the child (and, by negative implication, constructions of the proper role of satire). The problems of violence and authority, on the one hand, and of sincerity and innocence, on the other hand, make satire a generic hotspot of critical implications when it comes to the Romantic ideology in general.

Thus it comes as no surprise that among leading critics of Romanticism, Jerome McGann has for some time now, in various of his writings, noted the importance of the deeper, agonistic strain of Romantic satire. He has also acknowledged the full historical significance of decidedly un-Romantic, reactionary satirists such as Gifford and Polwhele and of their targets, the Della Cruscans and Bluestockings. On both fronts, the Romantic ideology as McGann has outlined it "privileges conventions of 'sincerity' over conventions of 'premeditation,'" and has thus "all but obliterated our received sense of the satiric traditions that were being worked between 1790–1832."[7] Satire and polemical verse, he argues elsewhere, work through "publicly installed dialogical operations,"[8] and therefore increased attention to these operations, he implies, can provide a useful way to reconsider the Romantic period as a whole. Likewise, Stuart Curran's magisterial *Poetic Form and British Romanticism* (1986) excluded satire for purely practical reasons (since it presents its own set of special problems and requires a more extensive treatment than even that book could offer) but also noted in the first chapter that satire is "an extremely vital mode in British Romanticism, one whose full dimensions have never been addressed by criticism."[9]

If traditional literary history successfully displaced the vibrant satiric activity of this most turbulent historical period, more recent literary history has begun to redress the imbalance. Several studies have since taken up McGann's and Curran's suggestions, as it were, and have begun the process of measuring the role and influence of Romantic-period satire. With recent books, such as Gary Dyer's comprehensive scholarly treatment of the extensive production of satire in the period (including an invaluable bibliography) and my own literary-historical argument about satire's relation to the construction of Romanticism, as well as with the publication of Kent and Ewen's shorter and Stones and Strachan's longer anthologies of Romantic-period parodies, satiric writing in the period has shifted from background to foreground, "context" to text, becoming available for mainstream critical attention as never before.[10]

≈

The essays in this collection appear, therefore, at an especially receptive moment in Romantic-period criticism. They examine a rich variety of satiric forms and they do so from widely diverse perspectives. For some, the critical understanding of Romanticism itself is enriched once its embedded satiric modes are recognized and understood. Thus Karl Kroeber finds Jane Austen's self-reflexive satire serving not only aesthetic but—strikingly—broad evolutionary purposes, a satire ultimately imaginative and Romantic in its rhetorical effects. For others, a basic skepticism or agnosticism regarding the existence within this period of Romanticism as a unitary phenomenon leads logically to greater attention to what that construct has excluded, to satire and other non-Romantic modes and discourses. Marcus Wood, for example, casts a revealing light on ribald and pro-slavery satires created by a kind of rhetorical violence against the slave body. These deeply disturbing works belong to a decidedly un-"Romantic" literary milieu perhaps best configured as the long eighteenth century.

Finally, for some (and I count myself among them), satiric modes often provide us with a dialectical counter-voice, even a counter-history, within the period, a dialectical perspective that has helped to construct and has been constructed by more conventional notions of the Romantic. Satiric works offer a way into the self-critical, rhetorically violent, or openly conflictual strains of Romantic-period texts themselves, while also marking a place outside Romanticism from which to assess its construction. Looked at in this way, many Romantic texts can be understood as counter-satires, works whose formal and ideological identities are often reflexively defined as what one form or another of satire is *not*. The greatest critical interest in these cases lies at the complex borderline between constructions of the Romantic and the satiric. For all of the contributors to this volume, it is fair to say, attention to satire increases the richness and complexity of our critical understanding of Romantic-period culture. The panorama of diverse evidence provided by this collection of essays serves as an eloquent argument in favor of further studies of this sort. It is our premise that making the critical effort to look with a satiric eye offers us a more capacious, detailed, and dialogically engaged picture of the Romantic period's literature and culture.

The essays that follow are loosely clustered in (very) rough chronological order, but they are also grouped according to affinity of medium or topic within those clusters (even when they can be read in dialogue or contention with one another). So the first four (Fulford, Gamer, Wood, and Trott), though written from diverse perspectives, focus primarily on works from the 1780s and 1790s (in one sense Trott examines the continuing reception of the *Lyrical Ballads* of 1798 as catalyzed by the *Poems, in Two Volumes* of

1807). In one way or another all four are also concerned with taste-making in the public sphere. The chapters in the second cluster (by Kroeber, Ruwe, and Curran), though again from very different perspectives, focus on women and children—as authors, readers, and characters—at what might be called the satiric scene of instruction. The problem of didacticism and of satire's ancient claims to improve and teach are reexamined in all three essays, with very different results. The final cluster (by Dyer, Grimes, Strachan, and Gaull) concerns topical and political satire in a variegated range of multi-media forms, mostly during the Regency period. Dyer's essay bridges the supposed gap between literary and popular forms by way of the subject of the Royal family, where gossip and political commentary overlap in reception. Both Grimes and Strachan focus on "low" forms in the public sphere with, on the one hand, serious political intent and, on the other hand, frivolous commercial purposes. Whereas Grimes zeroes in on the rhetoric of Hone's visual and verbal strategies, Strachan gives us a vivid sense of the trans-Atlantic circulation of satiric and commercial semiotics from an unexpected quarter—the barber shop. Gaull ends with the period's most characteristic theatrical form, the English pantomime, which flowered into an encyclopedic carnival for the stage (paradoxically) under the harsh censorship of the Regency, becoming at once a popular, topical, worldly, mythical, ironic, and consummately "Romantic" form of satire.

Notes

1. Wordsworth, "I wandered lonely as a cloud" (lines 15–16), in *Poems, in Two Volumes, and Other Poems 1800–1807,* ed. Jared Curtis (Ithaca, NY: Cornell University Press, 1983), 207–208.

2. See Carl Woodring, *Politics in English Romantic Poetry* (Cambridge, MA: Harvard University Press, 1970); David V. Erdman, *Blake: Prophet Against Empire* (New York: Doubleday, 1954; 1969); Jerome McGann, "Rethinking Romanticism," *ELH* 59 (1992): 735–54; Butler, "Satire and the Images of the Self in the Romantic Period: The Long Tradition of Hazlitt's *Liber Amoris,*" in *English Satire and the Satiric Tradition,* ed. Claude Rawson (London: Blackwell, 1984), 153–69; Butler, *Romantics, Rebels and Reactionaries* (New York and Oxford: Oxford University Press, 1982); hereafter cited in the text.

3. Michael Henry Scrivener, "The *Black Dwarf* Review of Byron's *The Age of Bronze,*" *Keats-Shelley Journal* 41 (1992): 42–48; Jon Klancher, *The Making of English Reading Audiences 1790–1832* (Madison: University of Wisconsin Press, 1987); Kevin Gilmartin, *Print Politics: The Press and Radical Opposition in Early Nineteenth-Century England* (Cambridge: Cambridge University Press, 1996); Iain McCalman, *Radical Underworld: Prophets, Revolutionaries and Pornographers in London, 1795–1840* (Cambridge: Cam-

bridge University Press, 1988); Marcus Wood, *Radical Satire and Print Culture, 1790–1822* (Oxford: Clarendon Press, 1994).

4. On *Don Juan* and the Pantomime, see Peter W. Graham, *"Don Juan" and Regency England* (Charlottesville and London: University of Virginia Press, 1990), 62–88; Moyra Haslett, *Byron's "Don Juan" and the Don Juan Legend* (Oxford: Clarendon Press, 1997), e.g., 59–60, 87–89; and Steven E. Jones, *Satire and Romanticism* (New York: St. Martin's/Palgrave, 2000), 169–97.

5. See Steven E. Jones, *Satire and Romanticism,* 186–89.

6. *Leigh Hunt's Literary Criticism,* ed. Lawrence Huston Houtchens and Carolyn Washburn Houtchens (New York: Columbia University Press, 1956), 144.

7. McGann, "Literary Pragmatics and the Editorial Horizon," in *Devils and Angels: Textual Editing and Literary Theory,* ed. Philip Cohen (Charlottesville: University of Virginia Press, 1991), 1–21 (13).

8. McGann, *Towards a Literature of Knowledge* (Oxford: Clarendon Press, 1989), 39.

9. Stuart Curran, *Poetic Form and British Romanticism* (New York and Oxford: Oxford University Press, 1986), 12–13.

10. Gary Dyer, *British Satire and the Politics of Style, 1789–1832* (Cambridge: Cambridge University Press, 1997); Jones, *Satire and Romanticism* ; David A. Kent and D. R. Ewen, eds., *Romantic Parodies 1797–1831* (London and Toronto: Associated University Presses, 1992); Graeme Stones and John Strachan, eds., *Parodies of the Romantic Age,* 5 vols. (London: Pickering & Chatto, 1999).

Chapter 1 ∿

"Getting and Spending": The Orientalization of Satire in Romantic London

Tim Fulford

> . . . where has commerce such a mart,
> So rich, so throng'd, so drain'd, and so supplied,
> As London, opulent, enlarg'd and still
> Increasing London? Babylon of old
> Not more the glory of the earth, than she
> A more accomplish'd world's chief glory now.
>
> (*The Task,* I, 715–24)[1]

With these words William Cowper encapsulated the deep unease that many Britons felt in the 1780s. Faced with the dazzling tide of commerce that was overwhelming their capital city, they recognized a culture of consumption and excess that put them in mind of the Oriental fleshpots of the Bible. London seemed the new Babylon, appropriately enough since its new wealth stemmed in great measure from the Oriental colonies that had, since Lord Clive's conquests in India, been pouring money into the coffers of the East India Company. According to Cowper, this Oriental wealth was responsible for a rise in consumption not only of goods but also of other people. Orientalism fostered capitalism that was as morally and politically dangerous as it was all-pervasive. Like despotic Oriental rulers, Britons were learning in the East to consume others in their greed for power and pleasure. "Hast thou," Cowper asked his nation,

> . . . though suckled at fair Freedom's breast,
> Exported slavery to the conquer'd East,
> Pull'd down the tyrants India served with dread,
> And raised thyself, a greater, in their stead?
> Gone thither arm'd and hungry, return'd full,
> Fed from the richest veins of the Mogul,
> A despot big with power obtained by rapine and by stealth?
> With Asiatic vices stored thy mind,
> But left their virtues and thine own behind,
> And, having truck'd thy soul, brought home the fee
> To tempt the poor to sell himself to thee?
>
> (*Expostulation,* lines 365–75)[2]

Cowper's solution to the Janus-faced process of commercialization and Orientalism was to satirize it from a safe distance. He took his critical stance in a rural retreat where he was, and could be seen to be, immune from the temptations and perversities of London. Like Virgil and Horace, Cowper used retirement to give himself the moral high (and simple) ground from which to attack urban vice. In doing so, he created a poetic method and position that would be lastingly powerful in Romantic-period satire. William Wordsworth, for instance, emulated Cowper not only in reviling "the increasing accumulation of men in cities, where the uniformity of their occupations produces a craving for extraordinary incident," but also in attacking London life from a position of self-conscious rural simplicity.[3] Crabbe would later do the same. All these poets knew very well, of course, that in so doing they were updating the procedure of the satirists of ancient Rome and that, for this very reason, they had more in common with Alexander Pope than they sometimes admitted.

In the case of the rural critics of Oriental London, satire's authority depended on its visible separation from the culture it criticized. But there was another, newer development in Romantic-era satire in which that separation was not so apparent. It is this development that I wish to discuss, looking first at its characteristic diagnosis of the times and then at its own implication in those times. This development was both a response to and a product of London's culture of conspicuous consumption, and it appeared in the topical verse that was written to be rapidly circulated in pamphlet, magazine, and handbill, and still more in the popular caricatures that were displayed in the windows of the new print shops and reproduced in engraved form.

What these poems and prints seized upon was the very phenomenon that made them successful—London's commercialism, its ability to display, disseminate, and absorb every kind of good. London, they said, was like no other place on Earth. It was a city of shows, teeming with the products of empire. As a Russian tourist remarked, it was like a "continuous fair"; its shops offered spectacular exhibits of "absolutely everything one can think of."[4] Exotic fruits and spices were displayed in shops and on stalls; so were rare animals. London made spectacles of human bodies, too. Indian jugglers swallowed swords; Mohawks performed the war-whoop, as Wordsworth discovered on his first visit to the city in 1791:

> . . . every character of form and face:
> The Swede, the Russian; from the genial south,
> The Frenchman and the Spaniard; from remote
> America, the Hunter-Indian; Moors,
> Malays, Lascars, the Tartar, the Chinese,
> And Negro ladies in white muslin gowns.
>
> At leisure let us view, from day to day,
> As they present themselves, the spectacles
> Within doors, troops of wild beasts, birds and beasts
> Of every nature, from all climes convened
>
> (*Prelude* [1805], VII, 244–47)[5]

Many of the foreign women now at home in London were, either in reality or by pretence, exotic dancers in new kinds of harems that Englishmen could penetrate and command for a price. The famous madam Charlotte Hayes advertised a live show featuring "a dozen beautiful Nymphs, unsullied and untainted . . . who breathe health and nature and who will perform the celebrated rites of Venus, as practised at Tahiti."[6] After witnessing the nymphs dance, the paying voyeurs were invited to join in. In London's great exhibition, beautiful women, like "savage" warriors, were on show and for sale. Wordsworth summed the city up as a "raree-show"—a place where everything was turned into a titillating commercial performance (*Prelude* [1805], VII, 236, 190). Fashion and show were not new. But London developed a culture of consumption and display on a scale never before seen. An unprecedented circulation of money and goods seemed to most observers to be a new and worrying trend that changed with dizzying speed.[7] The trend commodified foreigners and it commodified women in the image of foreigners—putting English girls on show in commercial displays that imitated Eastern men's harems, as described by travelers.

One such harem stood in central London from 1780 to 1783. For the princely sum of two guineas, one gained entrance to a "magical edifice," an

"Elysian Palace"[8]—the Temple of Health and Hymen. This institution was run by a man Wordsworth referred to as a "Scotch doctor, famous in his day"—Dr James Graham (*Prelude,* VII, 183). A French observer wrote about it with incredulity:

> Garlands, mirrors, crystal, gilt and silver ornaments are scattered about it with profusion, so that from all parts they reflect a dazzling light. Music precedes each lecture . . . when Dr. Graham presents himself vested in Doctor's robes. On the instant there followed a silence which is interrupted only at the end of the lecture by an electric shock given to the whole audience by means of conductors hidden under the cushions with which all the seats are covered. Whilst some jest at the astonishment of the others, a "spirit" is seen to emerge from under the floor of the room; it presents the appearance of a man of gigantic stature, thin and haggard, who, without uttering a word, hands the Doctor a bottle of liquor, which, having been shown to the company, is carried off by the spirit.[9]

Whatever was in the bottle, Graham's flair for ceremony and stage-setting made his medicine seem magical. And it needed to be, for what, ultimately, he was selling was his own power to cure impotence and infertility by channeling the "electric fluid." In Graham's practice, electricity would conjure potency from drooping patients (and profit for the doctor) as the ultimate trick in a display intended to stimulate their imaginations. Using "soft music" and "Arabian spices in the style of those in the Seraglio of a Grand Turk,"[10] Graham Orientalized his "temple." It seemed an erotic and private place, an intimate boudoir in which patients would be stimulated into arousal. Impotent Londoners would become, by association, Eastern potentates, their wives alluring harem-girls ready for action.

Graham, with a showman's instinct for exploiting the latest fashion, clothed his electrical medicine in the style popularized by the Arabian Nights—a style in which the East represents the exoticism, sensual excess, and sexual abandon of a culture skilled in the refinements of giving pleasure and power to the male. It was already widely thought that Englishmen had turned this style into reality in India. "Nabobs" were notorious for "turning Turk" in the subcontinent, living out their Orientalist fantasies by acquiring harems of their own. Samuel Foote satirized such men in his 1773 play *The Nabob,* in which Sir Matthew Mite, recently returned to London from India, declares, "I have thoughts of founding in this town a seraglio" to be guarded by "three blacks from Bengal."[11] Graham's "temple" had two tall fellows in turbans as doorkeepers. It seemed a truly royal Eastern harem, as an anonymous satirist noted in a work called *The Celestial Beds:*

> His high Priest Giants of the Street!
> All your sleepless nights shall prove

Nights of revelry and love;
Your bosoms, free from care and sighs,
And joy illume your radiant eyes!
Youth, beauty, pleasure, all your own!
And worthy of the Sultan's throne.[12]

Graham's "Turkish" seraglio attracted topical satire such as *The Celestial Beds* (published in pamphlet form) because it so blatantly epitomized the spirit of a commercializing and Orientalizing city. Graham offered Britons a cheap taste of the sexual power their nabob countrymen had enjoyed by virtue of the vast wealth they had acquired in the East. Just a mile away from Graham's Temple, one former Indian colonist set up house in Soho Square with his wife and six Indian concubines. They shared one bedroom, with the beds arranged in a circle allowing the nabob to make nocturnal tours.[13]

In the sensation-seeking culture of London there was almost no such thing as bad publicity (perhaps for the first time). Far from resenting such satires as *The Celestial Beds,* Graham matched their lurid descriptions with the language of his own advertising puffs, which was so inflated as to be self-parodic. Absurdity only piqued curiosity. Graham was an early master of hype, knowing that fantastical claims would make customers eager to see whether the reality could possibly live up to his exotic description. And it was exotic indeed, for Graham commodified sex in the image of the East. His Temple allowed Londoners to buy for a night the Oriental fantasy that nabobs could afford to live out permanently. Stepping past the doorkeepers, one entered a harem-world of luxury dedicated to proving the potency of the male. At its center was the "Celestial or Magnetico-electrico bed . . . the first and only ever in the world."[14] The bed featured a mirrored canopy, "ethereal spices, odours and essences," "celestial" music and a reservoir emitting "the exhilarating force of electrical fire." But its "chief principle" was "about 15 cwt. of compound magnets . . . continually pouring forth in an everflowing circle." For £50, clients could pass a night being attracted into coupling—or shocked rigid.

Many did. Graham's mixture of Oriental fantasy and scientific gadgets drew "overflowing audiences," including fashionable ladies who hid their faces from view.[15] Despite the disguises, some were identified, and the satirical author of *The Celestial Beds* addressed them publicly:

Sweeter, lovelier you'll seem
When you get a touch from him;
In your husband's doating eyes
You shall prove a precious prize;

His magnetic influence
Ev'ry hour new joys dispense.

(p. 20)

Through Graham, electrical and magnetic medicine had become firmly identified with decadent Orientalism, with salacious sexual touching and illicit—and extramarital—female desire.

As well as the delights of his bed, Graham offered lectures on sexual health assisted by a lovely and scantily clad "Vestina"—the goddess of health. Vestina's possible sexual availability was tacitly accepted to be part of the occasion. Her body was the site of a mystery intended to entice customers into paying to attend. Would or wouldn't the gentlemen who watched her fascinations be able to sample them in the flesh? Rumor had it that Emma Hart was one of those who played this role. Later, as Mrs. Hamilton, she was to become Nelson's mistress, having turned him on with a private show in which she played a series of "Oriental" temptresses including Dido and Cleopatra.

Emma wasn't the only courtesan whom the cartoonists and gossip columnists placed in the Temple of Hymen. Mary "Perdita" Robinson was the mistress of an even more august potentate than Nelson—of no less than the heir to the throne, George, Prince of Wales. She had attracted George by appearing in the theater, where she had performed on more than one stage, as the *Morning Post* of August 9, 1780, revealed. "There you shall see the famous Perdita of Drury Lane, sitting at the playhouse in the sidebox opposite the Prince of Wales. Look how wantonly she looks, Thinking, Gracious Sir! please to bestow one [shilling] upon a poor woman! Ho! ho! fine raree show!"[16] Like the satirist of *The Celestial Beds,* the newspaper journalist diagnoses London's culture as a matter of titillation and display, as the marketing of sex in only semi-disguised form. The play, it seemed, was not the thing—or not the whole thing, anyway. Robinson had turned the auditorium into her stage, exhibiting herself in the attitudes most likely to attract the wealthy Prince. As the phrase "raree show" suggests, she was an exotic commodity, a seemingly foreign spectacle, rarely seen and now viewable for a price. On sale to the Prince and his friends, Robinson was presented to the public as little different from Vestina in the Temple of Hymen or one of Hayes's "Tahitian" nymphs. To the newspaper, she was the embodiment of a new culture of commodified display that turned everything into a show for buyers—not so much sex and shopping as sex as shopping.

Robinson had first fascinated George by appearing in character on the stage rather than as herself in the gallery. But even when acting Perdita in *The Winter's Tale,* she was performing in a context that immediately associated her with Mrs. Hayes' nymphs and Graham's Vestina. Shakespearean actresses in the 1780s were not seen as being different in kind, but only in degree, from the more obviously sexually available performers of brothel and show. For gentlemen about town, both kinds of performance functioned as showcases of female charms that might subsequently be available for a price. Robinson's fellow actress Mrs. Jordan wittily acknowledged this when, after the King had complained of the money paid her by his son the Duke of Clarence, she replied, "No money returned after the raising of the curtain."[17]

What Jordan acknowledged, Robinson embodied. George had viewed and bought her at a raree-show and had gone to sample the delights of Graham's Temple with her. By appearing there, Robinson not only visibly linked classical theater with a London seraglio, but also revealed that a culture of commodification reigned—or at least threatened, literally, to reign—when the royal Prince succeeded his father. According to the author of *The Celestial Beds,* Robinson and "her Royal dear" were at the Temple to make her pregnant with a child that would be an heir to the throne:

> And shall not she, his joy and pride,
> Be for a pledge electrify'd?
> Yes, Graham shall exert his art,
> And give a bantling to her heart!
> The Muses' darling it shall be,
> The flow'r of royal progeny!
>
> (p. 26)

To the satirist, their child would represent the triumph, at the very pinnacle of British society, of a culture of, in Wordsworth's sexual pun, "getting and spending" in which even matters as intimate as sexuality were commodified in the image of the Orient. George would be the Sultan of an Easternized Britain; Robinson the favorite mistress of his harem.

To some commentators, this culture was a direct result of Britain's empire in the East. The colonization of India not only corrupted morals, but also turned Londoners into pampered buyers, conspicuous consumers of the foreign. They grew rich and corrupt by selling each other the products of the Orient—tea, coffee, china, and now women. The caricaturist Gillray expressed this view with biting wit in his "A Sale of English Beauties in the East Indies" (1786) (see figure 1.1). In this print, the British are shown as traders in sex, suppliers of Eastern harems. The East India Company's merchandise is all sexual. Not only does the auctioneer sell the women, whom a mixture of Indian and British buyers are sizing up, but he markets pornographic books, too. The packet in the foreground is labeled with the titles it contains "for the Amusement of Military Gentlemen"—"Fanny Hill," "Sophia," "Fe-

Figure 1.1. James Gillray, "A Sale of English Beauties in the East-Indies," 16 May 1786. Copyright the British Museum.

male Flagellant." Even the auctioneer's podium is a saleable commodity: it is a parcel of birches, of "British Manufacture," presumably for the use of the same military gentlemen who purchase the "Female Flagellant." Imperial trade, Gillray suggests, is perverse and corrupt: Britain prospers by commodifying desire and exporting it to feed the lust of the East, lust displayed by its own colonists as much as by Indians.

Gillray's women are not shown as victims, either of the Company that sells them or the Indians who buy them. These are not white slaves being bought by cruel Orientals. On the contrary, they participate in the process, cutting deals with their purchasers. Only those who have not found buyers and who are entering the "Warehouse for unsaleable goods" look unhappy. British women, Gillray suggests, willingly sell themselves in an empire where selling is the highest "good." Later, he was to draw Robinson as a similar commodity—as a naked and splayed whore depicted on a brothel sign.

It was not just her association with Graham's Temple that made Robinson an apt embodiment of the commodifying capitalism that Eastern empire was promoting. Her next lover was George's friend and mentor, the notoriously extravagant government minister Charles James Fox. Fox had introduced the Prince to a life of drinking and gambling. For this he was criticized. But what most annoyed satirists was the fact that he seemed to find women for his royal protégé and then take them off George's hands when the Prince tired of them. In July 1782 he took Robinson on in this secondhand way, just a few days after he had resigned from government. Even to friends, Fox seemed to be neglecting his political duty in favor of the expensive embraces of the Prince's cast-off mistress—"Charles saunters about the streets, & brags that he has not taken a pen in hand since he was out of Place . . . he lives with Mrs. Robinson" noted one.[18]

Fox's enemies were less sympathetic, and when he and Robinson visited Graham's Temple, he was depicted as a symbol of immorality. In a print of December 23, 1783, *The Aerostatick Stage Balloon,* both the profligate politician and the showgirl actress were linked to the latest fashionable novelty—balloon ascents. Also present were Graham, the beautiful "Vestina," and several notorious courtesans. Fox sits in the center next to Lord North, his long-time political enemy with whom he had suddenly entered a coalition. The implication is that by allying with his enemy in order to get back into government, Fox has turned his politics into the kind of raree show offered by such charlatans as Graham. Principles and morality are abandoned; the great Whig leader is a mountebank selling a cheap illusion to the people. Robinson's presence in this context says that Fox's political life, like his notorious love life, is promiscuous and immoral. She is a visual symbol of a new London: she does not figure in her own right but only as a sign of a culture of surfaces, in which an alluring and buyable exterior signals that the morals and principles that should lie within are, like the interior of the balloon, just hot air. The verses attached to the print conclude thus:

Spruce Graham launch Electric thunders
Vestina too—nor fear a fall
Sr Satans Net shall catch ye all
So said Monsieur in broken Brogue
And up they mounted whore and rogue.

Satires such as this used Graham and Robinson to make a conveniently reactionary reading of the capitalist culture of consumption, and of the political leaders who profited by that culture. At bottom, they suggested, the new science and the new politics of imperial Britain were about the oldest trade of all, the selling of a girl's body.

It was in 1783 that Fox appeared particularly Indian. In November, now the prime minister, he decided it was vital to root out the corruption that stemmed from the East India Company's rule in the subcontinent. Company officials had been enriching themselves by pillaging rich Indians. When these officials returned to Britain they and the Company itself used the ill-gotten gains to buy the support of MPs, thus corrupting parliament, too. The Duke of Portland commented, "the evil is grown so rank, all palliatives have been proved so ineffectual, the cure is of so much importance to the existence and character of the nation, that I pant for the experiment."[19] Imperial wealth put British liberty in danger at its very center—Westminster. Fox himself thought "the fate of the Administration & of the country" depended on destroying the corrupting influence.

Unfortunately for Fox, the bill that he drafted to effect the destruction only made him seem as greedy and corrupt as the Company that he accused of "rapacity." In order to stop the Company buying MPs, Fox proposed that a Board of Commissioners should decide who was offered the lucrative posts in imperial trade and administration that the Company had formerly doled out to its supporters. The Commissioners he proposed, however, were all his friends and political allies. Immediately it seemed that Fox was simply trying to transfer to his own party the ability to use Company loot to buy votes. Sir Francis Baring was staggered by what he judged to be the breathtaking hypocrisy of Fox's scheme:

> The Empire of Asia will remain completely & absolutely in the hands of Fox. . . . It is a system of influence & corruption as amazes me; it is however compleat, & if no other proof existed of the abilities & ambition of C. Fox, it will forever remain as a monument of the boldest and most artfull effort ever attempted by any subject since the restoration, for if he succeeds he will remain possessed of more real power & patronage than any future Minister can possibly enjoy.[20]

Caricaturists saw it Baring's way: Fox was pictured as Carlo Khan, emperor of India, triumphantly riding an elephant past the Company's London headquarters (see figure 1.2). He seemed, that is to say, as much a rapist and as much a despot lured by wealth as India's most notorious invaders—Mongol and British. Ruling by corruption, Fox was to be a Sultan, parliament his venal court. Graham's Temple of Health and Hymen had, after all, been the appropriate place in which to picture him since he would turn Britain's parliament into a capitalist version of a "seraglio of males,"[21] in which Oriental wealth would buy him whatever services he desired.

It never came to pass. The King used the unpopularity of the bill to maneuver Fox out of and Pitt into power. Fox and his followers did not regain it until 1806. Obsessed by their defeat, they ensured that imperial India shaped the pattern of British politics for the next quarter century. Pitt prospered, while the Foxites sought to show that they had tried to form "an English government

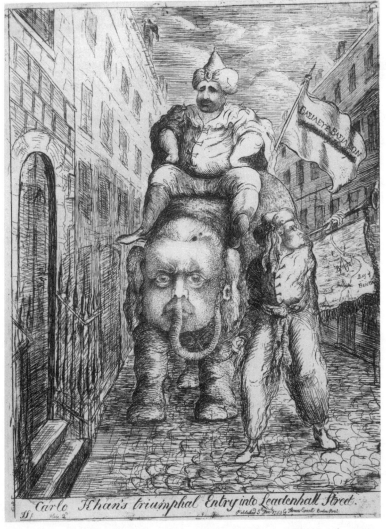

Figure 1.2. "Carlo Khan's Triumphal Entry into Leadenhall Street," 5 December 1783. Copyright the British Museum.

over India," whereas Pitt was establishing "an Indian [i.e., corrupt] government in England."[22] They impeached the governor general of the East India Company's colonies, Sir Warren Hastings, to show that, in order to keep the loot coming that allowed them to buy power in Britain, the "Court and Ministry" abetted a "tyranny, robbery and destruction of mankind" in India that was without historical precedent anywhere.[23] Hastings' trial was sensational, but few believed that his Foxite accusers were disinterested. And while they sought, year after year, to show that Hastings and the Crown, and not they themselves, had spread corruption from Britain to India and back again, Pitt cemented his control of government.

Again and again, satirists repeated the Orientalist diagnosis of Britain's ills. They attributed those ills, however, not to Pitt but to the Foxite aristocracy and above all to the monarch who had once been the Foxites' crony. Prince—subsequently King—George was the chief symbol of this corruption. In 1820, as the new King tried to force parliament to prevent his estranged wife becoming Queen and as he continued to live with his mistresses, an anonymous satire termed him Khouli Khan, the Asiatic emperor taking his ease under the Oriental domes of his latest pleasure palace–Brighton Pavilion. *Khouli Khan* combined verse with woodcut illustrations like a broadside ballad. Mixing its satiric media for maximum appeal, it was printed quickly and cheaply to hit the streets while the scandal lasted.[24] While it mocked George's excessive consumption it nevertheless depended for success on Londoners' willingness to consume. This was not aristocratic satire circulated among friends, nor the satire of a precocious young poet looking for a patron. It was not the slowly crafted moral verse that Cowper and Wordsworth penned in their rural fastnesses. It was a biting but ephemeral genre, written to sell cheap and fast, a product for and of a public who were as used to "getting and spending" on a minor scale as George IV was on a major one.

George certainly got and spent. Brighton Pavilion became a symbol of his extravagance and his arbitrariness because it revealed in stone his capricious desire to surround himself with the showiest Oriental style, only abruptly and on a whim to supersede that style with another. Draining the royal purse by tens of thousands of pounds at a time, George's architectural schemes turned the Pavilion into a hotchpotch of Indian and Chinese features. The *Monthly Magazine* archly declared that George "deemed it respectful to his Indian dependencies to exhibit a palace in conformity with their notions of architectural perfection."[25] What it meant was that empire had corrupted the judgment of the King himself: George was as tasteless and excessive as his Indian subjects. He was also as Oriental, if the satirical prints were to be believed, for they illustrated him as an Eastern

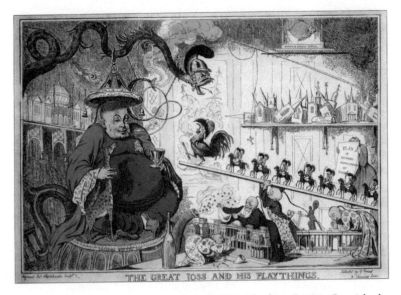

Figure 1.3. Robert Seymour, "The Great Joss and His Playthings," 1829. Copyright the British Museum.

ruler, complete with harem. In "The Great Joss and his Playthings" (1829) (see figure 1.3), the King appears as a pot-bellied Chinese deity, sitting on a huge example of one of the commodities that had made the East India Company wealthy—a China teapot. Out of it pour gold sovereigns. In the background is a model of the domes and minarets of Brighton Pavilion. The bloated King, a look of imbecilic contentment on his face, is stoned— for he is smoking a pipe of that other Eastern commodity that was enriching Britain, opium. George is surrounded with the "toys" that he so loves to buy and with the funds that are provided by a grateful ministry (pictured in the form of the Duke of Wellington as a cockerel). These include the models of his planned buildings, a collection of model soldiers, and a small giraffe (mocking the real one presented to the King by the Pasha of Egypt in 1827).[26] The satirist's message is that far from setting an example of paternal government, the King is a passive consumer of the exotic trinkets that empire brings to his chamber. George is an image of an Orientalized Britain reduced to voyeuristic torpor and stupefied satiety by its dependence upon commodities.

"The Great Joss" is a late example of the development that began in the 1770s and 1780s with the influx of goods and wealth from the East. It makes what was by 1829 a well-established link between commercialism and colonialism on the one hand and consumerism and Orientalism on the other. King George, once the youthful patron of exotic shows such as Graham's Temple, was now, in the words of William Hone's satire "The Joss and his Folly," "an old fat MANDARIN" who gloated over his exotic novelties in his Oriental pleasure dome.[27] Oriental imagery was a staple of the new satire, a graphic illustration of the conspicuous consumption engendered by empire and of the effects of that consumption on the body politic.

Such was the diagnosis that satirists such as Hone and Gillray made of the times. It was funny; it was perceptive; it was popular. Ironically enough, however, its popularity and its dependence on popularity put its authority in doubt. Whereas Cowper and Wordsworth satirized from a distance, Hone and Gillray succeeded in the very culture of display and consumption that they mocked. Prints, in particular, flooded into existence because a market of consumers who wished to buy them grew with dramatic speed.[28] Aiming to satisfy this market, artists such as Isaac and George Cruikshank, Thomas Rowlandson, and Gillray changed sides with frequency and rapidity—targeting politicians whose opponents they had attacked a month before. Gillray went so far as to take government pay to satirize Whigs and radicals—abandoning independence in all but outward appearance. But it was not primarily his compromised political position but his relationship to the public that was significantly new. He showed as much in the brilliant print "Very Slippy Weather" (1808) (see figure 1.4), in which Londoners are pictured gazing at a show of pictures. When we look closer, we can see that they are staring at prints by Gillray. The window-shopping voyeurs are ogling Gillray's caricatures in which Londoners are satirized. We, in turn, are ogling them doing so. Gillray, that is to say, self-referentially satirizes the process of looking at and consuming his own images. He laughs twice at his viewers, who are avidly inspecting satires on their voyeuristic avidity. But he also reveals the dependence of his popular art on the culture of consumption that it mocks. The last laugh is on Gillray himself, for he is a purveyor of displays for the consumption of a culture whose consumerism he satirizes.[29] In 1811 Gillray tried to kill himself by jumping from an upper window of the same shop pictured in "Very Slippy Weather."

Gillray was not alone in his insight into the complicity of the genre he had popularized with the culture it attacked. The anonymous artist who drew "Caricature Shop" (1801) also showed a crowd outside a print-shop window, satirizing the curious spectators and voyeurs. One of the grosser figures is a lecherous old man ogling a print of a voluptuous naked woman. This image reminds viewers that making, displaying, and con-

Figure 1.4. James Gillray, "Very Slippy Weather," 10 February 1808. Copyright the British Museum.

suming prints are activities close to the titillating sex shows operated by the likes of Graham and Hayes. Likewise Isaac Cruikshank's "Peepers in Bond Street, or the cause of the Lounge!!" (1793), depicts voyeurs hiding in order to view the bare ankles of ladies dressed in the latest Oriental fashions—the muslin gowns that Wordsworth remarked upon in *The Prelude*.

London is an endless display, a market of alluring commodities, which represent and substitute for the naked flesh.[30]

By 1818 Byron was also mocking such Oriental fashions. He belittled the Eastern poetry with which he had made his name by picturing himself as a salesman of exotic goods—a shop assistant pressing the latest fashion in chintz onto a customer:

> How quickly would I print (the world delighting)?
> A Grecian, Syrian, or Assyrian tale;
> And sell you, mixed with western Sentimentalism,
> Some samples of the finest Orientalism.
>
> (*Beppo: A Venetian Story,* LI)[31]

Publishing poetry in Regency Britain was like selling cloth—a commercial transaction all to do with exoticism and novelty and nothing to do with genius or morality.[32]

Byron was cynical but the result of this cynicism was the greatest satire of the era, a new satire in which Byron not only demonstrated Gillray's self-referential irony about his medium but also appreciated that there was no effective alternative. Byron was, in effect, one of the first to demonstrate that, as a commercial culture spread across the nation linking all Britons as consumers, there would be no rural retreat in which a satirist could find sanctuary from the trends he criticized. "Getting and spending," and the social mores getting and spending produced, were becoming so pervasive that only a hypocrite or a crank could claim immunity from them. And neither hypocrites nor cranks could legitimately possess the authority to castigate their fellow men. Byron implied that Wordsworth was both, and with devastating irony turned the symbols of Oriental corruption against the Lake poet.

> I'm fond myself of solitude or so,
> But then, I beg it may be understood,
> By solitude I mean a sultan's, not
> A hermit's, with a haram for a grot.
>
> (*Don Juan,* I, 87)

To be a Sultan is an Orientalist fantasy that brings the satires on the libidinous George IV to mind. Byron poses as a would-be nabob so as to read Wordsworthian solitude as an adolescent's sublimated sexuality. But Byron also simultaneously mocks the nabob by bringing him into conjunction with a hermit. Wordsworthian spiritual and Oriental sexual solitude turn out to be similar ego-driven fantasies. Both stem from the desire to be "a god indeed divine" (*Don Juan,* I, 88), an all-powerful exclusive consumer of others. But—and this is a further level of irony—only a writer who had played out *both* fantasies would be able to see through them in this way.

Byron had summed up what Oriental and commercial Britain meant for satirists: it meant that an effective dissection of the times would have to be written from within them, that commentators would have to accept—and turn to their advantage—the implication of their publications in the culture they criticized. A knowing and self-referential irony, Byron showed, was the necessary condition of credible critique. And the alternative—the solemnity of the satirist who spoke from beyond—was achievable solely by a degree of willful self-isolation that only those blinded by self-regard could achieve. Wordsworth was burying his head in his lake: he perversely manufactured his own innocence so as to produce a position of authority. What he created, however, was not innocence but naivety with the result that that his satires were not only pompous but too ignorant of the new world to hit the target. The truly powerful satirist of the Spirit of the Age, Byron showed, would not be naive but both experienced and disillusioned. He would be a man, like himself and like Gillray, who had risen to fame selling exotic images to Orientalist devotees and who therefore understood at first hand the glamor and the tawdriness of modern Britain. The Romantic satirist, in Byron's image, would have to have got and spent as fervently as his fellow Britons. He would have to have "lived in the world . . . and tooled in a post-chaise . . . In a hackney coach . . . In a gondola . . . Against a wall. . . . the *cant* is so much stronger than *cunt* nowadays; that the benefit of experience in a man who had well-weighed the worth of both monosyllables must be lost."[33] Only a man free from sanctimony could hold a mirror up to the age—and only then because that mirror also showed him his own face. Byron, as Don Juan, made himself both the Sultan and the salesman, the innocent and the rake of the raree-show that, the Romantics realized, was contemporary Britain.

Notes

1. *The Task* in *The Poems of William Cowper*, ed. John D. Baird and Charles Ryskamp, 3 vols. (Oxford: Oxford University Press, 1980–1995); hereafter cited parenthetically in the text.
2. In *The Poems of William Cowper*, ed. Baird and Ryskamp.
3. From the Preface to *Lyrical Ballads*, in *The Prose Works of William Wordsworth*, ed. W. J. B. Owen and J. W. Smyser, 3 vols. (Oxford: Oxford University Press, 1974), I, 128; hereafter cited parenthetically in the text.
4. Both quoted in James Walvin, *Fruits Of Empire. Exotic Produce And British Taste, 1660–1800* (Basingstoke: Macmillan, 1997), 158.
5. *William Wordsworth: The Prelude, 1799, 1805, 1850*, ed. Jonathan Wordsworth, M. H. Abrams, Stephen Gill (New York and London: Norton, 1979); hereafter cited parenthetically in the text.

6. Quoted in Neil Rennie, *Far Fetched Facts: The Literature of Travel and the Idea of the South Seas* (Oxford: Clarendon Press, 1992), 101.

7. On this rapid development of this culture at the time see Colin Campbell, *The Romantic Ethic and the Spirit Of Modern Consumerism* (Oxford: Blackwell, 1987) and Neil McKendrick, John Brewer, and J. H. Plumb, *The Birth Of A Consumer Society: The Commercialization Of Eighteenth-Century England* (London: Hutchinson, 1982).

8. Quoted in Roy Porter, *Health for Sale, Quackery in England 1660–1850* (Manchester and New York: Manchester University Press, 1989), 161.

9. Quoted in Porter, 160.

10. Quoted in Porter, 162.

11. Quoted in Lawrence James, *Raj: The Making and Unmaking of British India* (London: Abacus, 1997), 46.

12. Anon., *The Celestial Beds; Or, A Review of the Votaries of the Temple of Health, Adelphi and the Temple of Hymen, Pall-Mall* (London: G. Kearsby, 1781), 20.

13. Quoted in James, *Raj,* 208.

14. Graham's advertising pamphlet, quoted in Eric Jameson, *The Natural History of Quackery* (London: Michael Joseph, 1961), 119.

15. Quoted in Porter, *Health for Sale,* 160.

16. Quoted in Marguerite Steen, *The Lost One: a Biography of Mary (Perdita) Robinson* (London: Methuen, 1937), 153.

17. Quoted in Steen, 220.

18. Quoted in L. G. Mitchell, *Charles James Fox* (Oxford: Oxford University Press, 1992), 57.

19. Quoted in Mitchell, 63.

20. Quoted in Mitchell, 64.

21. Thomas Paine's phrase for the House of Commons, at a slightly later date, under the dominance of Pitt. The point holds, however, for Fox himself was to accuse Pitt of governing like an Indian ruler. Paine's remark appears in *The Rights of Man,* ed. Henry Collins (Harmondsworth: Penguin, 1969), 249.

22. Quoted in Mitchell, *Fox,* 77.

23. Quoted in Mitchell, 77.

24. *Khouli Khan; or, the Progress of Error* (London and Bristol: William Benbow, 1820).

25. *Monthly Magazine* (1819), quoted in Brian Goldberg, "Black Gates and Fiery Galleries: Eastern Architecture in *The Fall of Hyperion,*" *Studies in Romanticism* 39 (2000): 229–54 (235).

26. This information I take from Andrew Barlow's discussion of the picture in *The Prince and his Pleasures: Satirical Images of George IV and his Circle* (Brighton: The Royal Pavilion Libraries and Museums, 1997), 18.

27. Hone's satire quoted in Barlow, 20.

28. On the rapid expansion of print-publishing see Mark Hallett, "James Gillray and the Language of Graphic Satire," in Richard Godfrey, *James Gillray—The Art of Caricature* (London: Tate Publishing, 2001), 27–28.

29. On Gillray's complicity with London's display-culture see Hallett, 36–37.

30. Those prints are discussed in Diana Donald, *The Age of Caricature: Satirical Prints in the Reign of George III* (New Haven and London: Yale University Press, 1996), 103.

31. *Lord Byron, The Complete Poetical Works,* ed. Jerome McGann, 7 vols. (Oxford: Oxford University Press, 1980–86). All citations from Byron's poems are from this edition, hereafter cited parenthetically in the text.

32. On Byron's analogies between verse and Oriental cloth see Nigel Leask, "'Wandering through Eblis'; Absorption and Containment in Romantic Exoticism," in *Romanticism and Colonialism: Writing and Empire 1780–1830,* ed. Tim Fulford and Peter J. Kitson (Cambridge: Cambridge University Press, 1998), 165–88 (178–80).

33. Letter from Byron to Douglas Kinnaird, October 26, 1819, in *The Letters and Journals of Lord Byron,* ed. Leslie A. Marchand, 12 vols. (London: Murray, 1973–82), VI, 231–33.

Chapter 2 ～

"Bell's Poetics": *The Baviad,* the Della Cruscans, and the Book of *The World*

Michael Gamer

> I don't know anyone now who takes Della Cruscan writing seriously, and even its readers are rare. The received judgment—that it's trash— comes to us as naturally as the leaves to the tree. . . . [Yet e]very one of the so-called major Romantics was deeply marked by sentimental conventions of writing, and there is an important (unremembered) sense in which Keats, Shelley, and Byron are the supreme legacy of the Della Cruscan movement in particular.
>
> —Jerome McGann, "The Literal World of the English Della Cruscans"[1]

The most enduring legacy we possess of the group of poets dubbed "Della Cruscan" is the narrative of their rapid rise and rightful demise. It reports a group of nonsensical poetasters debauching British poetry for nearly five years before having their folly exposed by an eminent classicist and critic, William Gifford, in two satirical poems entitled *The Baviad* (1791) and *The Mæviad* (1795). That Jerome McGann's 1995 essay, quoted above, was the first unreserved defense of Della Cruscan writing in nearly two centuries stands as apt testimony to the story's durability and persuasiveness. McGann's wish to absolve himself from such a critical history stemmed in part from a warranted frustration with the criticism's perpetuation of basic factual errors and repetition of disparaging normative statements, from the *Dictionary of National Biography*'s characterization of the entire movement as "nonsense" to twentieth-century commentators' habit of using "Della Cruscan" simply as an adjective for bad poetry.[2] In response, the opening paragraphs of McGann's essay adopt the wide-ranging claims of a critical manifesto, pithily characterizing *The Baviad* as "Gifford's fustian" and dismissing that poem's legacy of "received judgment[s]" as quickly as his own critical predecessors had dismissed the Della Cruscans themselves.[3] With Judith Pascoe,[4] then, McGann argues for our unthinking dismissal of Della Cruscan writing as an emblematic moment of Romantic ideology, a critical rejection of a repressed but foundational discourse of Romanticism.[5] Both critics thus understandably shift their focus away from Gifford's two satires, and instead seek to explain Della Cruscanism's stylistic codes as central to, and definitive of, early British Romanticism.[6] Indeed, their insistence on the Della Cruscans' formidable proto-Romantic credentials is the only part of their foundational work that takes its cue from earlier studies.[7]

While sharing an interest in Della Cruscanism's ideological significance and cultural function, I wish to approach these same poets not from the vantage point of literary influence but rather from that of literary authority. To do this, I necessarily take up such "received judgments"—including Gifford's satires and their legacy—because they are essential to understanding the ways in which Della Cruscanism presented readers like Gifford with an alternative poetics and a fundamentally threatening model of authorship. Yet I also seek to challenge a more fundamental current of reading in commentaries on Della Cruscan writing, one that nearly always reads the Della Cruscans, whether positively or negatively, in terms of their relation to Romanticism and through the lens of Gifford's and subsequent satires. With *The Baviad* my ultimate object, I seek to render its relation to Della Cruscan writing mutually constitutive by placing Gifford and his poem under the same critical gaze we have usually reserved for the objects of his satire.[8]

Where satire has an explicit object we often neglect to ask the obvious question of why the satirist writes; Gifford wrote *The Baviad,* after all, to attack a group of poets called the Della Cruscans. Yet his reasons for writing the poem, and writing it so belatedly, differ greatly from those provided by the critical narratives we have inherited. Determinedly internationalist and materially hybrid, Della Cruscanism in England began as the product of a poetic tradition (Italian improvisation) and a literary social space (the Conversation) projected onto a specific kind of textual media (the periodical). While its initial productions were first privately printed in book form, the movement became known, its name coined, and its poetics established, through its affiliation with fashionable newsprint, and particularly with the newspaper entitled *The World*. As the poetry's popularity increased, *The World*'s publisher, John Bell, began to collect and republish it in book form, with dedications and advertisements praising the poems as lasting contributions to the nation's literature. It is within this transition, I argue—from improvisation to permanence, from newsprint to codex—that the Della Cruscans comprised their most serious threat to established notions of literary authority, and so my essay seeks to historicize Gifford's response to them as more than merely an aesthetic rejection of a supposedly corrupt poetical style.

Origins of Style

The story we have inherited of the Della Cruscans usually comes to us as a titillating narrative of origin, and publications from *The Baviad* to the *Dictionary of National Biography* to recent critical accounts of the movement have rehearsed its details. Usually these accounts focus on the newly remarried Hester Thrale Piozzi, her arrival in Florence and her founding a salon there, and her production of a volume of poetry entitled *The Florence Miscellany* (1785) with three other British tourists (Bertie Greatheed, Robert Merry, and William Parsons). Privately published and featuring works both in English and Italian by themselves and by Ippolito Pindemonte, Lorenzo Pignotti, Angelo D'Elci, and Giuseppe Parini, the book remains one of the first important eighteenth-century English engagements with Italian poetry, anticipating later English experimentation with Italian improvisation and with forms like ottava rima and terza rima.[9] Though privately printed and distributed, the volume quickly found its way into the hands of the editor of *The European Magazine,* who began publishing its contents at the rate of a few poems per month. Thus, when the Florence coterie disbanded several months later and its members made their separate ways back to England, they arrived to find themselves literary celebrities, Robert Merry adopting the self-consciously "Italian" style of the *Florence Miscellany* with the greatest success. Publishing poetry in a newspaper called *The World* under the sobriquet "Della Crusca," he quickly became the central figure within an expanded group of poets—the English Della Cruscans—who all published under pseudonyms in the same paper, using the pages of *The World* as an arena of literary flirtation and as a kind of virtual salon. The movement's defining moment came in July 1787 when the dramatist Hannah Cowley sent "To Della Crusca: The Pen" under the signature of "Anna Matilda" to *The World* in response to "The Adieu and Recall to Love," the first poem to which Robert Merry had affixed the signature "Della Crusca." Cowley's poem initiated a poetic love affair that helped to make *The World* the most successful newspaper of its time and inspired other poets, including Mary Robinson, Samuel Rogers, Miles Peter Andrews, and Edward Jerningham, to engage in similar pseudonymical correspondences in *The World* and other papers. The disease of Della Cruscanism continued to spread unchecked, we are told, until William Gifford published *The Baviad* in 1791, routing *The World*'s poets by exposing their folly and insignificance.

This is usually as far as we go with accounts of the Della Cruscans, perhaps adding a few choicely damning quotations by them before moving to Gifford's satire and recounting the group's demise. But what were *The World* and its poetry like? Returning separately to London during 1786 and 1787, the Florence coterie had arrived to find themselves identified as authors of a book already repackaged by London publishers.[10] Conspicuous among booksellers demanding further works was printer, newspaper editor, and circulating library mogul John Bell, who, having sold his shares of *The Morning Post* in January 1786, planned to publish a new daily at the beginning of the following year. He chose as his partner and editor Edward Topham, whose talents for elegant prose and dress combined well with Bell's gift for elegant printing. Over the next eighteen months the two produced lasting innovations in the history of newsprint. *The World*'s ornate gothic heading immediately became the norm for all London papers for over a century;[11] its elegant printing far outdistanced rivals and its advertisements boasted an inventiveness and ornateness usually reserved for fine books. As Lucyle Werkmeister notes, the result was an innovative style of journalism, the "success [of which] has no precedent in the history of newspapers."[12] Within this aesthetic and economic context, the group of poets that came to be known as the Della Cruscans played a pivotal role in shaping the paper's content and reputation. With Miles Peter Andrews already contributing as "Arley" and Edward Jerningham as "Benedict," Topham began to assemble additional poets, and Topham's rooms in the Beaufort Buildings became a fashionable meeting-place for young male poets and playwrights like Thomas Adney ("Mot Yenda"), Andrews, George Monck Berkeley ("The Bard"), Frederick Reynolds, and Thomas Vaughn ("Edwin"). Two years into *The World*'s existence, it would boast no fewer than thirty regular contributors, and it was the willingness of other writers to imitate Merry's success that transformed *The World* from a paper that periodically printed poems to one that specifically announced itself as "The Paper of Poetry."

While the Beaufort Building's core male coterie helped establish *The World*'s penchant for self-advertisement and exhibitionism, it was Merry and his female respondents who forged its increasingly Italian poetics. Part of this no doubt arose out of Merry's choice of pseudonym, but Merry's female respondents played an even greater role than he did in the paper's evolution.[13] Thus, Della Crusca's first poem, "The Adieu and Recall to Love," may address a listener (Cupid) and define consciousness as a state of feeling responsiveness—but it does not, as various commentators have suggested, call for a response. That characteristic of the poetry is instead established by Hannah Cowley's "To Della Crusca: The Pen," which redefines "The Adieu and Recall to Love" as the beginning of a correspondence while affirming Della Crusca's lyricism by responding in kind. In the lines that follow her opening, Cowley performs a series of rhetorical transformations and deft movements that would become typical of the exchange she is inaugurating:

> Thy golden quill APOLLO gave——
> Drench'd first in bright Aonia's wave:
> He snatch'd it flutt'ring thro' the sky,
> Borne on the vapour of a sigh;
> It fell from *Cupid's* burnish'd wing
> As forcefully he drew the string;
> Which sent his keenest, surest dart
> Thro' a rebellious frozen heart;
> That had till then defy'd his pow'r,
> And vacant beat thro each dull hour. (lines 5–14)[14]

The lines begin by presenting two separate events simultaneously. First, there is the act of Apollo snatching the golden quill out of the air, dipping it into the waters of the Ionian Sea, and giving it to Della Crusca to write with. Second, there is the more conventional act of Cupid piercing Anna Matilda's "rebellious frozen heart." These two actions are joined metaphorically through the figure of the quill pen, which functions as an emblem of Apollo's wand and of Cupid's dart and which, in both guises, thrills the heart. These same two events, however, are also joined metonymically through the body of Cupid, since the golden quill falls from his wing as he fires the arrow that pierces Anna Matilda's heart. If these multiple relationships between figures were not enough, the passage's final three lines create a further set of associations by gesturing back to the poem that inspired Anna Matilda's response in the first place. Della Crusca's "The Adieu and Recall to Love" first had banished Cupid and then, finding life without love a "frozen apathy" and a "cold vacuity of mind," had recalled him. "To Della Crusca: The Pen," in turn, represents Anna Matilda's heart as having the same symptoms of coldness, emptiness, and boredom before having her "vacant" and "rebellious frozen heart" awakened to love. The lines, then, associate the two hearts through shared sentiments and shared images, and imply that both, once inflamed, will burn with the same sympathy and with the same poetic brightness.

In Cowley's poem we see a number of the rhetorical gestures that would become definitive of Della Cruscan writing. The short couplets and the piling of tropes and sound patterns recall earlier poets like Jonathan Swift and Anne Finch, while the unusual mixture of conventional symbolism, sensual specificity, and sheer theatricality more closely resembles sentimental poetry after Gray.[15] Like the *Miscellany's* salon exchanges, the Della Crusca - Anna Matilda correspondence depends upon writerly dialogue, Cowley and Merry increasingly taking their cues not from past poets but from one another, appropriating entire passages of the other's poems as raw materials for further expression so each new poem arises, phoenix-like, out of the spent ashes of its predecessor. In later stages of the exchange, Cowley acknowledges these characteristics by repeatedly defining her own and Della Crusca's verse as spontaneous and improvisational. Her own missives frequently call attention to their own speed of composition, carrying subtitles like "Sent just forty hours after the publication of the preceding" and constantly placing Anna Matilda in the attitude of having just finished reading Della Crusca's own poem. She also is more than willing to reprimand Della Crusca for writing verse that is too finished, too serious, or too conventional:

> I hate thy tardy Elegiac lay—
> Chuse me a measure jocund as the day! . . .
> And be thy lines irregular and free,
> Poetic chains should fall before such Bards as thee.
> Scorn the dull laws that pinch thee round
> Raising about thy verse a mound,
> O'er which thy muse, so lofty! dares not bound
> Bid her in verse meand'ring sport;
> Her footsteps quick, or long, or short,
> Just as her various passion wills—
>
> (Dec. 22, 1787; lines 1–2, 13–20)

Later poems by Cowley consistently define poetry along these lines, presenting it as involuntary possession or as spontaneous, sincere, unplanned, and unlabored utterance. Deliberately consumable and temporary, they are perfectly suited to the disposable medium of newsprint.

Making a Proper Name

The name of an author poses all the problems related to the category of the proper name. . . . Obviously not a pure and simple reference, the proper name (and the author's name as well) has other than indicative functions. . . . it is, to a certain extent, the equivalent of a description.
. . . . .

> A [proper] name can group together a number of texts and thus dif-
> ferentiate them from others. A [proper] name also establishes different
> forms of relationships among texts.
>
> —Michel Foucault, "What Is An Author?"[16]

While *The Baviad* has never been described as spontaneous or unlabored, the poem's first reviewers differed from posterity in also considering it nei-ther original nor prophetic. Judged in its first years as unpleasantly topical and partisan, the poem's reputation shifted only with the turn of the nine-teenth century, its changing status connected to a concurrent rise in Gif-ford's own literary authority. Between 1791 and 1809, Gifford moved from being perceived as an indiscriminating satirist and partisan newspa-per editor (for *The Anti-Jacobin*) to a respected translator and prestigious journal editor (for *The Quarterly Review*). In these same years *The Baviad* came to be perceived as primarily an aesthetic critique rather than an eco-nomic and political one, acquiring the status of a respected satire and nec-essary defense of immutable critical law. The poem's ascent to the status of critical gospel, therefore, occurred quite early in the nineteenth century—as early as Byron's retrospective account to the Veronese poet Ippolito Pin-demonte "that they [the Della Cruscans] were 'all gone dead,'—& damned by a satire more than thirty years ago—that the name of their extinguisher was Gifford—that they were but a sad set of scribes after all."[17] This is the account, anyway, standardized at the turn of the twentieth century in the *Dictionary of National Biography*, which describes the Della Cruscans as "poetasters," "scribblers," and "fantastic coxcombs," and which, in the process, quotes, praises, and paraphrases Gifford's poem some dozen times in eight articles.[18]

Yet the immediate reception of Gifford's poem demonstrates, among other things, that this claim is not true. Gifford neither was the first to crit-icize the supposed excesses of Della Cruscan writings,[19] nor was he particu-larly successful in stemming the tide of poetry published in *The World* and its chief rival, *The Oracle*.[20] Published well after the Della Crusca - Anna Matilda correspondence had ended, *The Baviad* received sparing reviews that expressed significant reservations.[21] And throughout the 1790s he would be attacked repeatedly—in print by the targets of his satire and by pe-riodicals like the *Monthly Magazine*, and in person by the formidable John Wolcot ("Peter Pindar") in a bookshop brawl, the opposing accounts of which are so at odds with one another that they perfectly capture the ado-lescent nastiness of Gifford's poem and its reception.[22]

From its first publication, however, the poem also was enthusiastically promoted by Tory journalists and social conservatives, who saw in it qual-ities worth duplicating and celebrating. Thus supported and imitated, *The*

Baviad can be said to have invented its own subgenre of satire. Its cumbersome notes, elaborate classical buttressing, and merciless stream of abuse struck its supporters as a timely marriage of poetic form and rhetorical violence.[23] Its first lines, furthermore, presented a reductive yet fairly convincing critique of Della Cruscan poetics—one that categorized everything as either surface or depth, and that associated the latter category ("depth") with merit and truth and the former ("surface") with artifice and falsehood:

> Lo, Della Crusca! In his closet pent,
> He toils to give the crude conception vent.
> Abortive thoughts that right and wrong confound,
> Truth sacrificed to letters, sense to sound;
> False glare, incongruous images, combine;
> And noise and nonsense clatter thro' the line.
> 'Tis done. Her house the generous Piozzi lends,
> And thither summons her blue-stocking'd friends;
> The summons her blue-stocking'd friends obey,
> Lur'd by the love of Poetry—and Tea.[24]

This passage has proven so influential to critical opinion about Della Cruscan writing that its rhetorical strategies deserve scrutiny. It posits an analogy—that right is to wrong as truth is to letters (and, further, as sense is to sound)—before aligning Della Crusca with "sound" and its associates, "noise and nonsense." Gifford then shifts his critical ground slightly: rather than simply aligning Della Crusca with falsity and against truth, he accuses him of confounding the difference between the two in order to disrupt moral clarity through his "crude conception[s]." The passage's most inventive act, however, is the one of substitution that follows. Having constructed two oppositional sets of terms (right and wrong, truth and letters, sense and sound, real poetry and Della Cruscan poetry), Gifford animates the latter, illegitimate set of terms in the form of Piozzi and her "blue-stocking'd friends," who act as embodiments of the "false glare [and] incongruous images" of "the Bard" Della Crusca's poetic style:

> The BARD steps forth, in birth-day splendour drest,
> His right hand graceful waving o'er his breast;
> His left extending, so that all may see,
> A roll inscrib'd "THE WREATH OF LIBERTY." ...
> And now 'tis silence all. "GENIUS OR MUSE."
> Thus, while the flowry subject he pursues,
> A wild delirium round th' assembly flies;
> Unusual lustre shoots from Emma's eyes,

Luxurious Arno drivels as he stands,
And Anna frisks, and Laura claps her hands.

(lines 45–48, 53–58)

The aim here is to represent the scene of the Della Cruscan salon as a travesty of a real poetry reading, where a false poet reads a poem full of false glare
and false politics to an audience with false pretenses to taste. Both the political and the masculine heft of the Continental salon are systematically denied here. The gathering's pretense of critical engagement and intellectual
conversation hides motives at once more trivial ("Tea") and more dangerously erotic and bacchanalian, as Gifford associates the "liberty" of Della Crusca's poem with the "unusual lustre" and "frisk[ing]" of an overwhelmingly
female company.

After *The Baviad* was published, Gifford made his authorship known
through various channels despite the numerous advantages of remaining
anonymous.[25] It is easy to see why. A poem claiming to defend classical
virtue and neoclassical aesthetics, that champions unfettered indignation
and transparency of signification, requires, at least through private channels
of communication, an authorizing signature. These considerations also
begin to explain Gifford's Augustan invocation of "critics' laws," his obsessive Latin quotations, and his decision to write the poem as "a paraphrastic
imitation of the first satire of Persius," printing it in its first edition side-by-
side with its Latin source text. Built on this solid foundation, the satire itself
deploys similar assumptions and logic, representing the Della Cruscans as a
"thousand nameless names"[26] who produce "laboured nothings" (26)—and,
in the passage below, insisting on *reattaching* the pseudonyms of Merry, Jerningham, Piozzi, Cowley, and Robinson to their middle-aged bodies in order
to render the youthful eroticism of the fictional personae ridiculous:

Yet when I view the follies that engage
The full-grown children of this piping age;
See snivelling Jerningham at fifty weep
O'er love-lorn oxen and deserted sheep;
See Cowley frisk it to one ding-dong chime,
And weakly cuckold her poor spouse in rhyme;
See Thrale's grey widow with a satchel roam,
And bring in pomp her labour'd nothings home;
See Robinson forget her state, and move
On crutches tow'rds the grave, to "Light o' Love"

(lines 19–28)

The poem thus aligns assumed names with assumed taste, and casts pseudonyms as illegitimate adulterations of authorial dignity. The bastardized

writing produced under them is fit only for "prurient ears" that at best can bestow "transitory fame." Such passages demand that writers write only as themselves and that they "author" their work in that word's most literal sense—with their physical persons and legal identities.

Beginning with Thomas James Mathias, whose poem *The Pursuits of Literature* (1794–1797) transformed Gifford's fondness for footnotes into an end in itself,[27] *The Baviad* was extolled over the next decades by party faithful in verse and in prose. Mathias, for example, had praised Gifford lavishly while aligning his own project with that of *The Baviad*,[28] and the notoriety of both poems produced other tributes: *The New Morality* (1798) extolled Gifford and Mathias as Pope's true heirs; *The Unsex'd Females* (1798) featured a dedication to Mathias with complimentary notes to Gifford; *Innovation* (1799) vowed to continue both writers' vigilance; and *Cordelia; Or, A Romance of Real Life* (1799) lampooned Della Cruscan writing in language borrowed from *The Baviad and Mæviad*.[29] On the other side of the Atlantic, William Cobbett reprinted *The Baviad and Mæviad* and *The Unsex'd Females* in American editions, calling Gifford a man of "genius and taste";[30] and when news of Merry's death in Baltimore reached England, *The Gentleman's Magazine,* in a stunning piece of partisan reporting, published an abusive "obituary" that took most of its text from *The Mæviad*'s preface and Mathias's *Shade of Alexander Pope on the Banks of the Thames* (1798).[31]

While the reciprocal blandishments of these Tory satirists resemble practices Gifford originally had attacked in the Della Cruscans, they had lasting effects on Gifford's reputation. They were aided, furthermore, by a number of unforeseeable events. The death of Merry in 1798 and Robinson in 1800, the unsuccessful late publications of Piozzi, and the effective ceasing of literary activity after 1796 by Cowley, Greatheed, Topham, and Parsons meant that the literary careers of the most important Della Cruscans had effectively ended by 1800.[32] After 1802, while *Baviad*-inspired satires like *The Simpliciad* (1807) and *The Modern Dunciad* (1814) continued to abuse the Della Cruscans in Gifford's terms, no sustained defenses of the movement appeared, so that Gifford's swaggering claim to having "scattered" the Della Cruscans, it seems, had become either received truth or at least accepted fantasy. A decade after Byron's report to Pindemonte, Walter Scott would write in his *Journal* that Gifford's "translation of Juvenal is one of the best versions ever made of a classical author and his Satire of the *Baviad* and *Mæviad* squabashd at one blow a set of coxcombs who might have humbugd the world long enough."[33]

As Scott's entry suggests, Gifford's publication in 1802 of *The Satires of Decimus Junius Juvenalis* played an even greater role in elevating *The Baviad* than the absence of dissenting pro–Della Cruscan voices after 1800. The translation earned him immediate acclaim and, with his later edition of Massinger, established him as a classicist and scholar rivaling Dryden, Johnson, and Malone.[34] This shift in cultural status is registered earliest in the *Juvenal* edition's reviews, where Gifford is treated generously and read painstakingly. Byron's praise of Gifford as "the first satirist of the day," both in his correspondence and in *English Bards and Scotch Reviewers* (1809), is a fairly good indicator of his status after 1805.[35] And while Gifford never entirely rid himself of his taste for literary brawling, the prestige of these publications led, by 1809, to his being offered the position of editor of *The Quarterly Review,* later becoming publisher John Murray's confidential critical advisor as well—positions he maintained until the year of his death.[36]

The acclaim accorded to the *Juvenal,* however, does not entirely explain the name Gifford made for himself in these years or the ironies attending it. Here the reviews provide an instructive barometer of reputation, and what the positive notices share without exception is their strong association of Gifford with Juvenal that extends beyond textual to personal, and even bodily, virtues. Part of this no doubt stemmed from Gifford's decision to include an autobiographical memoir along with one of Juvenal, and his readers were quick to note the similarities between the two. Explaining the project's long delays and the hardships of his early life, Gifford's account in many ways attracted even greater attention than the translation itself. Thus, we find *The Monthly Review* representing Gifford as both ventriloquist and medium, and *The Gentleman's Magazine* praising Gifford for his ability to assume Juvenal's voice "with peculiar energy . . . [h]e has insinuated himself completely into the nature of his author's style and opinions, tracked his latent meanings, and caught his spirit."[37]

It is this preoccupation with "spirit" and its relation to authorial identity that ultimately propels the institutionalization of Gifford and his satires in nineteenth-century literary criticism. With Gifford's earlier political satires forgotten, the reviews shift the focus of their analysis, no longer reading Gifford in his immediate political context and instead reading his early partisan attacks as essential traits of his Juvenalian style. This move from context to style carries with it an essentializing poetics that transforms materiality into detritus, redefining context as a waste product of genuine Romantic inspiration. Yet what is most striking here is the power of "spirit" to effect material changes in context and in literary reputation—changes all the more ironic given the Della Cruscans' own reputation for writing airily and striving after sublimity and idealism. More than any other consideration, then, Juvenal's spiritual essence vindicates *The Baviad* by claiming a kind of underlying authenticity and cultural authority for it that no "paraphrastic imitation" can achieve.[38] Both Byron's *English Bards and Scotch Reviewers* and Francis Hodgson's *Childe Harold's Monitor* (1818), for example, call upon

Gifford the translator and editor to break his satirical silence, the latter arguing that "nature placed him [Gifford] for the stay and support of the yet remaining taste [on] that throne of moral satire."[39] In Foucault's terms, one might imagine this process—first of bestowing authorial status and second of rereading a writer's works through the lens of that status—as a specific kind of "author-function," one that imposes authorial coherence and consistency upon a career that need not be governed by such principles.[40]

But this is not the only kind of function or effect at work here. If Gifford's earlier condemnations of the Della Cruscans become in some sense "owned" by Juvenal, then the same thing can be said of Gifford's own literary identity. With increasing regularity, the same reviews that marveled at Gifford's ability to "out-Juvenal Juvenal" also began to project Juvenalian traits upon him. Thus *The British Critic* infused Gifford with Juvenal's "vigorous and masculine wit"[41] as a way of explaining Gifford's combativeness, while *The Monthly Review* extended these same traits beyond character even to physical presence.[42] Repeatedly we see the sickly and partially disabled Gifford represented as "manly," "robustly virtuous," "vigorous," and "masculine." Such a process is taken to its logical conclusion in places like Martin Shee's *Rhymes on Art* (1805) and Byron's correspondence, where both writers refer to Gifford simply as "Juvenal."[43]

To happen upon these moments of identification is to witness at once a typical moment of authorial self-fashioning and something more unsettling, since Gifford's acquisition of the name "Juvenal" marks the replacement of his own authorial identity with that of an earlier writer. This strikes me as at once the most ancient of models of literary authority and a curiously modern one. On one hand, it is based in imitation of the classics; on the other, it registers in ways similar to the marketing of twentieth-century paperbacks or late-eighteenth-century circulating library books. Here the *Baviad,* in effect, is repackaged after 1802 as being "by the author of *Juvenal.*" The effect, moreover, seems familiarly Della Cruscan in its linking of persona to inspired poetic performance, not to mention the way that Juvenal's name here functions, like that of "Della Crusca," both as a kind of trademark and as a delimiter of style. It is a similarity no doubt worth savoring for its irony; yet the differences here tell us far more about the competing theories of authorship represented in each case. For far from being a Della Cruscan "nameless name"—as Gifford puts it—"Juvenal" is cultivated by Gifford because Juvenal is a *name with a name*—a name with recognizable and largely unassailable authority. Based in languages to which few have access, Gifford's model of authorship seeks to banish all writers from the domain of authorship but a small group of learned gentlemen. Piozzi's own comments in her *Thraliana,* furthermore, confirm that what is at stake in the difference between Della Cruscanism and older models of authorship are these issues of access and authority:

This Fashion makes well for us Women however, as Learning no longer forms any part of the Entertainment expected from Poetry—Ladies have therefore as good a Chance as People regularly bred to Science in Times when *fire-eyed Fancy* is said to be the only requisite of a Popular Poet.[44]

Applying Piozzi's analysis of gender and educational access to Gifford, we find *The Baviad* less a critique of Della Cruscan style than an attempt to stifle dissent and deny access to authority. It inflicts an ungentle assault on a group of writers presumed to have at best an imperfect grasp of the languages in which they are being attacked. Gifford's *Juvenal*, then, is all the more remarkable for how it adds to these ideas an embracing of economic conservatism and a rejection of market publishing. In narrating his own ascendance from cobbler's apprentice to scholar, Gifford's memoir not only provided the illusion that such paths of learning were open to all who had merit, but also suggested that the only way to achieve authorship with propriety was through the patronage of a worthy nobleman and benevolent subscribers. In this light, we begin to understand how strange and ultimately stifling an authorial construct Gifford's "Juvenal" is to other modes of writing—particularly to a mixed, significantly female Della Cruscan coterie possessing little classical education and writing under fictitious pseudonyms. Looking to writers like Mary Robinson, who wrote under multiple personae of both sexes, we can at the very least perceive the threat that Della Cruscanism posed to prevailing literary establishments. And it is this threat to literary authority—to books and authors, publishing and patronage—that produced *The Baviad* in the first place.

"Bell's Poetics"

If my analysis of the changing status of *The Baviad* has demonstrated anything, it is the extent to which a text's authority and reputation depend upon its medium and presentation—that the reputation of one work can transform another and in effect repackage it. In this essay's final section, therefore, I move from questions of style and models of authorship to the wider context of market publishing, since the final questions that remain—about *The Baviad*'s timing, form, and tone—cannot be answered otherwise.

Here, Gifford's introduction to *The Baviad* provides a useful starting point, since his stated reasons for attacking the Della Cruscans are at once suggestive and fundamentally evasive. Alternately inconsequential and dangerous, the Della Cruscans present a threat to public taste and morals not because of their own malice but because of an innovation in newspaper publishing:

Yendas, and Laura Marias, and Tony Pasquins, have long claimed a prescriptive right to infest our periodical publications: but as the Editors of them never pretended to criticise their harmless productions, they were merely perused, laughed at, and forgotten. A paper, therefore, which introduced their trash with hyperbolical encomiums, and called upon the town to admire it, was an acquisition of the utmost importance to these poor people, and naturally became the grand depository of their lucubrations. . . . [T]he first cargo of poetry arrived from Florence . . . [and] was given to the public through the medium of this favoured paper. There was a specious brilliancy in these exotics which dazzled the native grubs. . . . From admiration to imitation is but a step. Honest Yenda tried his hand at a descriptive ode, and succeeded beyond his hopes; Anna Matilda followed. . . . The fever turned to a frenzy: Laura Maria, Carlos, Orlando, Adelaide, and a thousand nameless names caught the infection; and from one end of the kingdom to the other, all was nonsense and Della Crusca.[45]

Both this passage and Gifford's account in general are remarkable for their density of critical metaphor. In less than two pages he represents Della Cruscan poets as fairly harmless vermin, as invading foreign insects, and as infectious fever. He then attaches further metaphors of sexual contagion and disease to this narrative by appending to the above passage an outrageous quotation from Juvenal's second satire that, in its original context, had chastised homosexual "transmission" between Roman philosophers.[46] Within such an array of representations one begins to wonder where the real threat lies—whether in the poetry itself, in the ease of its transmission, or in its means of delivery. Certainly a portion of Gifford's outrage lies in what he represents as a breakdown of editorial responsibility. Pseudonymical newspaper poetry, the passage suggests, would be better left unprinted but is harmless enough when left to founder in its own hackneyed conventionality. Here, however, the threat of Della Cruscanism is not stylistic. Rather, it stems from two separate transgressions upon this status quo, each disguising the poetry's lack of merit: its importation of foreign, "exotic" forms; and its editors' interloping upon critical prerogative by lavishly praising it. The "infection" becomes an epidemic, then, because of editorial malpractice and misuse of authority. Rather than discouraging contact between diseased poets, the editors of *The World* have encouraged a promiscuous assembly of them, thereby necessitating the intervention of an indignant satirist.

Gifford's explanation and *The Baviad*'s indignation, however, are curiously belated. Published in December 1791, *The Baviad* appeared well after Hannah Cowley ceased writing poetry under the name "Anna Matilda" and over two and a half years after Merry had shed the pseudonym "Della Crusca." Gifford's own account of why he waited so long to publish his poem, furthermore, is hardly convincing:

> Even THEN, I waited with a patience which I can better account for, than ex-
> cuse, for some one (abler than myself) to step forth to correct the growing de-
> pravity of the public taste, and check the inundation of absurdity now
> bursting upon us from a thousand springs. As no one appeared, and as the evil
> grew every day more alarming, (for bed-ridden old women, and girls at their
> samplers, began to rave,) I determined, without much confidence of success,
> to try what could be effected by my feeble powers; and accordingly wrote the
> following poem.[47]

The explanation, of course, "accounts for" little; instead, with a comic gesture to those reliable bugbears old women and young girls, Gifford simply
describes the "evil" as growing "every day more alarming." Yet if we are to
judge from the pages and circulation figures of *The World*, we find the Della
Cruscan "epidemic" either exaggerated or decidedly receding by the time
that Gifford penned *The Baviad*. While immensely successful well into
1789, *The World* by the time of *The Baviad*'s publication was foundering and
less than a year away from ceasing production due to poor circulation.[48] Reviews of its poetry were for the most part positive but reserved. For most of
1789 and 1790, moreover, *The World*'s principal poetic draw had been the
very un - Della Cruscan letters of "Simpkin the Second to his Brother Simon
in Wales" reporting the trial of Warren Hastings. The particulars of Gifford's
narrative, then, are less about the period 1790–91 than 1787–89—meaning
that, if we accept the explanation of Gifford's introduction that the primary
evil of Della Cruscanism lay in Merry and the pages of *The World*, *The
Baviad* at its publication was nearly years out of date. Given that Cowley,
Merry, and many of the other Della Cruscans had abandoned their correspondences and their pseudonyms by the late 1780s and moved on to other
projects, why did Gifford wait over two years, until late in 1791, to publish
his attack? And why attack in such excessive and vitriolic terms?

This question of *The Baviad*'s belatedness, I think, begins to be answered
when we cease exclusively to focus on *The World*'s poets and consider as well
its publisher, John Bell. Critical accounts of the Della Cruscans rarely mention Bell other than in passing; yet in *The Baviad* he is attacked more often
and at greater length than any other target. Often, the Della Cruscans function as mere satellites of Bell's larger empire—as "Bell's ever-jingling train"—
while *The World*'s effusive introductions to their poems are personified as
puffs from the "critic Bell." Even more striking is Gifford's representation of
Della Cruscan poetic style:

> Some love the verse that like Maria's flows,
> No rubs to stagger, and no sense to pose;
> Which read, and read, you raise your eyes in doubt,
> And gravely wonder—what it is about.

These fancy "BELL's POETICS" only sweet,
And intercept his hawkers in the street;[49]

"Bell's poetics" may signify the same privileging of sound over sense that we earlier saw directed at Merry's poetry, but the above passage supplements this with the additional element of trade. Just as Gifford had insisted on reattaching Della Cruscan pseudonyms to the aging bodies of their writers, here he does the same with the poems themselves, reconnecting them to the newspaper "hawkers" who originally sold *The World* to the public. Later in *The Baviad* Bell acquires an almost institutional presence resembling modern multinational corporations, a sense echoed in Stanley Morison's account of him as being "a syndicate in himself, responsible for a [fundamental] change in books and newspapers, and in the types in which they were printed."[50]

Backed by Bell, then, the Della Cruscans comprised something more than merely a confederation of poets with an identifiable poetics. For Gifford, they made up part of a more general threat—not only to literary taste but also to the bookselling and reviewing institutions that supposedly defended and regulated it. Thus, when Gifford attacks "Bell's poetics," he is not merely attacking Della Cruscan poets but also the printing and publishing empire backing them.

Given Bell's history in the London book trade, it is not difficult to see why. Like most eighteenth-century entrepreneurs, Bell is a shadowy figure. Leigh Hunt's description of Bell as "a speculator in elegant typography [with] a certain liberal instinct, and a turn for large dealing" is the only contemporary account of any length we have of him.[51] In an age obsessed with personalities Bell is known to us almost exclusively through his actions and publications. The first available records of him are in 1769 as successor to Bathoe's circulating library in the Strand, which he eventually renamed Bell's British Library.[52] He was most famous in his own day for his role in publishing *The Morning Post* in the 1770s—the first newspaper to make a significant business out of bribery and extortion, systematizing and expanding these practices so until they became its principal source of revenue. Bell made his most lasting reputation, however, through inexpensive pocket reprints of British poets and dramatists published in the wake of the landmark case *Donaldson v. Becket,* the 1774 decision by the House of Lords that implemented the 1710 copyright act of Queen Anne, thereby ending perpetual copyright in Britain. Bell's *Shakspeare* (11 vols., 1774) and Bell's *British Theatre* (20 vols., 1774–76) were both successful; but when Bell announced *Poets of Great Britain from Chaucer to Churchill* (109 vols., 1777–82), a group of thirty-six London booksellers, calling themselves "the trade," boycotted Bell's edition and announced a rival one, *Works of the English Poets* (60 vols., 1779), with biographical essays by Samuel Johnson.[53] The success of the collection—known, like other Bell collections, by its "Bell" brand name and through its advertised name of "*Bell's British Poets*"—effectively broke up the monopoly of London booksellers on reprints, and it is for this reason that Charles Knight refers to him as "the very Puck of booksellers."[54]

Thus, when Bell decided to collect the verse of Della Crusca, Anna Matilda, and others in book form under the title of *The British Album* late in 1790, he did so with the greatest fanfare possible. Like other Bell books, this was to be elegantly bound and ornately printed. Bell's own advertisements in his new paper, *The Oracle,* informed "the LOVERS of POETRY, and ADMIRERS of FINE PRINTING and ENGRAVING . . . that the[se] Volumes will associate properly with BELL's CLASSICAL ARRANGEMENT of FUGITIVE POETRY, which is so universally admired for the purity of the Collection, and the very beautiful manner in which it is executed."[55] Carrying the imprint "J. Bell, at the British Library," Bell's *British Album*—in its size, printing, arrangement, and engravings—was meant to resemble Bell's other anthologies, especially *Bell's Fugitive Poetry, Bell's British Theatre,* and *Bell's British Poets.* The implication made through the book's printing and title, needless to say, is that the poets contained in Bell's *British Album* possess a merit at least analogous to the poets of other Bell books. We see a similar swagger in its dedication to Richard Brinsley Sheridan, which stated the book's contents "to possess intrinsic merit, and to deserve their fame, which have received the sanction of the best Critic, the first Scholar, and the most admired Genius of the Age."[56]

While my earlier discussion of *The Florence Miscellany* suggested that its contents might have been read differently when transmitted from book to periodical, Bell's *British Album* forces us to ask, among other things, what happens when this direction of transmission is reversed. What happens when newspaper poems, through a change of medium, rapidly ascend literary hierarchies and are printed in a form that attempts to bestow upon them canonical status? What happens when they reappear, showered with the most lavish praise, and appearing in a form reserved only for the greatest and most anthologized of England's national poets?

In a sense, I think we need go no further in order to understand what moved Gifford finally to write *The Baviad.* But I wish to end this essay by stressing the extent to which we misunderstand the erasure of Della Cruscan poetry from literary canons after 1800 if we see that erasure of "Bell's Poetics" merely as the rejection of a literary style. Looking back to Gifford's poem and notes one final time, we find them representing Bell in nearly every instance as a transgressor not only upon authorial but also upon critical privilege. Thus, in addressing Della Crusca, Gifford attributes his poor poetry and bad taste to his being duped, like the public at large, by Bell's praise:

> O fool, fool, fool!—But still, thou criest, 'tis sweet
> To hear "That's HE!" from every one we meet;
> That's he whom critic Bell declares divine,
> For whom the fair diurnal laurels twine;
> Whom Magazines, Reviews, conspire to praise,
> And Greathead calls the Homer of our days.[57]

Part of the reason that *The Baviad* has struck most twentieth-century ears as strangely paranoid and merciless, then, lies in our misunderstanding of the conspiracy of praise that it imagines. Already proprietor of a circulating library, a press, a newspaper, and a train of writers ready to declare each other's productions divine, John Bell—above all other things—presented a threat to Gifford's notion of a print culture regulated by a professional critical audience. He threatened to bypass this regulatory institution through the economic control he exercised over all aspects of literary production, including advertising, circulation, and reception. Thus, if I ultimately locate the origin of Gifford's *Baviad* and its successors in Bell's publication of *The British Album*, it is because *The British Album* presented the first instance in which the Della Cruscans appeared in high cultural packaging accompanied by unqualified assertions of their unquestionable merit. Outraged at Bell taking poetry from its original newsprint and republishing it in book form as a permanent contribution to the nation's literature, Gifford was moved to attack the movement with vigor and with abandon, presenting himself as a defender of British letters, British publishing, and, most of all, the British book. For Gifford, then, Bell's attempts to repackage Della Cruscan verse into high cultural artifacts amounted to multiple usurpations of literary authority: of the poetic "work" by improvised, self-consuming verse, of book by newspaper, and of critic by bookseller.

Notes

1. See Jerome J. McGann, "The Literal World of the English Della Cruscans," in *Fins de Siecle: English Poetry in 1590, 1690, 1790, 1890, 1990,* ed. Elaine Scarry (Baltimore and London: Johns Hopkins University Press, 1995), 96–97.

2. See, for example, *Dictionary of National Biography* articles on William Gifford, Robert Merry, and Mary Robinson. See also John Mark Longaker, *The Della Cruscans and William Gifford* (Philadelphia: University of Pennsylvania Press, 1924), 44; Roy Benjamin Clark, *William Gifford: Tory Satirist, Critic, and Editor* (New York: Columbia University Press, 1930), 36–80; W. N. Hardgreaves-Mawdsley, *The English Della Cruscans and Their Time 1783–1828* (The Hague: Martinus Nijhoff, 1967), 179.

3. McGann, "The Literal World of the English Della Cruscans," 96.

4. See Judith Pascoe, *Romantic Theatricality: Gender, Poetry, and Spectatorship* (Ithaca, NY: Cornell University Press, 1997), 68–94.

5. See Jerome McGann, *The Romantic Ideology: A Critical Investigation* (Chicago: University of Chicago Press, 1983), 1–3.

6. See Pascoe, *Romantic Theatricality,* 71; and McGann, "The Literal World of the English Della Cruscans," 96. While Pascoe argues that we cannot understand "interconnections between Della Cruscanism and an evolving Romantic ethos" without attending to gender, McGann is more sweeping in seeing the Della Cruscans as proto-Romantic: "Every one of the so-called major Romantics was deeply marked by sentimental conventions of writing, and there is an important (unremembered) sense in which Keats, Shelley, and Byron are the supreme legacy of the Della Cruscan movement in particular."

7. For earlier studies that assert the Della Cruscans' ties to the Romantic movement, see Longaker, *The Della Cruscans and William Gifford,* 44–46, 62; Roderick Marshall, *Italy in English Literature* (New York: Columbia University Press, 1934), 180; James L. Clifford, "Robert Merry—Pre-Byronic Hero," *Bulletin of the John Rylands Library* 27 (1947): 74–96; Edward E. Bostetter, "The Original Della Cruscans and the *Florence Miscellany,*" *Huntington Library Quarterly* 19 (1956): 277–78, 298; and Hardgreaves-Mawdsley, *The English Della Cruscans and Their Time,* 43, 56–59.

8. For a study taking a similar approach to the relation of the Della Cruscans to second-generation Romanticism, see Steven Jones, *Satire and Romanticism* (New York: St. Martin's Press, 2000), 110–38.

9. For accounts of *The Florence Miscellany's* experimentation with Italian verse forms, see Marshall, *Italy in English Literature,* 176–91; Bostetter, "The Original Della Cruscans and the *Florence Miscellany,*" 296.

10. Appearing piecemeal in the pages of the *European* and *Gentleman's* magazines, the *Miscellany* remained unknown to British readers as an intact collection—its contents excerpted by the *European* and *Gentleman's* magazines and the excerpts themselves chosen as evidence of Piozzi's celebrity abroad. The *Gentleman's Magazine,* for example, printed Piozzi's preface in January 1787 and in March printed five poems that portray the group as pleasantly convivial: Piozzi's "To Wm. Parsons, Esqr."; Parsons' "To Mrs. Piozzi in Reply"; Merry's "To Mrs. Piozzi"; Greathead's "When Emma first I saw"; and Piozzi's "Conclusion." See *The Gentleman's Magazine* 57 (1787): 3, 257–58. When we look to the much larger selection of twenty-eight poems published by *The European Magazine* between February 1786 and April 1787, moreover, we see there the same principles of unrepresentative selection at work. Many of these same poems had earlier been reprinted in the *London Chronicle* on February 14–16 and May 30 to June 1, 1786, and were again reprinted only a few weeks later in *The World.* It is through this kind of repetition of the same poems across multiple publications that we begin to understand why Gifford, having never read the volume in its entirety, dismissed *The Florence Miscellany* as harmless folly.

11. The claim is from Stanley Morison, *Captain Topham 1751–1820* (Cambridge: Cambridge University Press, 1933), 19–20; my own sampling of late-eighteenth- and nineteenth-century newspapers confirms the assertion. See as well Nicholas Barker, *Stanley Morison* (Cambridge, MA: Harvard University Press, 1972), 294: "When the *Daily Universal Register* became *The Times* in 1788, its title was in decent roman capitals. But within three months John Walter changed it to imitate a rival. . . . *The World's* taste in titling."

12. Lucyle Werkmeister, *The London Daily Press 1772–1792* (Lincoln: University of Nebraska Press, 1963), 158.

13. Here also see Pascoe, *Romantic Theatricality,* chapter 3.

14. Hannah Cowley, "To Della Crusca: The Pen," in *The World,* July 10, 1787.

15. For extended discussions of Della Cruscanism's use of embodied symbols and romance images, see McGann, "The Literal World of the English Della Cruscans," 106–108; and Jacqueline Labbe, *The Romantic Paradox: Love, Violence and the Uses of Romance, 1760–1830* (Basingstoke and New York: Macmillan/St. Martin's Press, 2000), 55–62.

16. Michel Foucault, "What Is an Author?" in *Language, Counter-memory, Practice: Selected Essays and Interviews,* ed. Donald F. Bouchard (Ithaca, NY: Cornell University Press, 1977), 113–38 (121, 123).

17. Byron to John Murray, June 4, 1817, in *Byron's Letters and Journals,* ed. Leslie A. Marchand, 12 vols. (London: John Murray, 1973–82), V, 233–34; hereafter *BLJ.*

18. See *DNB* articles on John Bell, Hannah Cowley, William Gifford, Bertie Greatheed, Robert Merry, Hester Thrale Piozzi, Mary Robinson, and Edward Topham.

19. See Clark, *William Gifford,* 53. For reviews of Della Cruscan works that anticipate Gifford, see *The English Review* 12 (Aug. 1788): 126–36; *The Monthly Review* 2nd series, 4 (January 1791): 56–60; and *The Monthly Review* 6 (Sept. 1791): 21–4. Gifford's own satire not only drew from the criticisms expressed by these reviewers, but also took at least its title from *Modern Poets: A Satire: To which is prefixed a dedication to the Monthly, the Critical, and the Analytical Reviewers* (London: J. Ridgeway, 1791), 30:

> An artificial fame our Poets raise,
> With zeal they praise, for 'tis themselves they praise.
> *Laura Maria* sings sweet *Arno's* powers,
> And *Arno* the soft dews of flatt'ry showers.
> *Yenda* to *Evelind,* and, back again,
> Fair *Evelind* returns th'abundant strain.
> 'Tis "*Muse immortal*"—'tis "*O Bard divine—*"
> 'Tis "*your mellifluous strain*"—"*your magic line!*"
> With such profound respect, so grave a face,
> They treat themselves, some sweat they're *Popes* and *Grays;*
> Congenial souls, the Muse can wish no ill!
> May every *Bavius* find his *Maevius* still!

20. Clark, *William Gifford,* 61, 72–74; and Bostetter, "The Original Della Cruscans," 298. Even Mathias, in the "Epistle to a Friend" that prefaces the complete edition of *The Pursuits of Literature* (Dublin: J. Milliken, 1798), notes that "the Bavian drops from Mr. Gifford have fallen off, like oil, from the plumage of the Florence and Cruscan geese [and] his success is imperfect. I am told, that Mr. Greatheed and Mr. Merry yet write and talk; and Mr. JERNINGHAM (poor man!) still continues *sillier than his sheep"* (p. xxiv).

21. See *The English Review* 19 (May 1792): 349–53; and *The Monthly Review* 8 (May 1792): 93–96.

22. Clark, *William Gifford,* 19–22; see as well *The Monthly Magazine* 7 (1799): 255–58.

23. For an informative and extended treatment of both Gifford and especially Mathias, see Gary Dyer, *British Satire and the Politics of Style, 1789–1832* (Cambridge: Cambridge University Press, 1997), esp. chapters 1–2.

24. William Gifford, *The Baviad* (London: R. Faulder, 1791), lines 35–44. All quotations from the text of this poem will be quoted parenthetically in the text, and cited by line number.

25. In 1794 Thomas James Mathias was especially vocal about the advantages to anonymity in the first dialogue of *The Pursuits of Literature:* "He has divulged his name *imprudently.* Such compositions require secrecy for their effect; especially if they are published at an early period of life, and still more if the poet commences his career with satire. See [Thomas James Mathias], *The Pursuits of Literature; A Satirical Poem in Four Dialogues; With Notes; The Fifth Edition, Revised and Corrected* (London: T. Becket, 1798), 9n.

26. Gifford, *The Baviad,* xiii.

27. Mathias's *The Pursuits of Literature,* for example, applauded Gifford in four separate passages between 1794 and 1797; his notes, furthermore, explicitly aligned the project of the poem with that of *The Baviad.*

28. See Mathias, *The Pursuits of Literature,* Dialogue 1, lines 17–24 and note to line 17; Dialogue 2, lines 35–6, 269–76; Dialogue 3, lines 287–96; Dialogue 4, lines 89–92.

29. See [George Canning and John Hookham Frere], "The New Morality," in *Poetry of the Anti-Jacobin* (London: J. Wright, 1799), especially lines 29–54; [Richard Polwhele], *The Unsex'd Females: A Poem, Addressed to the Author of the Pursuits of Literature* (London: Cadell and Davies, 1798), 6n; [Thomas Gisborne], *Innovation: A Poem* (London: Cadell and Davies, 1799), 7; [Sophia Fortnum], *Cordelia, or, A Romance of Real Life, by Sophia King,* 2 vols. (London: Minerva Press, 1799), esp. 50–53.

30. William Gifford, *The Baviad and Mæviad; To which is Prefixed, a Poetical Epistle to the Author by an American gentleman* (Philadelphia: William Cobbett, 1799); Richard Polwhele, *The Unsex'd Females; A Poem, Addressed to the Author of The Pursuits of Literature; To Which Is Added, a Sketch of the Private and Public Character of Peter Pindar* (New York: William Cobbett, 1800). The quotation is taken from Clark, *William Gifford,* p. 59.

31. *Gentleman's Magazine* 69.1 (March 1799): 252–54. The obituary, while having next to nothing positive to say about Merry, praised Gifford as the "most *correct* poetical writer since Pope," and as one who had exposed "the pernicious tendency [of] the influence of the CRUSCAN SCHOOL upon our taste in poetry" (253). Merry was to receive similar treatment in *Literary Memoirs of Living Authors*, 2 vols. (London: R. Faulder, 1798), I, 205–206; II, 42. Given the similarities in the two entries, it is likely either that both texts are written by the same author, or that *The Gentleman's Magazine* plagiarized significant selections of the entries for Gifford and Merry in *Literary Memoirs*.

32. The opposing obituaries of Merry in *The Gentleman's Magazine* and *The Monthly Magazine* demonstrate the extent to which Della Cruscan writing could still produce fairly entrenched and partisan responses as late as 1799. See *Gentleman's Magazine* 69.1 (1799): 252–54; and *The Monthly Magazine* 7 (1799): 255–58. While *The Gentleman's Magazine* mocked Merry's poetry and took most of its material from Gifford and Mathias, *The Monthly Magazine* praised Merry for his "beautiful verses" and "witty epigrams" and did not mention Gifford at all.

33. Walter Scott, entry for January 17, 1827, in *The Journal of Walter Scott*, ed. W. E. K. Anderson (Oxford: Clarendon, 1972), 265.

34. On the mediated reception of Gifford's *The Satires of Decimus Junius Juvenalis*, 2 vols. (London: W, Bulmer et al, 1802), see Steven E. Jones, "Intertextual Influences in Byron's Juvenalian Satire," *Studies in English Literature 1500–1900* 33 (1993): 772–73; and *Shelley's Satire: Violence, Exhortation, and Authority* (Dekalb: Northern Illinois University Press, 1994), 153–54.

35. See *BLJ*, II, 249. Byron praises Gifford in the preface and text of *English Bards and Scotch Reviewers*, lines 93–96, 699–706, 741–44, 777–82, and 818–30. See Byron, *The Complete Poetical Works*, I, 227–64.

36. See *BLJ*, XII, 92, which tracks, under the index entry for "Gifford," Gifford's critical advising at length.

37. *The European Magazine* 43 (1803): 149; *The Gentleman's Magazine* 72:2 (1802): 994, 898.

38. See Dyer, 174 n54.

39. Byron, *English Bards and Scotch Reviewers*, lines 699–706 and 818–30; Francis Hodgsden, *Childe Harold's Monitor* (London: J. Porter, 1818), 92–93; quoted in Dyer, 174 n54.

40. Foucault, "What Is an Author?," 130.

41. *British Critic* 20 (1802): 616.

42. *The Monthly Review* 40 (1803): 13.

43. See Martin Archer Shee, R.A., *Rhymes on Art, or, The Remonstrance of a Painter* (London: John Murray, 1805; Philadelphia: John E. Watson, 1811), pt. 2, lines 19–40. Shee calls Gifford "Thou Juvenal of more prolifick times!" (pt. 2, line 22). My thanks to Gary Dyer for this reference. See also Byron to Robert Charles Dallas, August 25, 1811 (*BLJ*, II, 80): "I also have

written to Mr. Murray my objection to sending the M.S. to Juvenal, but allowing it to show it to others of the calling."

44. Piozzi, *Thraliana*, 730.

45. Gifford, *The Baviad and Mæviad*, xi.

46. Gifford's quotation from Juvenal *Satires* 2.80 is "labem / Hanc dedit in plures, sicut grex totus in agris Unius scabie cadit, et porrigine porci." [Contact has given you this disease (homosexuality), and will pass it on to others, just as a whole flock will be destroyed through the scab or mange of a single pig."]

47. Gifford, *The Baviad and Mæviad*, xiv.

48. The Bell-Topham partnership dissolved early in 1789, and by June Bell had founded the rival *Oracle*. For information on *The World* and *The Oracle*, see Werkmeister, *The London Daily Press 1772–1792*, chapter 4; Sumbel, *Memoirs of Mrs. Sumbel*, I, 56–105; and Morison, *John Bell*, 7–30 and *Captain Topham*, 11–21.

49. Gifford, *The Baviad*, lines 181–86.

50. Morison, "John Bell," pamphlet advertisement for First Edition Club printing of *John Bell, 1745–1831*, 2.

51. Leigh Hunt, *Autobiography* (New York: Chanticleer Press, 1948), 151–55 (151). See as well Morison, "John Bell," 3.

52. William J. Cameron, "John Bell (1745–1831): A Case Study of the Use of Advertisement Lists as Evidence in Publishing History," *Humanities Association Review* 26:1 (Winter 1975): 201.

53. See Bonnell, "Bell's *Poets of Great Britain*," 142.

54. Charles Knight, *Shadows of the Old Booksellers* (New York: R. R. Bowker, 1927), 248. A. S. Collins, in *The Profession of Letters: A Study of the Relation of Author to Patron, Publisher and Public, 1780–1832* (London: Routledge, 1928), 59, calls Bell one of "the greatest educational force[s] of the last decade of the century."

55. *The Oracle*, December 17, 1789.

56. *The British Album*, n.p.

57. Gifford, *The Baviad*, lines 77–82.

Chapter 3 ∾

Black Bodies and Satiric Limits in the Long Eighteenth Century

Marcus Wood

The last thirty years have seen satire become significantly and centrally reintegrated into the heart of Romantic studies. The old literary historiography set out a master narrative. Satire was a magnificent neo-classical structure that decayed from the perfection of high Augustanism, becoming increasingly tatty through the late Augustan slump, to lie as an art of neglected ruins in the Romantic period. Byron alone among the major Romantic poets was seen as the central torch carrier for satire as high art. In this familiar story he emerged triumphant from his struggle with the shadow of Pope to create the distinctly robust and modern voice of *Don Juan,* the first satiric tertiary epic. This story has now been changed. The pioneering work of Jerome McGann and Marilyn Butler, and of cultural historians, all of whom ultimately originate with and return to E. P. Thompson, has encouraged Romanticists to think in new and more complicated ways about the definitions and operations of satire.[1] The extraordinary range and diversity of satire generated by the radical reform movement has been given its due. The role of parody has begun to be appreciated; viewed from within contemporary sites of literary contestation even the major bedrocks of the Romantic poetic canon have now been shown to be engaged in advanced forms of parody that are essentially satiric.[2]

In Romantic studies satire is back with a bang, and yet at least one area central to parody in the Romantic age appears to maintain an almost total resistance to being opened up by the pioneers of parodic and satiric theory. For all the laudable developments in satire studies, slavery, the slave body, and the associated subjects of slave trauma and interracial sexuality have apparently continued to lie beyond the pale.[3] In this chapter I think about what might be done with such a significant silence. I take a series of test cases, satiric poems written in the late eighteenth and early nineteenth centuries that take the black body and slavery as their central themes. The works that form the focus for the main body of this analysis were written from pro-slavery positions, or—perhaps more dangerously—from a position of amused detachment. What these works reveal is the weird and highly charged status of the slave body as a subject for satiric writing during the long eighteenth century. What they also reveal is that satire provided an unusually open space for the expression of white sexual pathologies related to the slave inheritance.

I want to frame this discussion by thinking about the strangeness of treating the black body in satire, whether that satire is written for or against slavery. The slave body is a peculiar subject for satire for several reasons. The first relates to the essentially abstract nature of the representation of African slaves during this period; both pro-slavery and anti-slavery rhetorics at the time constructed African slaves in ways that were essentializing, generalizing, and abstracting.[4] This consequently means that one of the central resources of the satirist, ad hominem (not to mention ad feminam) attack, is simply not an option. Individual white abolitionists, slavers, or plantation owners may be conventionally attacked, or defended, but black Africans or their descendants within the British sugar colonies are not. Individual slaves are not singled out in pro-slavery satire; clearly they cannot be taken that seriously. But anti-slavery satire also tended to ignore the slave, focusing upon the objects of vilification, the slave-trading sailors, the planter power, and their parliamentary supporters and representatives. It is only, in fact, within print satires of the late eighteenth and early nineteenth centuries that black persons, frequently ex-slaves, occasionally appear *as individuals* in collective satires directed against abolition, or more occasionally the activities of Radical reformers.[5] The tendency to abstract the slave body in anti-slavery literature comes out in extreme form in William Cowper's anti-slavery verse. Cowper wrote a huge variety of poetry on the theme of slavery and the slave trade. The subject dominated his religious and philosophical poetry from an early date.[6] Yet when he comes to treat the African body in satire, odd things happen to his rhetoric. Take for example what is probably the most bitter of the English satires written about the details of the Middle Passage, *Sweet Meat Has Sour Sauce: or, the Slave Trader in the Dumps.* In this poem Cowper attacks the enormities of the trade by creating a dramatic monologue in which through his speaker he in effect plays the role of slave trader, lamenting the effects of abolition on his industry. Obviously the satire works on the premise that the monstrous inhumanity of the trader is revealed in the callousness of his tone. Cowper's fictive trader can describe the most horrific tortures with a comic detachment, and speaks about the slaves as if they are animals:

> When a Negro his head from his victuals withdraws,
> And clenches his teeth and thrusts out his paws,
> Here's a notable engine to open his jaws,
>   Which nobody, &c. . . .
>
> . . . 'Twould do your heart good to see 'em below,
> Lie flat on their backs all the way as we go,
> Like sprats on a gridiron, scores in a row,
>   Which nobody, &c.[7]

Clearly the poem works as a satire through the device of simple inversion, on the premise that the black slaves are not what the slave trader perceives them to be. There is an implied pressure on the reader to reinvent the satiric subject as its opposite, to see the slaves as humans, not as creatures with paws, or even more weirdly as dead sprats. Yet the very rhetorical power of the verse paradoxically lies in its utter transformation of the slave body from human to animal, and finally to dead animal/fish. What Cowper's vision leaves us with, despite the suggestion that it is our duty not to accept this vision, is the animalized and finally abstracted slave body. The slave may be human but in this satiric world s/he cannot be fleshed out and presented as such because of the very imaginative mechanism that demands that we see the world through the slave captain's vision. This is essentially a problem in the politics of representation. When does irony end and complicity begin? It depends on the reception, we might suggest—on who the reader is and what they want to get out of the poem.

When Cowper is not playing parodic Devil's advocate, but speaking through his own satiric persona, things are no more straightforward. Take for example the following punchy little "Epigram from the Northhampton Mercury":

> To purify their wine some people bleed
> A *Lamb* into the barrel, and succeed;
> No Nostrum, Planters say, is half so good
> To make fine sugar, as a *Negro's* blood.
> Now lambs and negroes both are harmless things,
> And thence, perhaps, this wondr'ous Virtue springs,
> 'Tis in the blood of Innocence alone—
> Good cause why Planters never try their own.[8]

This is certainly clever, and is hard-hitting at the expense of the generalized "Planter." But look again at what is going on in the presentation of the black body. The black man is presented as a symbol of innocent suffering, precisely aligned with the Chistologically ambient Lamb of God. Yet that summary statement, "Lambs and negroes both are harmless things," contains the mechanism that both enables abolition to construct a black fiction and disempowers the slave as historical victim. Slaves were of course known in the slave trade to be far from "harmless things," which is why they had to be chained down in the ships and continually terrorized through the violence of the slave codes in the plantations. It is only within the carefully constructed mechanics of abolition thought that slaves are manufactured as "harmless things." The assumption was that they had to be constructed as passive victims in order to be accepted by a sceptical and easily frightened British readership. Slaves as black lambs to be petted and pitied are acceptable figures, slaves as uprooted Africans with the capacity to organize a revolution are imagined images falling completely outside the terms of Cowper's satire. But if anti-slavery satire could only see the slave as objectified victim, what options were open for the appropriation of the slave body in *pro*-slavery satire?

Pro-slavery verse satire provides ample demonstration of the extraordinary degree to which the abstraction and simultaneously pornographic exploitation of the slave body may operate within polite modes of social discourse. It also needs to be emphasized that interracial sexuality involving the white male domination of black—and white—females is treated in these works with a figurative excess that is, apparently, contained by no limits. Two poems serve as particularly condensed demonstrations of the bizarre qualities that inhabit Romantic-period forays into interracial intersexualities: James Boswell's *No Abolition of Slavery; or the Universal Empire of Love (Addressed to Miss——)*, and Isaac Teale's earlier *The Voyage of the Sable Venus*. Boswell's poem is a peculiarly challenging hybrid. It is both a love poem addressed to the white lady who is the object of Boswell's amorous obsession and, simultaneously, a detailed and quite cleverly viperous assault upon the leading abolitionists of the day. Teale's poem, written some twenty-five years earlier but finally published in 1793, is also a love poem, this time one directed at the idealized figure of the female African slave, and a satire on the absurdity of the project of writing such a poem in the first place.

As a young man James Boswell wrote a good deal of conventional and aesthetically unimpressive love poetry. A strain running throughout this woeful doggerel was to provide one half of the dialectic base for his later *No Abolition of Slavery; or the Universal Empire of Love,* a work that has a good claim to be the strangest pro-slavery satire ever created. The second section of the unpublished manuscript of Boswell's poetic juvenilia is entitled

"Amorous" and contains many verses constructed around the trope of the lover enslaved by his desire for the beloved. Sometimes the slavery is presented as the (almost) desirable fantasy of bondage through marriage, as in this platitudinous quatrain from the *Song to Mira:* "O, were I with my Mira bound / In Hymen's silken chain, / In transports we should run life's round / And scarcely think of Pain."[9] Pain is killed by the gentle chains of marriage; voluntary enslavement to the object of desire is presented in other contexts as a total sacrifice of will-power, an effacement of personality by the lover: "You say my charmer, that I swore, / When sighing at your feet, / That I should have a will no more. . . ."[10] Captivity and enslavement are imagistically made more explicit in later poems in the sequence: "While I was held by Chloë's chains, / And felt fierce love's fantastic pains, / Ah! What a wretched swain was I / Who dragg'd a life of misery!"[11] Boswell's linking of slavery and love climaxes with the warning that enslavement to beauty is contingent, and that when beauty fades this form of bondage ends: "Think not, fair one, that your slave / Vainly means in verse to rave; / Friendship only bids me say, / Love and beauty have their day."[12] Unremarkable as these little *jeaux d'amour* are as love poetry, they do indicate the extent to which a late-eighteenth-century literary gentleman and libertine felt at his ease linking the metaphorics of enslavement with the love lyric.

Enslavement through love is, of course, an old trope, most fully and ironically searched in Shakespeare's *The Tempest.* Shakespeare sets off Caliban's, and later Ferdinand's, enslavement by Prospero against Ferdinand's amorous fantasies of enslavement, through love, to Miranda.[13] In devolved and far less challenging forms the "slave to love" formula was repeated in innumerable seventeenth-century lyrics, climaxing in the love poems of the Cavalier poets. Boswell's youthful appropriations of this tradition are the fag end of a well-worn tradition. Yet in the early 1790s Boswell entered the slavery debates, and gave the love-as-slavery trope a cynical and clever new twist. Boswell was a staunch supporter of the planters' lobby in parliament. He decided to publish a satiric verse-attack upon the leading abolitionists and further to defend the property rights of the West India planters. One of the dangers inherent in writing pro-slavery satire is that of taking the slave too seriously as a subject. Merely by deciding to write satire on the subject of the abolition of the slave trade the satirist runs the danger of placing African enslavement center-stage as a social and human rights issue. Boswell's cynical formula for avoiding this danger lay in the facetious coupling of his amorous bondage fantasy with the serious political issue of abolition of the slave trade. He manages in this way to produce a poem that is saturated with strange sexual tensions, tensions that extend finally beyond the presentation of his own attempts at seduction and into his presentation of the leading abolitionists.

The love/slavery conceit frames the argument, occupying the first eight and the last forty lines of the poem. Boswell opens by addressing the young woman as a force that potentially controls the poet's troubled soul, yet even at this stage Boswell is playing with sexual imagery, although attention to contemporary etymology is required to see what he is up to:

> Most pleasing of thy sex,
> Born to delight and never vex;
> Whose kindness gently can controul
> My wayward turbulence of soul[14]

"Kindness" was a particularly charged word at this time, and the act of being kind when applied to a woman carried a range of meanings.[15] The obvious meanings as outlined in the OED would be "behaving with natural affection, lovingly," or "naturally well disposed; having a gentle, sympathetic, or benevolent nature" (OED, kind a, 4 c, d). Yet the word could also mean "pleasant or agreeable to the recipient," and to be kind could describe forms of pleasure that spill over into sexual innuendo. The OED cites a plethora of examples where to be kind means to have casual sex, often via prostitution. "Kind" meaning "the character or quality derived from birth or natural constitution" (OED, 3) extends to a specifically sexual connotation "to perform the sexual function" (OED, 3C) and in obsolete usage "kind" was a word for "the sexual organs" (OED, 6B) and "the semen" (OED, 6C). Again as an adjective "kind" is charged with sexual innuendo meaning "fondness" carried to extremes, "affectionate, loving, fond, on intimate terms, also euphemistically" (OED, 6). The dictionary's wonderfully arch "euphemistically" covers a wide range of sexual meanings. In several quoted examples to be "kind" means simply to have casual sex.

The kind of "kindness" Boswell is after is about control, and loss of control. Having set out the poem's premise (namely seduction of the mistress into the act of "kindness" whereby he will "controul" the poet's mad desire or "wayward turbulence of soul" through sexual release), Boswell then turns to contemporary politics and the abolition debate, asking the young woman if she ever reads the newspapers. After a lengthy verse peregrination around familiar arguments justifying the slave trade, the poem finally circles back to its opening theme to argue that Boswell's enslavement to this young woman through sexual desire proves the inevitability of slavery as part of the human condition. Abolition is consequently an impossible dream:

> My charming friend! It is full time
> To close this argument in rhime;
> The rhapsody must now be ended,

My proposition I've defended;
For Slavery there must ever be,
While we have Mistresses like thee!

(lines 293–298)

Yet before reaching this pat conclusion Boswell moves through a series of fantasies describing the process of enslavement though love. He produces an account of his imagined acceptance by the young woman in terms of a detailed parody of abolitionist accounts of the slave trade's operation:

By your keen roving glances caught,
And to a beauteous tyrant brought;
My head with giddiness turn'd round,
With strongest fetters I was bound;
I fancy from my frame and face,
Thou thought me of th'Angola race:
You kept me long indeed my dear,
Between the decks of hope and fear;
But this and all the *seasoning* o'er,
My blessings I enjoy the more.

Contented with my situation,
I want but little REGULATION;
At intervals *Chanson à boire*
And good old port in my *Code noire.*

(lines 275–288)

Here the process of falling in love and then getting married is mapped in terms of a slave's progress through the Atlantic slave trade. The process begins with kidnapping in Africa, Boswell identifying himself with a type of African slave who, as his footnotes set out, was seen as the most rebellious. He then relates his transportation below decks on the Middle Passage in a state of fear, his subsequent "seasoning" on the plantation, and final labor and torture ("REGULATION") on the plantations under the conditions of the slave code. Boswell in placing himself in competition with the slave victim through this curiously precise parodic narrative is making a move that is unnervingly close to that of many of the abolitionists. Boswell's ridicule is in fact extremely clever in terms of contemporary literary dialogics because his assumption of mimetic proximity to the slave's suffering, and his desire to appropriate (via the empathetic process) that suffering, runs so close to the imaginative moves that enable so much sentimental abolition literature.[16]

Boswell's cynical ingenuity is capable of exploiting the spaces opened up by his amatory apparatus in a series of ingenious ways within the central part of the poem. Packaged within his elaborate frame Boswell appears to rehearse a series of familiar pro-slavery arguments. He attacks the Clapham sect abolitionists for their sanctimoniousness, and as enemies of trade. He runs through the familiar arguments that the slaves are better off than the suffering poor in Britain, whether in urban centers, or the agricultural poor of Scotland. Yet throughout the meat of the argument a weird sexual dynamic, enabled by the poem's opening and its ending, is deliberately exploited. The argument concerning trade, for example, reaches a climax in an attack on Wilberforce:

> No longer to the Senate cackle,
> In strains which suit the Tabernacle;
> I hate your little wittling sneer,
> Your pert and self-sufficient leer,
> Mischief to Trade sits on thy lip,
> Insects will gnaw the noblest ship;

> (lines 27–32)

In this strange verse Boswell sets upon, and satirically feeds off, Wilberforce's facial expressions, the emphasis upon his "sneer" and "leer" feeding into the subsequent lip imagery. The oral imagery eats into the final metaphor whereby Wilberforce becomes literalized as an insectival pest. Yet the "noble ship" he is seen feeding off, and simultaneously destroying, is a slave ship. Wilberforce is thus represented as a big bug biting at the heart of British sea trade. His jealousy of the very nobility of the slave trade, the satire argues, is what motivates Wilberforce to plan its destruction. Yet in the idea of the "self-sufficient leer" there is the inference that Wilberforce attacks the trade out of a sense of his own frustrated libidinousness. What after all is a "self-sufficient leer" but an expression of desire that cannot be satisfied except by self-stimulation? For Boswell, abolition activity focused on desire for the slave and emerges as a form of self-sufficient but self-destructive masturbation. According to the verse, abolition's unhealthy sexual solipsism is set in opposition to Boswell's healthy desire for a respectable (and white) woman.

In this poem the attacks on individual Clapham sect abolitionists repeatedly turn to themes of licentiousness and repressed libidinousness. There are many examples, but the attack on Sir William Dolben is particularly extreme in its perverted sexual metaphorics. Boswell uses Greek, and an elaborate scholarly apparatus, in order to introduce a particularly nasty little pun on the concept of "planting":

> Drawcansir DOLBEN would destroy
> Both slavery and licencious joy;

Foe to all sorts of *planters**, he
Will suffer neither *bond* nor *free*.

*Diogenes being discovered in the street in fond intercourse with one of
those pretty misses whom Sir William Dolben Dislikes, steadily said,
"Φυτευ Ανδραζ—I plant men."

(lines 47–50n)

Here Boswell, with a knowing disgracefulness, couples prostituted sex and
plantation slavery as areas that allow the white male to prosper. "Slavery and
licencious joy" coexist as opportunities for the fully empowered white male.
Dolben is set out, with a quite deliberately literal perversity, as a kill-joy.
Dolben's activities within the Evangelical Societies for the Suppression of
Vice, attempting to keep a lid on street prostitution in urban centers in England, are set against his activities in support of abolition of the slave trade.
"Planting" sperm in a prostitute, a habit to which Boswell, according to his
own rather overstrained confession, was addicted throughout his adult life,
and planting plantations in the colonies, are bizarrely aligned as legitimate
areas of activity/productivity for an English Gentleman.[17] In this strange
world of English literary satire, slave trade abolition somehow becomes synonymous with prudery, and slavery exists in the same company as a good
night in a bawdy house, or worse. The final crudity is wrapped up in Greek
and put into the mouth of Diogenes the Cynic; thus Dr. Johnson's great bi-
ographer attempts to displace the responsibility for his own satiric sickness.
So where did such a sickness—such satire—come from?

   Boswell was writing in a literary milieu in which Atlantic slavery and
the trope of amorous enslavement were not an untried combination. The
Jamaican planter and pro-slavery apologist Bryan Edwards had, in 1793,
printed a long parodic love poem entitled *The Voyage of the Sable Venus,
from Angola to the West Indies*. The title consequently constitutes a poetic
locution for what was to become notorious as "the Middle Passage." This
poem by Isaac Teale was written for Edwards and ironically celebrated
the delights of interracial sex between sailors and black women (slave
rape) on the Middle Passage and then of slave owners and black women
within the Caribbean. The poem is published at the precise historical
moment when the groundswell within Quaker, Evangelical, and some
Radical circles was just beginning to build up against the immorality, in-
efficiency, and moral inexcusability of the slave trade. Yet it was written
at a point when the trade was still seen by many as legitimate business,
and when the great fact-finding missions of the abolition movement in
the late 1780s had not yet exposed the full enormity and scale of the
trade to a wide readership.

It is above all the tone, the ability to deal with such utter abuse in such an utterly frivolous manner, that leads the way for Boswell. Yet in taking the black female form, in sexual terms, as both highly charged and ultimately comic, Edwards was looking back to, and in many ways perverting, a well-established Renaissance tradition. From the late fifteenth century through the late seventeenth century, commonplace books regularly contained playful and punning experiments set on the premise of white men wooing black women, and less regularly black women wooing black men, or sometimes boys. (Black men wooing white women is a romantic premise that apparently did not hold any attraction.) Many of these poems circling around the topic of interracial sexuality appear to be exercises in rhetorical sophistication and in the art of playing with oppositions and inversions. Some have an overtly satiric edge, but many others do not. Some appear to have as their overriding motivation the aesthetic celebration of black over white.[18] With the exception of Dunbar's "Ane Blacke Moire," which is much earlier than the other poems, and far more cynical, none of them is built upon the satiric exploitation of black-white power relations—and none of these works deals explicitly with the social power relations growing out of slavery. What differentiates Teale's *Voyage of the Sable Venus* from this earlier body of work is the confidence with which it asserts the absolute right of the white male to use the body of the black woman. The poem extends this right across the slave Diaspora, whether dealing with the West Indian male in the plantation or with the British sailor during the Middle Passage.

Teale's satire is a terrifying assertion of white male cynicism, cast in the form of a mock celebration of the sexual desirability of black women. The poem abounds in cocksure innuendoes and never loses touch with an ironic baseline that trivializes the theme of black beauty with a ludic consistency and cruelty. Behind the poem lies the amused certainty that it is a ridiculous creative premise to celebrate black female beauty according to the conventions of the English love lyric. The gesture of writing about a black woman, albeit a black figure abstracted from a white neoclassical goddess of love, is consequently parodic. The disjunction between form and subject constitutes the primary satiric mechanism. The greater the levels of hyperbole employed to celebrate the charms of the essentialized "Sable Venus," the bigger the joke. The poem is a cleverly modulated and, finally, obscenely cruel celebration of black female sexual exploitation and white male empowerment. Neoclassical satiric and amatory convention is appropriated to provide a sneering yet voyeuristically charged account of the rape of a black woman on the Middle Passage. Along the way the verse plays games with the dynamics of love poems and master-slave relations. Power floats strangely as the rape of the slave woman is presented as the direct result of the manner in which the Sable Venus has enslaved white male hearts. Consequently, the poem casts the effects of the black woman's desirability as an effect of empowerment. When the Sable Venus is shown to leave Africa, her native shore, it is as a conqueror, albeit of white men's hearts: "When thou, this large domain to view, / Jamaica's isle, thy conquest new, / First left thy native shore, / Bright was the morn, and soft the breeze."[19] After the enforced sexual union described on the slave ship, the Sable Venus arrives in Jamaica, and touches off a sexual frenzy in the island:

> But when her step had touched the strand,
> Wild rapture seized the ravished land,
>   From every part they came:
> Each mountain, valley plain, and grove
> Haste eagerly to show their love;—
>   Right welcome was the dame.
>
> Port-Royal shouts were heard aloud,
> Gay St. Iago sent a crowd,
>   Grave Kingston not a few:
> No rabble rout,—I heard it said,
> Some great ones joined the calvalcade—
>   The muse will not say who.
>
> (lines 115–126)

At the heart of the satire is the mechanism whereby disempowerment is presented as its opposite. The Sable Venus is shown to be the sexual magnet that draws the crowds of men, including "some great ones." Yet an often repeated scene related to the realities of slave trading and the Middle Passage lies behind this image of the arrival of the frenzied crowds to greet the slave ship. It was not uncommon, on the arrival of a slave ship, for the captain to prepare the slaves for sale, and then allow potential purchasers to rush on board and fight for possession of the most likely bargains. The experience by all accounts caused the slaves, and the women and children in particular, an indescribable terror.[20] Yet in this poem, as the sexually obsessed men swarm around her, the Sable Venus is again shown to be patronizingly in control of the situation: "Gay Goddess of the sable smile! / Propitious still, this greateful isle / With thy protection bless!" The poem ends with the author, Teale, claiming that he will pursue sexual encounters with slave women throughout the Caribbean plantation systems:

> Try every form thou canst put on,
> I'll follow thee through every one;
> So staunch I am, so true.

Do thou in gentle Phibba smile,
In artful Benneba beguile,
In wanton Mimba pout;
In sprightly Cuba's eye look gay,
Or grave in sober Quasheba,
I still shall find thee out.

(lines 142–150)

Slavery-parody and slavery-satire can take some extremely bizarre turns. What is to be done with this work now? Isaac Teale, a man in late middle age, composes a poem for the amusement of, and at the instigation of, his friend, the pro-slavery planter Bryan Edwards. The poem climaxes with a claim that because of the beauty of the Sable Venus it is the author's manifest duty to take any black woman in the slave Diaspora he can get his hands on—and the women are of course assumed to desire this domination: this violent male fantasy is the oldest rape "defence" in the world, Mimba "pouts" and is "wanton."[21] Types of female beauty are introduced in a sort of plantation pastoral that substitutes the Phyllises and Cynthias for Bennebas, Quashees, and Mimbas.

Shocking as these parodic substitutions may seem, they are not the exclusive preserve of plantocratic gentlemen playing literary games with each other. No less a literary light than William Wordsworth was capable of deploying them. Wordsworth was disengaged from any direct concern with the abolition movement as he observed its operations after his return from France in the early 1790s. The San Domingo revolution seems to have passed him by, with the exception of the relatively detached sonnet on Toussaint L'Ouverture.[22] Yet when that revolution had run its course and led to the disastrous dictatorship of Henri Christophe, he did engage with the downfall of the Christophe regime by adopting a satiric voice very much in the spirit of Boswell and Isaac Teale.

The dictatorship of Henri Christophe, self-appointed Emperor of Haiti, ended in rebellion and his suicide in 1820. His wife and daughters came to England and stayed with the Clarksons (Thomas Clarkson had conducted a voluminous correspondence with Christophe).[23] The arrival of the ex-slave family was the occasion for much hilarity in the newspapers of the day, and evidently among Dorothy, Sara and William Wordsworth as well.[24] Wordsworth's view of the Haitian revolution, which began with the representative appropriations of the sonnet to Tousaint, ends by participating in the general racist bathos. Wordsworth is recorded as composing the following three-stanza poem amid bursts of hilarity with Sara Hutchinson in the drawing room.

The poem itself is a precise parody of a little song of Ben Jonson's celebrating Queen Elizabeth in *Cynthia's Revels*. The stanzas are set out alternately below beginning with Wordsworth's rewriting and with Jonson's original interpolated in italics:

Queen and Negress chaste and fair!
Christophe now is laid asleep
Seated in a British Chair
State in humbler manner keep
Shine for Clarkson's pure delight
Negro Princess, ebon bright!

Queen and huntress, chaste and fair,
Now the sun is laid to sleep,
Seated in thy silver chair,
State in wonted manner keep:
Hesperus entreats thy light,
Goddess excellently bright.

Lay thy Diadem apart
Pomp has been a sad Deceiver
Through thy Champion's faithful heart
Joy be poured, and thou the Giver
Thou that mak'st a day of night
Sable Princess, ebon bright!

Lay thy bow of pearl apart,
And thy crystal-shining quiver;
Give unto the flying hart
Space to breathe, how short soever:
Thou that mak'st a day of night,
Goddess excellently bright.

Let not "Wilby's"[25] holy shade
Interpose at Envy's call,
Hayti's shining Queen was made
To illumine Playford Hall[26]
Bless it then with constant light
Negress excellently bright!

Earth, let not thy envious shade
Dare itself to interpose;
Cynthia's shining orb was made
Heaven to clear, when day did close:
Bless us then with wished sight,
Goddess excellently bright.

The joke is fundamentally the same as that elaborated in the conclusion of the *Voyage of the Sable Venus;* the elevated diction and classical allusion of the Renaissance love lyric, in this case respectfully celebrating the young Elizabeth, are here turned on the black ex-revolutionary matriarch. Wordsworth is also playing with the old Renaissance conceits involving love and light, blackness and love, and the supposed paradox that black beauty can be radiant. Yet, like Teale, he departs from the innocent and celebratory playfulness that typify Renaissance approaches to the themes of interracial love. This poetry is finally not seriously interested in its subject, and does not want its subject to be taken seriously. Wordsworth is more concerned to pursue a frivolous line in order to enforce the lowest, most banal assumptions of popular racism. The spirit of the humor, and the context for the humor, are finally effortlessly in line with that of popular visual satire, which had from the start shown Wilberforce and Clarkson to be figures fixated with, and the fixation of, big black women. The "joke" underlying this lyric is monumentally crude, in line with Gillray's brilliantly disturbing *Philanthropic consolations on the Loss of the Slave Bill.*[27] White abolitionist males and black slave (or ex-slave) females are involved in a relationship of mutual desire that is somehow hopelessly funny to the white audience. The substitutions are critically instructive. Christophe replaces the setting sun, a solid British chair replaces Elizabeth's "Silver Chair," Clarkson replaces Hesperus. The idea that a black ex-empress from Haiti could even be discussed in the very language invented by Jonson to celebrate England's Virgin Queen is supposed to be seen as preposterous and hilarious. Sara Hutchinson and Wordsworth got their reported laughs because the parody was created from the absurd extremity of the imagined substitution. Yet as so often with humor produced by whites and focused on miscegenation, there is also a discernible hysterical anxiety lying behind the verse, and maybe even an underlying terror at what had been done in the verse. After all, on one level Wordsworth, then poet laureate, had in the parody transformed the notoriously white Virgin Queen into the black ex-empress and matriarch. One is left asking (as so often in English satire focused on the black body): was he really in control of what he was doing?

Notes

1. The book that has opened a pathway into considerations of the relationship between satire and canonical Romanticism is Steven E. Jones, *Satire and Romanticism* (New York, St. Martin's/Palgrave, 2000). The book that in many ways has enabled all subsequent work reading Romanticism against the (canonical) grain is Jerome McGann's *The Romantic Ideology: A Critical Investigation* (Chicago and London: University of Chicago Press, 1983).
2. The central studies to open up the full range of satiric publishing during the Romantic period are Olivia Smith, *The Politics of Language 1791–1819* (Oxford: Oxford University Press, 1984); Marcus Wood, *Radical Satire and Print Culture 1780–1822* (Oxford: Oxford University Press, 1994); Gary Dyer, *British Satire and the Politics of Style 1789–1832* (Cambridge: Cam-

bridge University Press, 1996). Marlon Ross's *The Contours of Masculine Desire: Romanticism and the Rise of Women's Poetry* (Oxford: Oxford University Press, 1989) is important for having suggested that the operations of parody and relational constructions within Romantic literatures are limitless. For print satire and its relation to Romantic thought, see Ronald Paulson, *Art and Revolution* (New Haven, CT: Yale University Press, 1983); Diana Donald, *The Age of Caricature: Satirical Prints in the Reign of George III* (New Haven and London: Yale University Press, 1996).

3. For an overview of developments in this area see Marcus Wood, "William Cobbett, John Thelwall, Radicalism, Racism and Slavery," *Romanticism on the Net* 15 (August 1999), <http/www/users.ox.ac.uk/~scat0385/thelwall.html>.

4. The best overviews of these tendencies are Marcus Wood, *Blind Memory: Slavery and Visual Representation in England and America 1780–1865* (London and New York: Manchester University Press and Routledge, 2000); Srinivas Aravamudan, *Tropicopolitans Colonialism and Agency, 1688–1804* (Durham, NC and London: Duke University Press, 1999). For primary sources see also Srinivas Aravamudan, ed., *Slavery, Abolition and Emancipation: Writings in the British Romantic Period,* Vol. VI (London: Pickering and Chatto, 1999).

5. For individual slaves in print satires see Wood, *Blind Memory,* 151–174.

6. For a detailed analysis of Cowper's varied approaches to the theme of slavery throughout his oeuvre see the chapter "Slavery, testimony, propaganda: John Newton William Cowper and compulsive confession" in my forthcoming *Slavery, Empathy, and Pornography* (Oxford: Oxford University Press, 2002). For *Charity,* see David Brion Davis, *The Problem of Slavery in the Age of Revolution 1770–1823* (Ithaca, NY: Cornell University Press, 1975), 368–73.

7. William Cowper, *The Poems of William Cowper,* ed. John Baird and Charles Ryskamp, 3 vols. (Oxford: Clarendon Press, 1980–1995), III, 15–16.

8. Cowper, *Poems,* III, 183.

9. James Boswell, *Boswell's Book of Bad Verse (A Verse Self Portrait) or 'Love Poems and Other Verses by James Boswell,'* ed. with notes by Jack Werner (London and New York: White Lion, 1974), 54. "Song to Mira," ll. 25–28.

10. Boswell, *Bad Verse,* 54. "Song," ll. 1–4.

11. Boswell, *Bad Verse,* 55. "Song," ll. 1–4.

12. Boswell, *Bad Verse,* 57. "To Miss Kitty Colquhoon," ll. 15–18.

13. For an analysis of this and passing reference to Boswell see Wood, *Blind Memory,* 58.

14. James Boswell, *No Abolition of Slavery; or the Universal Empire of Love: A Poem* (London, 1791), reprinted, in *Slavery, Abolition, and Emancipation: Writings of the British Romantic Period,* Vol. IV, ed. Alan Richardson (London: Pickering & Chatto, 1999), 170–191, ll. 1–4; hereafter cited parenthetically in the text.

15. For Jane Austen's punning on this use of "kindness" in the context of Fanny Price and Sir Thomas Bertram see the chapter "Canons to the right of them canons to the left of them: *Mansfield Park, Jane Eyre* and memorial subversions of slavery," in Marcus Wood, *Slavery, Empathy and Pornography.*

16. For the extended treatment of this theme and its relation to pornography see the chapter "Slavery, empathy and pornography in John Gabriel Stedman's *Narrative of a Five Years Expedition Against the Revolted Negroes of Surinam*" in my *Slavery, Empathy and Pornography.*

17. For Boswell's fraught and frantic sexual antics and accounts of his venereal diseases see Peter Martin, *A Life of James Boswell* (New Haven and London: Yale University Press, 1999), 73, 75, 120–23, 198, 234–38, 242, 247–48, 255, 257, 370, 395, 424, 440.

18. The most detailed analysis of this body of love poetry is Gordon McMullan, *Renaissance Configurations Voices / Bodies / Spaces, 1580–1960* (London: Macmillan, 1998). A representative body of amatory poetry focused on black-white conjunction and desire is reprinted, chronologically arranged as an appendix titled "Poems of Blackness," 269–90.

19. Isaac Teale, *The Voyage of the Sable Venus* (1765), reprinted in Robert Young, *Colonial Desire* (London: Routledge, 1994), 153–157; hereafter cited parenthetically in the text.

20. For a discussion of the slave "scrambles," see James Walvin, *Black Ivory,* second edn. (Oxford: Blackwells, 2001), 53–55; for an extended account of boat sale procedures throughout the Diaspora, see Hugh Thomas, *The Slave Trade,* 431–42.

21. On this form of rape fantasy see Brenda Love, *Encyclopaedia of Unusual Sex Practices* (London: Abacus, 1992), 265–67.

22. For an extended analysis of this poem in the context of contemporary verse treatments of Toussaint, and for Wordsworth's highly ambivalent stance over slavery generally, see the chapter "Slavery and the English Romantics" in my *Slavery, Empathy and Pornography.*

23. See *Henry Christophe and Thomas Clarkson: A Correspondence,* ed. Earle and Leslie Griggs (Berkeley: University of California Press, 1952).

24. For the text of Wordsworth's poem, "Queen and Negress chaste and fair!," its background and composition, see *Last Poems 1821–1850,* ed. Jared Curtis (Ithaca, NY and London: Cornell University Press, 1999), 24–25 and notes.

25. "Wilby" is a mocking reference to William Wilberforce, parliamentary spearhead for the abolition movement. Dorothy Wordsworth wrote in the margin of her letter of October 24, 1821, to Catherine Clarkson, and containing the parody, "Mrs. Wilberforce calls her husband by that pretty diminutive—'Wilby'—you must have heard her."

26. Playford Hall: in the same letter Dorothy explained the poem's genesis in the "lively picture I shaped myself of the sable Queen with her sable daughters beside you on the sofa in my dear little Parlour at Playford."

27. James Gillray, BM 8793, *Philanthropic consolations on the Loss of the Slave Bill.* For the political context for this print see Draper Hill, *Fashionable Contrasts* (London: Phaidon, 1966), 146; for the poem, see Wood, *Blind Memory,* 158–59.

Chapter 4 ~

Wordsworth and the Parodic School of Criticism

Nicola Trott

Literary historians once cast Romanticism as a reaction against the eighteenth century, and, primarily, against Pope. Wordsworth stood at the vanguard, leading what James Chandler has nominated "arguably the canonical canon controversy in English literary history" (p. 481); and critics like Hazlitt (who actually admired Pope in many ways) followed, seeing a poet with "none of the enthusiasm of poetry" (p. 71): it was only a short step from that to Matthew Arnold's dismissing Pope (and Dryden) as "classics of our prose" (*Essays in Criticism,* p. 42).[1] Robert J. Griffin has recently argued persuasively that the construction of "Wordsworth's" Pope was really accomplished by the Warton circle much earlier in the century,[2] but it is the undoubted firmness of its establishment by the time of the Romantics that matters here. For Byron, the follies of his poetical contemporaries were indivisible from their rejection of the neoclassical excellences of "the little Queen Anne's Man."[3] And the most prominent reviewers, Francis Jeffrey among them, agreed that some kind of would-be revolution had been started, intent on overthrowing the old school: the newly formed "*sect* of poets . . . are *dissenters* from the established systems of poetry and criticism," and their works marked by a "splenetic and idle discontent with the existing institutions of society."[4]

But the precise nature of the relationship between the Romantics and their eighteenth-century forbears has lately come in for a good deal of revisionary thinking. Jerome McGann, for example, in *The Beauty of Inflections,* usefully draws attention to "an interesting, and neglected, aspect of Romanticism: that its ideologies share important attitudes with the ideologies of

Neo-Classicism"[5]—an observation that, coming from the critic of the Romantic Ideology, is worth pausing over. McGann's counter-hegemonic criticism no doubt arises in part from his long and distinguished career as a Byronist: Byron was the poet who would not fit in M. H. Abrams' *Natural Supernaturalism,* an otherwise awesomely syncretic account of the period, and the relative proximity of Byron (and sometimes of Shelley) to certain strains in neoclassical feeling has often enough been detected.[6] But can we find such a sharing of attitudes in the apparently less promising ground of the "first-generation" Romantics as well?

One place where we might look is the genre of satire. I suppose nothing could seem more incorrigibly Augustan, more the work of the Pope whom Hazlitt thought "was in poetry what the sceptic is in religion" (p. 71). And certainly, nothing about the Romantic period feels more like the work of a tenacious old sensibility deploring the new than does the satirical onslaught launched upon Wordsworth, especially, by the new reviews, as though he were a modern-day Colley Cibber. But, especially with McGann's *aperçu* in mind, we might wonder whether the opposition between satirical review and Romantic bard is as neatly antithetical as it might seem (and as its protagonists might have pretended). Wordsworth's own phase as a satirist saw him imitating Juvenal—a "Juvenalian spirit" Coleridge envisaged as part-and-parcel of his later plan for a philosophic epic[7]—and nominating as "great names" the unlikely trio of "Boileau and Pope and the redoubted Peter [Pindar]."[8] By 1839, the sixty-nine-year-old poet could afford to boast of having committed to memory "several 1000 lines of Pope."[9] As Robert Griffin observes, even "while overtly attacking Pope and his allies, Wordsworth covertly draws upon Pope's satiric authority by means of allusion" (p. 93). However, my concern here is not with Wordsworth the hidden satirist; rather, it is with the intersection between two emergent literary forms of the early nineteenth century. I want to argue that the "new school of poetry" that so displeased the reviewers was in fact not the antagonist of their "new school of criticism," but effectively its collusive partner—joined in mutual labor within the precincts of a new nineteenth-century institution, the "Critical Journal," and preeminently Jeffrey's own *Edinburgh Review.* ("Nor know we when to spare, or where to strike, / Our bards and censors are so much alike," said Byron, in *English Bards and Scotch Reviewers* [lines 91–92].) The reviewers' satire and the Romantics' poetry interacted during the period in extremely intricate ways; and one of the most shrewdly audacious strokes of the satirists was to see Wordsworth as, in some incongruous sense, his own best parodist. Thus the new criticism often gained a helping hand from another rising form of the day, parody—a form that, as Gary Dyer observes, "established itself in this period as a distinct genre," yet the "development" of which, he suggestively continues, "does not ensure that the line between it and satire is uniformly clear."[10] It is that wavering or blurred line that is pursued, to brilliant effect, in the critical journals; and that I hope to retrace here. Why *Wordsworth* should be the focus of such complexly satirical feelings is another question, one that I end the essay by addressing.

Wordsworth in the Nursery

In *Biographia Literaria,* Coleridge recalled that Wordsworth's poems "were for a long time described as being" "silly" and "childish things."[11] If we ask where Coleridge might have come across such a description, there is one simple answer: Richard Mant's anonymous *Satirico-Didactic Poem, The Simpliciad* (1808), began by lamenting that the art of poetry had lived "to see the high-soul'd Muse / Condemn'd in leading strings to pipe, and cry, / And lisp the accents of the nursery" (lines 10–12).[12] Placing the work alongside Gifford's satire of the poetic follies of the 1790s, the *British Critic* recognized *The Simpliciad* as a "new Baviad" (33 [February 1809], 180)—aware, perhaps, that William Gifford was at this very moment assuming editorship of the new, Tory *Quarterly Review* (whose first number also appeared in February). Mant had signaled his model, first by the form of his title, then by taking up the dialogue between "P" and "F"—Pasquin and Foulder—and yet again by openly citing Gifford's assault on the Della Cruscans (lines 60–65). However, since current fashions were arguably tending in the opposite direction to the Della Cruscan, *The Simpliciad* imitated Gifford's imitation of the Satire of Persius to different ends. Mant's argument went as follows: even though genuinely "artless bards" have already provided baby with an ample supply of the "ditty simple," a still "simpler lay / Wrests from their grasp the nursery prize away." For instance, while old-style versifiers sing "Cock Robin," the new go one better and "call Cock Robin brother," a clear step up in silliness (lines 133, 135). In short, the traditional "brethren of the cradle and the crib" are "Less worthy far of go-cart, pap, and bib" than the most babyish of all bards—the "Bards of the lakes" (lines 124–27, 128–31).

The Simpliciad, for its part, is demonstrably in the leading strings of Francis Jeffrey: The *Edinburgh Review* had used its founding number to open hostilities against what it dubbed the "new school of poetry" (1 [October 1802], 71), and Mant's subtitle names as its target the very same *Scholars of the New School.* What is more, to the stigma of "simplicity" the *Edinburgh* had recently added the slur of infantilism: Wordsworth's 1807 volumes reminded Jeffrey of the "Childishness" of the *Lyrical Ballads,* while a review of Crabbe, in early 1808, provided him with a further opportunity for castigating the "ambitious fraternity" of "the Wordsworths, and the Southeys, and Coleridges," this time for "labouring to bring back our poetry to the fantastical oddity and puling childishness of Withers, Quarles, or Marvel" (*Edinburgh Review* (*ER*) 11 [October 1807], 214; 12 [April 1808], 133). Mant notably refers to modish Simplicity as a "puling, puny child," and singles out the "babyish style and phrase fantastical" of Coleridge's poem "To A Young Ass" (*Simpliciad*, 25, 234). His Dedication, meanwhile, addresses itself "To Messrs. W-ll—m W-rdsw-rth, R-b-rt S—th-y, and S. T. C-l—r-dg-" (*Simpliciad*, p. iii); and the couplets that follow present their poetry—quoted at the foot of each page in a continuous ironic citation of "Authorities"—as a modern and more juvenile sort of nursery rhyme.

An Anglican clergyman, Mant objected to the Lakers' open-air nature-worship and déclassé innovations. But it is not irrelevant, perhaps, that he too had recently been receiving an indifferent press—one that had come, curiously enough, from the *Edinburgh Review* itself, which effectively gave Mant warning not to repeat the experiment of publishing his *Poems* (1806) lest he "put himself in the way of more unmerciful critics" (11 [October 1807], 171, unattributed).[13] The *Edinburgh's* discouraging treatment had prompted Edward Copleston, Professor of Poetry at Oxford and a tutor at Oriel, where Mant had also held a Fellowship, to produce an anonymous pamphlet of *Advice to a Young Reviewer* (1807). There he imagined what a contemporary hack would have made of a poem of Milton's. *L'Allegro*, were it suddenly to appear, would surely be censured for "trite images of rural scenery, interspersed with vulgarisms in dialect, and traits of vulgar manners . . . dress[ed] up . . . in a sing-song jingle."[14] The similarities with current responses to Wordsworth, Richard Mant's included, are rather striking. Mant's parodic verse followed hard on the heels of Copleston's parodic review; but *The Simpliciad* occupied much of the same ground in order to satirize the "new school of poetry" and not "the new school of criticism"—as Southey would call it, when deploring *Edinburgh* tactics in the *Quarterly Review* (6 [December 1811], 412). That Mant should return to the lists with a poem based on *Edinburgh* dicta may seem perverse, given his own treatment; but he might have taken comfort in the thought that Wordsworth was far more culpable even than he: as luck would have it, Jeffrey's assault on Wordsworth's *Poems, in Two Volumes* appeared last of all in the very same number in which his own collection had gained its dubious notice.

This little episode suggests how readily the specific material, and the wider literary culture, of the leading Review (see Morgan, p. 6) crossed over into other publishing formats—or, putting it slightly differently, how readily those formats became a way of reviewing by other means. A precisely similar case is met with in Byron, who, like Mant, suffered at the hands of Scotch reviewers: indeed, his *Hours of Idleness* led Jeffrey to "counsel him, that he do forthwith abandon poetry" (*ER* 11 [January 1808], 286). Like Mant, Byron reacted by turning from personal poetry to a verse satire in which the Lakers were accused of writing "childish verse," fit only to "lull the babe at nurse." Unlike *The Simpliciad,* however, *English Bards and Scotch Reviewers* (1809) directed its animus against the critics as well as the poets and made a self-conscious attempt to seek out a formal alternative to the Whig Review:[15] "Moved by the great example, I pursue / The self-same road, but make my own review: / Not seek great Jeffrey's" (lines 59–61, 48–88, 528–39, 917–18).

The Simpliciad, on the other hand, can be seen simply to have versified the formulae of the "new school of criticism." In this respect, it was continuing the work of Peter Bayley's *Poems* (1803), which, much to Wordsworth's dismay, had used the *Edinburgh*'s first salvo against "The followers of simplicity" (1 [October 1802], 65) to parody "The Idiot Boy." Lest the point be missed, Bayley's note to "The Fisherman's Wife" had compared its "simple" verse with "The simplicity of that most simple of all poets, Mr. W. himself" (*EY,* p. 413n; and p. 455). It was not long before the copy and criteria of the "Scotch Reviewers" were in general circulation. *The Simpliciad* adopted an *Edinburgh* perspective, and, for all its editorial rivalry with the "new school of criticism," the older, Tory *British Critic* responded to *The Simpliciad* in the terms already laid down by Jeffrey: "Of this new school [of poetry] the chief teacher was Mr. W. Wordsworth, who in pursuit of an object laudable in judicious use, went so far into the familiar and even infantine style, as to become frequently ridiculous" (*British Critic* 33 [February 1809], 180). More inventively, a pseudo-documentary magazine article, "The Bards of the Lake,"[16] picked up a phrase from *The Simpliciad* (line 128) and, using the device of an admiring witness to the Lakers' outdoor pursuits, applied *Edinburgh* charges of sectarianism and sans-culottism to a medley of prose reportage and impromptu song. One by one "the bards arose" and sang, after the spontaneous manner of their primitive Blairite ancestors—a flatulent visionary (Coleridge) "burst[ing] forth" with broad humor in "Breeches. An Ode," a childish "genius" (Worsdworth) versifying a hermit's address to a snail, whose "original simplicity" leaves his audience at a loss to know "in what class of poetry to place it."

Mant's innovation was to combine the two staples of negative reviewing— simplicity and childishness—into a single idiolect, of "babyish simpleness in nonsense drest" (*Simpliciad,* line 361). This sort of baby-speak soon hardened into the set-piece of a new parodic repertoire. And it too can be dated fairly precisely. Four years on from *The Simpliciad,* and baby was back, in another anonymous production, the *Rejected Addresses: or The New Theatrum Poetarum* (1812), written and published in six weeks by that facetious metropolitan duo, the brothers James and Horace Smith. Their mise-en-scène was provided by a competition to commemorate the reopening of Drury Lane after a fire; and their imitations of contemporary authors proposed to represent those authors' unavailing efforts to submit the winning entry. In real life, as many as 112 such addresses were turned down by the committee. But none of these genuine failures, excepting Horace's own, is in the volume.[17] For the most part, the Smiths burlesque the leading poets of the day, rather than its occasional versifiers: Byron (who in the end agreed to compose the real address), Moore, Scott, Southey, Coleridge, Crabbe—and Wordsworth. The offering "By W.W.," entitled "The Baby's Debut," was immediately seized on by Jeffrey as an opportunity to repeat and reinforce his contempt for the *Poems* of 1807: "We hope it will make him ashamed of his Alice Fell, and the greater part of his last volumes"—the reason for hope being that it "has succeeded perfectly in the imitation of his maukish affectations of childish simplicity and nursery stammering" (*ER* 20 [November 1812], 438).

"The Baby's Debut" is "*Spoken in the character of Nancy Lake, a girl eight years of age, who is drawn upon the stage in a child's chaise, by Samuel Hughes, her uncle's porter.*" Nancy's vehicle infantilizes the mailcoach in which Alice Fell traveled, even as her surname indicates the geography that Jeffrey had made synonymous with Wordsworth. Her casual talk of "poor brother Bill" brings "We Are Seven" into the picture, and the poem borrows its stanza-form from "Ruth" and makes a passing reference to "The Thorn." But its larger purpose is to make a Cockney out of a Laker, and, though it plays with the dramatis personae of the lyrical ballads, the Smiths' double-act downplays specific Wordsworthianisms in favor of the theatrical occasion. Having been deprived of a trip to Drury Lane as a punishment for bad behavior, Nancy is rescued and taken center-stage by her uncle "Sam," Mr. Lake's porter and shoe-blacker (and suspiciously reminiscent of another well-known Samuel, currently lecturing on the London circuit). Her "Address" rehearses the whole domestic saga, up to the point of her unexpected debut:

> At first I caught hold of the wing,
> And kept away; but Mr. Thing-
>   umbob, the prompter man,
> Gave with his hand my chaise a shove,
> And said, Go on my pretty love,
>   Speak to 'em little Nan.
>
> You've only got to curtsey, whisp-
> er, hold your chin up, laugh and lisp,
>   And then you're sure to take:
> I've known the day when brats not quite
> Thirteen got fifty pounds a night;
>   Then why not Nancy Lake?

The nonce-name and haplessly run-over line-endings—"Mr. Thing- / umbob," "whisp- / er"—are new departures. So too is the knowing construction of a child-persona by an adult minder: "You've only got to . . . laugh and lisp, / And then you're sure to take." The prompter-man's image of a child-star derives from "the young Betty mania" of 1803–05, when a boy-actor of that name was the cause of public disorder, an early adjournment of parliament, and takings at Drury Lane amounting to "17,210l. 11s." over "twenty-eight nights."[18] Even Wordsworth had hopes that "the young Roscius," as he was known, would "restore the reign of . . . Nature" to the stage (*EY,* pp. 518–19). Betty started at the age of twelve; Nancy is making her first appearance at no more than eight, and an archly bashful performance it is: her last act is to "curtsey, like a pretty miss" and "blow a kiss" to her audience. Amid this slightly sinister bit of theatrical business, a mock-Wordsworthian poetics emerges, involving the dramatizing and marketing of the "artless" and "infantile" to urban theatergoers hungry for youth and innocence. The poet's "little Actor" (*Ode,* line 102) is all set to become a London pro.

Off-stage, Nancy is anything but innocent, however.[19] The story of how she came to break a windowpane as she and her "brother Jack" destroyed each other's birthday presents ensures that a counter-Wordsworthian childishness of temper competes with a "Wordsworthian" childishness of speech. The sight of her family leaving in a hackney coach produces some choice instances of the latter sort of banality and redundancy: "one horse was blind, / The tails of both hung down behind, / Their shoes were on their feet." Together, Nancy's "two voices" perform the alienating deflection of their model, which parody requires in order to do its work. Yet "The Baby's Debut" contrives to be playful. Simon Dentith has rightly placed the *Rejected Addresses* at the "ludic" end of the "two extremes" of parody, the other, "corrective," pole being occupied by the poetry of the *Anti-Jacobin.*[20] When Judge Jeffrey reviewed the *Addresses,* however, he tellingly refused to see these same publications as anything other than "comparable," and fastened upon the "Debut" as a way of bringing Wordsworth before the bench once more (*ER* 20, 434). His intention, presumably, was to fix the poet back in the anti-Jacobin moment, with only its satirico-political hardmen for company; and, indeed, the Address itself furnished some unexpectedly savage material in the shape of an epigraph from the dramatist Richard Cumberland: "The Baby's Debut" was headed by lines declaring "hat[red]" for "Thy lisping prattle and thy mincing gait . . . Nature's true Ideot I prefer to thee." This baby had teeth.

Namby-pamby Jack-a-dandy

The *Edinburgh Review* cast Wordsworth's *Poems, in Two Volumes* as "furnishing themselves from vulgar ballads and plebeian nurseries" (*ER* 11 [October

1807], 218). But the first critic to rock the poet's cradle in 1807 was not Jeffrey but Byron. Still himself a minor, the noble reviewer had taken a dim view of Wordsworth's more "trifling" pieces. Quoting the lines written "at the Foot of Brother's Bridge"—"The cock is crowing, / The stream is flowing, / The small birds twitter, / The lake doth glitter . . ."—he passed judgment as follows:

> this appears to us neither more nor less than an imitation of such minstrelsy as soothed our cries in the cradle, with the shrill ditty of
>
> "'Hey de diddle,
> The cat and the fiddle [. . .]"
> *   (Monthly Literary Recreations* 3 [July 1807], 65–66)

Byron has started what rapidly becomes a classic technique in the critic's sport of Wordsworth-baiting—namely, juxtaposing offending lines from the poet with some genuine "cradle" verses, and thereby equating the two. Typically, it is the "double rhyme"—the rhyme that Dryden had identified with burlesque[21]—that provides the hostile reviewer with an opening (not until Byron himself took it up, to macho-satirico effect, in *Don Juan,* would the feminine ending be rescued from mockery). Once again, what begins in the reviews carries over into the parodies.

Take John Hamilton Reynolds, for example, whose preemptive strike against *Peter Bell* (1819) sends Peter on a tour of Wordsworth's lowlife characters, all of whom are "rurally related"[22] and all, it turns out, dead in their graves—thus in macabre fashion pointing to their author's oblivion in the final stanza. When Reynolds's country bumpkin of a poet-narrator pauses to echo the same verses as are quoted by Byron, he mischievously rhymes the moon's "pretty glitter" in a waterfall with the rubbishy "litter" in Lucy Gray's "baby-house" (*Peter Bell,* lines 13–16). Reynolds had learnt his lesson in nursery Wordsworth from Keats, who in September 1817 had written to his friend quoting the identical lines of Wordsworth as an instance of how the poet "sometimes, though in a fine way, gives us sentences in the Style of School exercises," before himself turning to do a parody of the whole poem in the form of a comic "description" of Oxford, the seat of grownup learning where Keats was then staying.[23] Or, again, take Peacock's pseudonymous *Sir Proteus: A Satirical Ballad,* by P. M. O'Donovan, Esq. (1814), written in the wake of Wordsworth's accession to the post of Distributor of Stamps, lavishly dedicated to Byron, and printed for the Hookhams, publishers also of Shelley. Although the principal aim is to caricature the new Laureate in a "burlesque of Southey's most elevated style,"[24] the subtitle guys at Wordsworth. "A Satirical Ballad" wears its anti-"lyrical" intentions on its sleeve;

and when the garrulous Laker duly appears, he is made to chime his own ballad folk with their siblings (and metrical equals) in the nursery:

> . . . he chattered, chattered still,
>   With meaning none at all,
> Of Jack and Jill, and Harry Gill
>   And Alice Fell so small.[25]

"The Baby's Debut" had already insinuated a nursery rhyme element in the shape of Nancy's "brother Jack"; and on his return, as Mr. Paperstamp in *Melincourt* (1817), Peacock's Wordsworth—who is "chiefly remarkable for an affected infantine lisp in his speech, and for always wearing waistcoats of duffil grey"—names himself the greatest genius "since the days of Jack the Giant-killer."[26] His nursery connections, who run from "scarlet" Mother Goose to "little Jack Horner," are model con artists rather than children's entertainers; and, as "Peter Paypaul Paperstamp, Esquire, of Mainchance Villa," the poet leads his cronies in a song celebrating the allegorical meaning of the peculator's rhyme: "Jack Horner's Christmas Pie my learned nurse / Interpreted to mean the *public purse*" (ii.396–98, 418).

The most significant aspect of Byron's review is its exact identification of the critical tradition within which all of these different opponents of the infantine Wordsworth are operating. Having adopted an aggressively grownup line with the senior Laker, his review asks, "what will any reader or auditor, out of the nursery, say to such namby-pamby[?]" (p. 66). "Such namby-pamby" would have taken Byron's reader straight back to the culture wars of the early eighteenth century.[27] A hundred years earlier, the phrase had been coined to represent a child's efforts to get his tongue round the name of Ambrose Philips. Philips, having been on friendly terms with Pope and Swift, chose to attach himself instead to Addison and the Hanoverian cause, and so became the irresistible butt of his former associates.[28] Scriblerian opportunities for revenge arose with Philips's complimentary verses to the offspring of various patrons, among them these frankly cringing lines "To Miss Margaret Pulteney, daughter of Daniel Pulteney Esq; in the Nursery" (April 27, 1727):

> Dimply damsel, sweetly smiling,
> All caressing, none beguiling,
> Bud of beauty, fairly blowing,
> Every charm to nature owing [. . .]

The name Namby Pamby soon appeared in the following verse, said to have been written in Swift's handwriting—

Namby Pamby, Jack a Dandy,
Stole a piece of Sugar-Candy
From a Grocer's Shoppy-Shop,
And away did Hoppy-hop[29]

—and a version of the same lines also appeared as an epigraph to the first outing of Philips under his new name, in a poem called *Namby-Pamby. A Panegyric on the New Versification, addressed to A——— P———, Esq.* This, the most "lethal parody" of Philips, was not by Swift, Pope, or Gay, "but by a writer of musical farces named Henry Carey"—on this occasion presenting himself in the guise of a Captain Gordon.[30]

To judge from Carey's subtitle, then, there was nothing new in Jeffrey's disdainful proclamation of the "new"—nor, indeed, in the various ironies he and others leveled at the Lake School, such as the call to poetic "reform" ("All ye poets of the age [. . .] Crop your numbers and conform"), or the satirical allusion to bona fide nursery-verse ("Now he sings of Jacky Horner"), or even the invention of an infantilect:

Now the venal poet sings
Baby clouts and baby things [. . .]
Little playthings, little toys,
Little girls and little boys.
As an actor does his part,
So the nurses get by heart
Namby-Pamby's little rhimes,
Little jingle, little chimes,
To repeat to missy-miss,
Piddling ponds of pissy-piss [. . .]

(Carey, cited in Macdonald, pp. 25–27)

A man who was nicknamed Namby Pamby, who wrote poems to children "in the Nursery," and had mock nursery rhymes circulated in his honor: the inference seems clear enough. The "namby-pamby" tag was intended to cast the contemporary hostility to Wordsworth in something of the same light as the Scriblerian war against Philips. It implied the very continuity of culture that Wordsworth had rejected; and it found grounds for condemnation equally in his violations of political allegiance, linguistic propriety, and poetic dignity. Resurrecting Philips had the effect of placing Wordsworth within an established and hierarchical poetic order, whose codes and criteria—as much social as literary—he had wholly failed to fulfill.

Though Byron hit on the perfect persona for a "simple Wordsworth,"[31] it was Jeffrey who made the negative spin possible. Already in 1802 he had referred in passing to the new school's predilection for "the *innocence* of Ambrose Philips" (*ER* 1 [October 1802], 64). And Byron's pointed reference to Wordsworth's "*innocent* odes of the same cast" (66) clinches the connection. Jeffrey's own review of the 1807 *Poems* emerged, three months after Byron's, in October, and with impeccable timing: exactly five years had passed since the *Edinburgh*'s first, founding attack. It noted, with studied casualness, that "By and by, we have a piece of namby-pamby 'to the Small Celandine,' which we should have taken for a professed imitation of one of Mr Philips's prettyisms." And then again, of "The Kitten and the Falling Leaves," "There is rather too much of Mr Ambrose Philips here and there in this piece also" (*ER* 11, 220). Wherever Francis Jeffrey went, the rest were sure to follow: the *British Critic* was soon remarking on the "*namby-pamby* brethren" of the 1807 volumes (33 [March 1809], 298); and not long after that, the juvenile poetics of the "nursery bards" were turned into nursery-verse: when Mant refers to "numbers shilly-shally, shally-shilly, / So very feeling and so very silly" (*Simpliciad,* lines 151–52), the ghost of Ambrose is haunting the sound and rhyming patterns; and, sure enough, such metrical vulgarities are eventually assigned their proper name, as the poets of the *Simpliciad* "Trip it in Ambrose Philips's trochaics" (line 279).

The tense of *Biographia Literaria* (Wordsworth's poems "were [. . .] described as" "silly" and "childish") suggests that, by the mid-1810s, his infantalization was a thing of the past; but this was far from the case. Even as *Biographia* was being printed, Jeffrey was using a review of *Christabel* to repeat his old attack on "the new school, or, as they may be termed, the wild or lawless poets," whose writings appeared to vie with one another in the production of "the unmeaning or infantine" (*ER* 27 [September 1816], p.59). And, as Reynolds's *Peter Bell* attests, the "infantine" Wordsworth was still going strong in 1819. The poet's latest "Lyrical Ballad" having been advertised but not published, Reynolds was bound to find an early model. In his case it was "The Idiot Boy,"[32] a favorite with parodists, since it tended to make a village idiot of Wordsworth. If anything, the publication of the real *Peter Bell* only settled the matter—thanks partly to its inevitable mediation by Reynolds' "burlesque," and partly to a probable self-review by the parodist himself, in the *Alfred* for May 11, 1819, which argued that his mockery had been limited to the poet's "infantine follies."[33] This pre-publicity seems to have sealed the fate of Wordsworth's poem. Classing *Peter Bell* as an "infantine pamphlet," the *Monthly Review* pronounced that "No lisping was ever more distinctly lisped than the versification of this poem; and no folly was ever more foolishly boasted than that of the writer. . . . The . . . style [is] of Mr. Newbery's best gilded little volumes for nurseries. . . ."[34] John Newbery was a children's writer and bookseller, who incidentally made a habit of assuming juvenile pseudonyms. His "Collection of pretty poems for the amusement of children" (1800), for instance, was issued as "By Tommy Tagg, Esq."

The trick of Ambrose Philips's satirists—to identify the poet with a child-persona—was played and replayed by the reviewers of Wordsworth; and, so familiar was Namby-Pamby in connection with "the Lakeiest Poet" (Reynolds, *Peter Bell,* 196), that the critic for the *Monthly* had merely to utter the double-rhyming exclamation of "unmeaning prittle-prattle" to repeat the association, appealing as he did so from the art of the ballad to life in the nursery: "We can only say that, if a nurse were to talk to any of their children in this manner, a sensible father and mother would be strongly disposed to dismiss her without a character" (*MR,* p. 422). Thus Wordsworth's poem is dismissed along with the nurse; and, in the following month's review of the *Waggoner* volume, double-rhyme and nursery-verse combine to ridicule "that unrivalled Sonnet, ycleped The *Wild Duck's Nest*": "Oh 'Goosy-goosy-Gander!' friend of our infancy, resign thine honours! [. . .] before an author who wishes (almost) to lay aside *humanity,* at the sight of a wild duck's nest!" (*MR* 90 [September 1819], 40).

Significant in all these responses is their commitment to the *Lyrical Ballads* phase of Wordsworth's career as an interpretative paradigm for subsequent developments. Significant, too, is the fact that, even though the *Ballads* were the obvious means of attacking Wordsworth, the critical method that made them so emerged only on the publication of *Poems, in Two Volumes.* The first feeding-frenzy came in the reviews of 1807, and produced Mant's *Simpliciad;* the second followed in the wake of the *Rejected Addresses,* which went through sixteen editions in seven years and, by the time of its eighteenth, in 1833, had spanned an entire generation of nursery rhyme parodists.[35] The Distributor of Stamps episode provided a third occasion for satire; and a fourth and last concentration surrounded the publication of *Peter Bell.* Throughout, the role of Jeffrey was crucial. Launched in late 1802, the *Edinburgh Review* had to hold much of its fire on *Lyrical Ballads* until the *Poems, in Two Volumes* permitted Jeffrey his first direct review of Wordsworth. This delayed reaction to the poet's already well-established reputation for childishness had important consequences for the reception of the later work: Wordsworth, it might be said, was never allowed to grow up. The 1807 volumes were made to seem continuous with the output of an earlier poetic self—a critical assumption that ironically coincides with the poet for whom the child is father to the man. And, as we have seen, another sort of continuity ensured that the 1807 *Poems* were absorbed into a preexisting critical idiom. In his role as a modern Namby-Pamby, Wordsworth found himself the principal, though wholly unintentional, reviver of an entire Augustan satirical tradition.[36] Wordsworth also, in the process, became the medium through which the "new school of criticism" established its own distinctive procedures and techniques.

The Parodic Method of Reviewing

Reviewers of Wordsworth pursued their poet not (as did the Sriblerians) in privately printed broadsides, but in publicly circulated journals. Yet their Augustan inheritance was of a kind that led them to make invidious comparisons between Lake poems and nursery rhymes. The effect was to turn their perception of the "ridiculous" *in* Wordsworth's style into a more active "ridicule" *of* his style. Reviewing, it seems, was drawing on the resources of parody. In this development, as in others, Jeffrey had a critical role to play. And, as it happens, the subject of Wordsworth's reception in the *Edinburgh* later became the occasion for Coleridge to draw an explicit connection between parody and criticism, when a "Selection From [his] Literary Correspondence" published in *Blackwood's* pointedly coupled "the Buffoons of parody, and the Zanies of anonymous criticism" (*Blackwood's* 10 [October 1821], 259). A similar coupling had emerged a decade earlier. Two years after it was founded in opposition to the *Edinburgh,* the *Quarterly Review* gave Southey an opportunity of settling scores on behalf of the "new school of poetry" (among whose members Jeffrey had repeatedly numbered Southey himself). Southey's review of the poetry of James Montgomery was really a reply to Jeffrey's own, which had "thought proper to crush the rising poet" in "the usual strain." Accordingly, Southey attempted to name and shame the "new school of criticism," first by retorting upon the *Edinburgh* its label for the Lakers, then by exposing its "mischievous" manner of proceeding:

> A burlesque description of the contents of the volume follows, together with a few passages, most easily susceptible of ridicule, as specimens of the poetry; and the critique is thus wound up. "We cannot laugh at this any longer. [. . .] When every day is bringing forth some new work from the pen of Scott, Campbell, Rogers, Baillie, Sotheby, Wordsworth, or Southey, it is natural to feel some disgust at the undistinguishing voracity which can swallow down three editions of songs to convivial societies, and verses to a pillow."
>
> (*Quarterly Review* 6 [December 1811], 412–13;
> quoting *ER* 9 [January 1807], 354)

The method of the *Quarterly's* great antagonist is explicitly identified as "burlesque." The irony of finding Wordsworth for once in its favor is also dryly observed: *Edinburgh* "Critics . . . will praise one poet in pure malice to another," and "Even Mr. Wordsworth himself is mentioned with praise when the object is to run down Montgomery" (*Quarterly,* 407). In fact, the irony is still sharper, for Jeffrey on Montgomery is almost identical to Jeffrey on Wordsworth (the point being that the former case is subsumed within the latter, "that great sinking fund of bad taste, which is daily wearing down the debt which we have so long owed to the classical writers of antiquity" [*ER*, 347]). Just nine months later, the *Edinburgh's* review of Wordsworth shows the same closed circle of parodic interpretation: having made themselves "ridiculous," the 1807 volumes are deservedly subject to "ridicule," Jeffrey advising that "the composition in which it is attempted to exhibit" their typically forced "associations"

> will always have the air of parody, or ludicrous and affected singularity. All the world laughs at Elegiac stanzas to a sucking-pig—a Hymn on Washing-day—Sonnets to one's grandmother—or Pindarics on gooseberry-pye; and yet, we are afraid, it will not be quite easy to convince Mr Wordsworth, that the same ridicule must infallibly attach to most of the pathetic pieces in these volumes.
>
> (*ER* 11 [October 1807], 218)

Now it is Wordsworth (rather than Montgomery) who has acquired an "air of parody" by his burlesque proximity to unpoetic subjects, be they pies or pillows. In addition, "Wordsworth" has been made to stand alongside, and thus to represent, a whole class of déclassé and largely "Jacobin" poetry: Southey's "Gooseberry-Pie. A Pindaric Ode," and his "colloquial poem," "The Pig"; Lloyd's sonnets "on The Death of Priscilla Farmer, by her grandson," and Barbauld's "Washing-Day" (this last a coded reference also to "The Blind Highland Boy," whose infamous washing-tub provokes outrage later on in Jeffrey's review).

In Jeffrey's words, the effect of the "peculiarities" of the 1807 volumes is "to render them ridiculous": the perception that Wordsworth is ridiculous becomes associated with the attempt to render him so—and, with him, the "new school" of which he is declared head. This transition is partly a matter of applying parodic techniques—Jeffrey's satirical italicizing and pointing of Wordsworth quotations, for instance,[37] or his juxtaposition of the "pathetic" and "ludicrous" in poetry. Elsewhere, as we have seen, a similar effect is achieved by placing authentic and nursery verses side by side. These local examples of parodic reviewing practice involve larger critical assumptions. If, as Jeffrey has it, Wordsworth's method of "composition" is such as "will always have the air of parody," then for its part Jeffrey's method of criticism assumes that the new school is *itself* already parodic. Richard Mant, once again in line with *Edinburgh* thinking, makes much the same point in his Dedication to *The Simpliciad*:

> I do truly affirm my belief, that in attempting to excite ridicule, I have employed no unfair exaggeration; that the [new] school is incapable of caricature; and that, if a smile be raised by my illustrations, it will be heightened by a perusal of the originals whence they are drawn. (*Simpliciad*, p. v).

The parodic critical method operates a kind of double bluff: wherever possible, the representation of the poetry under review is referred back to the originals from whence it came. Whatever is parodic in the response is merely a reflection of the text's existing parodic features. The source of parody lies not in the critic, but in the poet himself.

Coleridge recognizes just this element of feigned mimesis, and its connection to a disguised or displaced genre of parody, when, in *Biographia Literaria,* he names as identical phenomena the "parodies and pretended imitations" of Wordsworth's early poems (II, 9). And, indeed, the technique of pretended imitation is central to the reception of Wordsworth, and to the transition from the review to parodic reviewing and verse parody. The criticism of Wordsworth's "imitation of such minstrelsy as soothed our cries in the cradle" (to quote Byron's review of the 1807 *Poems*) leads over five years to an appreciation of how the Smith brothers had "succeeded perfectly in the imitation of his . . . nursery stammering" (to quote Jeffrey's review of "The Baby's Debut"). That is, Wordsworth's nursery imitations give rise to parodic imitations of the nursery Wordsworth that the reviewers themselves invented.

This pretended imitation passes from prose review to verse parody, and back again to the reviews: "We hope," says Jeffrey of "The Baby's Debut," "it will make him ashamed of his Alice Fell, and the greater part of his last volumes—of which it is by no means a parody, but a very fair, and indeed we think a flattering imitation" (*ER* 20 [November 1812], 438). So infectious is the mock-imitation that Coleridge records its persistence among "some affected admirers" of Wordsworth, "with whom he is, forsooth, a *sweet, simple poet!* and *so* natural, that little master Charles, and his younger sister, are *so* charmed with them, that they play at 'Goody Blake,' or at 'Johnny and Betty Foy!'" (*BL,* II, 158–59). Even Wordsworth's admirers are unwittingly parodic. Alternatively, of course, Coleridge may be parodying the very method of pretended imitation on which Wordsworth's critics depend. That both possibilities occur shows how close the admiring and ridiculing varieties of the poet's "simplicity" are to one another; and how in either case the assumption of childishness rests upon anecdotal appeals to his adaptation for or by children.

When responding to Wordsworth parody, in "The Baby's Debut," Jeffrey ensures that review and verse are alike joined in an ironic consensus to disclaim any intention to parody: the method of pretended imitation must feign innocence of a genre that of necessity gestures toward and yet deflects, or is deflected away from, an original. When responding to Wordsworth himself, in *Poems, in Two Volumes,* however, Jeffrey transforms an apparently innocuous act of "imitation" into a poetry that is synonymous with a parodic, or namby-pamby, tradition: "the Small Celandine," we recall, is "taken

for a professed imitation of one of Mr Philips's prettyisms." Even more star-
tlingly, the poet becomes an "imitator"—and a *bad* imitator—of his own
Lyrical Ballads style:

> Even in the worst of these productions, there are, no doubt, occasional little
> traits of delicate feeling and original fancy; but these are quite lost and ob-
> scured in the mass of childishness and insipidity with which they are incor-
> porated; nor can any thing give us a more melancholy view of the debasing
> effects of this miserable theory, than that it has given ordinary men a right to
> wonder at the folly and presumption of a man gifted like Mr Wordsworth,
> and made him appear, in his second avowed publication, like a bad imitator
> of the worst of his former productions.
>
> (*ER* 11 [October 1807], 231)

As Coleridge would later concur, it is the theory's fault (*BL* I, 70–71; II,
119–20). However, where he attempts to show a Wordsworth who is instinc-
tively free of his theoretical commitments, Jeffrey insists that they are both in-
escapable and "debasing." Another passage from the same review (quoted
above) surrounded Wordsworth's "pathetic pieces" with the offensively ludicrous subjects of other poets—sucking-pigs, grandmothers, and gooseberry-
pie. Here, similarly, poetic values are "lost and obscured in the mass of
childishness and insipidity with which they are incorporated." In either instance, Jeffrey seeks to "attach" to Wordsworth a "ridicule" that has been established through his criticism's parodic relationship to the poetry. What's
more, Wordsworth in 1807 is declared to be a pale imitation of Wordsworth
in 1800. The throwback to *Lyrical Ballads* appears to have a function beyond
that of tying the Laker to a juvenile poetics and persona. Its other point is to
make him go from bad to worse—in short, to make him *self*-parodic.

The Self-parodic School of Poetry

In Leigh Hunt's *Feast of the Poets*, Wordsworth is found "spouting"

> some lines he had made on a straw,
> Shewing how he had found it, and what it was for,
> And how, when 'twas balanc'd, it stood like a spell!—
> And how, when 'twas balanc'd no longer, it fell!
> A wild thing of scorn he describ'd it to be,
> But he said it was patient to heaven's decree:—
> Then he gaz'd upon nothing, and looking forlorn,
> Dropt a *natural* tear for *that wild thing of scorn!*[38]

Like other members of his circle, Hunt had mixed views about Wordsworth,
and was by no means univocally unappreciative. However, he did share in

the wider cultural distaste for the poet's experiments in "childish" ballads[39]—an antipathy that is signaled by his choice of anapestic rhyming couplets. In its repetitions, Hunt's verse is itself doubly mischievous, since it performs the parodist's echo of a (fictitious) text, even as it parodies the redundancies associated with Wordsworth's own habits of tautology. The final exclamatory emphasis—"*that wild thing of scorn!*"—corresponds to Jeffrey's manner of drawing attention, by italicized quotation, to whatever seems most self-evidently laughable in the poet's style. For all their differences, the editors of the *Edinburgh* and *Examiner* make common cause here. *The Feast of the Poets* first appeared in the Hunts' *Reflector* (1811). On being lifted out of its magazine format for separate publication, the work gained 110 pages of notes. Directed as much at the poet's fan club as at the poet himself, the note to the lines just quoted reads: "I am told, on very good authority, that this parody upon Mr. Wordsworth's worst style of writing has been taken for a serious extract from him, and panegyrized accordingly, with much grave wonderment how I could find it ridiculous!" (*Feast,* p. 87n19).

Hunt's disingenuousness could certainly have been learnt from Jeffrey: his *Autobiography* confesses to having been "then unacquainted" with Wordsworth's writings "except through the medium of his deriders."[40] And Jeffrey for his part seems gleefully to have seized upon the possibility, laid out by Hunt, that Wordsworth parody could swap places with Wordsworth poetry;[41] his review of *The White Doe of Rylstone* has almost as damning an opening as his infamous article on *The Excursion:*

> This, we think, has the merit of being the very worst poem we ever saw imprinted in a quarto volume. . . . It is just such a work, in short, as some wicked enemy of that [new or Wordsworthian] school might be supposed to have devised, on purpose to make it ridiculous; and when we first took it up, we could not help fancying that some ill-natured critic had taken this harsh method of instructing Mr Wordsworth, by example, in the nature of those errors, against which our precepts had been so often directed in vain.
>
> (*ER* 25 [October 1815], 355)

Once again, the anniversary of October—that Glorious Twelfth of the *Edinburgh*'s Lakeland calendar—is observed. The poet's anti-progress has now reached a nadir of debasement. Wordsworth's latest poem is represented as so far gone in self-parody as to be mistaken for the work of a hostile critic: so thoroughly "bad" an imitation could be attributable only to a source outside the "school" itself. That this mock-Wordsworth should have been "devised, on purpose to make it ridiculous," is of course a precise description of the aims and contrivances of the parodic reviewer himself, and of his long-running opposition to the new school. Yet all the while, it is the real Wordsworth who is under review, and whose poem is exposed as the last and "worst" of his *self*-imitations.

The sly jest of "fancying . . . some ill-natured critic" seems at once to be responding to, and claiming a degree of responsibility for, the "harsh method of instructing Mr Wordsworth, by example," which emerged in *The Feast of the Poets,* published the previous year. In Hunt's annotation, a parody Wordsworth is said to have been taken by admirers for the genuine article; in Jeffrey's review, the genuine article is purportedly assumed to be the work of "some wicked enemy." Jeffrey capitalized on *Rejected Addresses* by using the imitative model of criticism to pretend that the Smiths' parody or pretended imitation of Wordsworth was a true imitation of the poet. That was sufficiently entangling, perhaps; but the shrewder application of the model comes about when both he and Hunt turn to Wordsworth himself, and play off their own parodic intentions against another, imaginary audience—be it the gormless admirer or the malevolent critic.

Either way, it is the business of parodic reception and reviewing to ensure that parody usurps the place of poetry. Both Hunt and Jeffrey can be seen as giving formal recognition to the requirements of their "method of instructing . . . by example." The usurpation of Wordsworth's poetry by parody acts out its usurpation by criticism, or by the critical stance that is implicit in its parodic representation. With this in mind, it follows that Reynolds's "antenatal Peter" (as Shelley christened it) was merely publishing or literalizing a priority of parody to poetry that was already normative in the adverse criticism of Wordsworth. To put it another way, parody had become the original of which the poems were the imitators.

Issued by Keats' publishers, Taylor and Hessey, on April 16, 1819, Reynolds' "skit" upon *Peter Bell*[42] was the apotheosis of pretended imitation. The poem declared itself to be "a Lyrical Ballad," and ironically vouched for its own authenticity with the words "'I do affirm that I am the real Simon Pure.'" Reynolds' epigraph is adapted from act V of *A Bold Stroke for a Wife* (p. 86), Susanna Centlivre's pro-Hanoverian comedy of 1718: "the real" is his addition to the text. At this point in the play, the male lead, Colonel Fainwell, is speaking to a Quaker preacher called Simon Pure, after he has assumed the latter's identity in order to trick the pious guardian of Miss Lovely into allowing them to marry; and from this situation arose "The compound *simon-pure,* meaning *genuine.*"[43] Apart from their metrical symmetry, the names Peter Bell and Simon Pure may well have rung a bell with Reynolds because the two had recently been linked by Peter Pindar, in one of whose Odes "The gossiping Peter telleth a strange Story," in which "Truth" features as "a plain Simon Pure, a Quaker preacher, / A moral mender, a disgusting teacher, / That never got a sixpence by her speeches!"[44] As well as twitting Wordsworth with its claim to be the genuine article, then,

Reynolds' epigraph insinuated the poet's tendency to dogmatism of a sanctimonious or prudish—and impoverishing—kind (something Shelley afterward developed in *Peter Bell the Third* and that, as it turned out, was curiously apposite to the methodistical aura of the Wordsworth poem).

Reynolds' equation of "Peter Bell" with "Simon Pure" drew attention to the fact that his poem was prompted by Wordsworth's summoning of "those ridiculous associations which vulgar names give rise to."[45] The issue of poetic naming was also one of poetic class, and Reynolds had risen to the bait that the "lyrical ballad" ostentatiously threw in the way of contemporary taste. Later in 1819, Wordsworth doggedly took the idea of a classless poetic to his parodists and critics. Quoting the motto to the *Waggoner* volume—"'What's in a name? / Brutus will start a spirit as soon as Caesar!'"—the *Monthly Review* was quick to reach the logical conclusion: "and, *therefore*, 'the Waggoner' will do as well as Brutus" (*MR* 90 [September 1819], 36). While Shakespeare's play casts the shadow of Brutus' overthrow upon Caesar's greatness (*Julius Caesar* I. ii.144–66), Wordsworth implies a challenge to an inherited poetic constitution, or at the very least the equality for poetry of different names. In this context, Reynolds' epigraph has had a further point to make: behind the innocent and successful impostures of Centlivre's Colonel Fainwell lurks the failed attempt of the Stuart Pretender, in the first Jacobite Rebellion of 1715, to overturn the Act of Settlement, which secured the throne for a Protestant succession under George I. An active supporter of the Hanoverian Whigs, Centlivre used her play both to defuse and recast this Jacobite plot, and to "Convince our unthinking Britons by what vile arts France lost her liberty."[46] A hundred years later, and the ground of pretence has shifted in the direction of the literary, and the legitimacy (or otherwise) of aspirants to the throne of literature. Significantly enough, when Lamb wrote to Wordsworth about the "mock" *Peter Bell,* he asked, "Is there no law against these rascals? I would have this Lambert Simnel whipt at the cart's tail."[47] Lambert Simnel was one of two pretenders to the throne of England during the reign of Henry VII.

Though Reynolds was clearly a pretender, so too, in his own way, was Wordsworth, since he introduced into poetry claimants to poetic interest who formerly had had no place there. In pretending to be Wordsworth, Reynolds undertook to "feign" as well as Centlivre's Colonel. Yet, in selecting his epigraph, he raised the very questions of authorship and authorization that his pseudonymous spoof ostensibly proposed to evade. "Simon Pure" gave a name to the deliberately provoking ways in which his *Peter Bell* simultaneously asserted, and cast doubt on, the poet's validity and identity. A "Preface" signed "W.W." warned readers to beware of impostors, "As these are the days of counterfeits."[48] A follow-up squib, "Peter Bell *v.* Peter Bell," launched an authorial suit, but only facetiously, distinguishing "The

Burlesque,—by its having a meaning" from "The Real,—by its having an Ass" (lines 1–2, 13–16).

Coleridge's classification of the period's "pretended imitations" recognized both the pretence and how the parody might get taken for real. In Reynolds, that threat of displacement was realized: imitation Wordsworth usurped genuine Wordsworth in a text of the same name. Reynolds provided the impetus—and possibly was himself responsible[49]—for yet "another fling at Mr. Wordsworth" in *The Dead Asses,* whose gruesome newspaper-derived tale of two animals left to starve did not deter one reviewer from feigning to detect the hand of the poet himself before ceding priority to his parodist: "The verses . . . are written so much in Mr. Wordsworth's style, that we should certainly have taken it for one of his productions, had not the pseudo Peter Bell convinced us that this lyrical ballad belonged to the same author" (*New Monthly Magazine* 12 [October 1819], 332). The trick of putting the parodic cart before the poetic horse (or ass) has been around in the reviewing of Wordsworth for some time; and it is interesting, though not surprising, that the reviews reacted to the *Peter Bell* phenomenon by seizing on it as a confirmation and extension of their existing parodic methods. The *Eclectic Review* set the tone, archly demanding, "from whom but Mr. Wordsworth could we expect to receive any other than a burlesque poem under the title of Peter Bell?" (11 [May 1819], 475). That does little more than take up the opportunity provided by Reynolds, of treating "The Real" *Peter Bell* as though it were "The Burlesque." The intriguing thing, though, is that this review is immediately followed by a parody—a parody, as it happens, of Hunt (475–78). It is as though the whole frame of Wordsworth's reception has become parodic. And something like a deliberate journal policy does seem to have been at work. A few months later, in consecutive numbers of the *Monthly Review,* notices of Wordsworth poems go hand-in-hand with notices of their parodies. The August 1819 issue places its articles on the two *Peter Bell*s side-by-side (*MR* 89, 421–23). The September number (*MR* 90, 36–42) does precisely the same with reviews of *The Waggoner* and the anonymous parody, *Benjamin the Waggoner*—which, despite its title, was also *Peter Bell*–inspired, and thought to be by Reynolds.[50]

The parodic method of reviewing has acquired a formal dimension, achieving a sort of simultaneous transmission of poem and parody in which it is the latter that provides the determining context for Wordsworth's reception. Reviewing *The Waggoner,* Wordsworth's half-ironical, half-indulgent critic "exhort[s] him to cultivate his talent for the ridiculous" on the grounds that "nature has plainly designed him, 'the Prince of Poetical Burlesque'" (*MR* 90, 39). Having delivered a harsher judgment on the "infatuated poetaster" of *Peter Bell,* the *Monthly* turns swiftly to the wider parodic context:

We really waste *words,* however, on what is scarcely *Word's-worth* . . . Some well-meaning, and, in one case, witty individuals have published parodies of Peter Bell, the potter, and of his brother, the Waggoner. We shall be required briefly to notice these parodies, as well as their originals: but in fact the originals themselves are the parodies, or rather the gross burlesques of all that is good in poetry. It is like travestying Cotton's Travesties of Homer and Virgil, to parody Wordsworth's own parodies of other illustrious poets. Nay, he is the buffoon of Nature herself; and . . . presents to some a *ludicrous,* and to all an *unfaithful* portrait of his pretended original. We say pretended; for in fact it is not Nature, but his own narrow, whimsical, unpoetical idea of Nature, which this strange writer worships.

(*MR* 89, 421)

Wordsworth is parodic twice over: a burlesquer "of all that is good in poetry," he is also "the buffoon of Nature herself." In this inferior relation to "his pretended original" he becomes himself a pretender of the lowest rank. If Wordsworth is parodic, then his parodists are doubly so. The spectacle of the parody parodied is provided by Charles Cotton, whose seventeenth-century buffooning led to a travesty of Virgil *In English Burlesque*—"I *Sing the Man* (read it who list), / A *Trojan* true (as ever pist,)"—which was itself a redressing of Paul Scarron's *Virgile Travesti.* Similarly, his *Lucian's Dialogues Newly put into English Fustian* made for a *Burlesque upon Burlesque: or, the Scoffer Scoff'd.* Like Byron and Jeffrey's resurrection of Namby Pamby, the *Monthly's* citation of the tradition of *Mock-Poem* belittles Wordsworth by putting him low in a neoclassical hierarchy. This is the parodic school of reviewing as the sprightly guardian of reactionary taste.

The New School of Criticism

Parody, which sings alongside another poem, is etymologically disposed to resemble the art of criticism. If, as Marilyn Gaull remarks, the Romantic is the period in which parody "comes of age,"[51] it is also the period that sees the beginnings of professional criticism. The truism that parody is a form of criticism[52] can be thought of as having been applicable in culturally specific and documentable ways. A few of these intricate lines of relationship have been traced here. In passing, it has been striking how many of the verse-parodists discussed were themselves, like Gifford and Canning in the 1790s, journalists or journal editors. Perhaps, then, Romantic verse parody is properly to be regarded as taking up a variety of positions within a "new school of criticism." Not only are parody and criticism intimately related at their rise, they also interact, each sharing the other's techniques and often copy space. Suggestive in this regard are the multiple crossings-over of form or format within both the reviews themselves—the habitual switches from prose to verse and back again—and the mixed-genre journalism of *The Satirist* or *Blackwood's*.

Reversals are dear to parody; but the parodic reception of Wordsworth appears to have had a specialized interest in those involving his authority, identity, and originality—taking genuine Wordsworth for parody, or counterfeit Wordsworth for true coin. These too had formal equivalents, most obviously in the promiscuous blending of real with fake Wordsworth in the Prefaces and annotations to the *Peter Bell* parodies—such forms being best adapted to mock-solemn declarations of authorial priority and purpose. A blend of this type arises in "The Nose-Drop: A Physiological Ballad" (1821), which was published under the poet's initials but also, via a "Note, by the Editor," as a posthumous production (a trick picked up from Reynolds, whose Peter Bell comes upon his author in a suicide's grave). In prefacing this, the last of all his literary labors, Wordsworth is found boasting about the juvenility that marked his very first collection of poems:

> I have taken as much pains to avoid what is usually called *poetic diction,* as others ordinarily take to produce it; and, restricting myself from the use of those cut-and-dry figures of speech which have long been regarded as the common inheritance of poets, I have converted their Parnassus into a nursery, and exchanged the winged Pegasus for a hobbyhorse, and the mantle of the Muse for the bib and tucker of a baby.[53]

This return to the nursery puts Wordsworth back where he began, and takes me back to where my chapter started. I want to end with a reversal of my own, serving partly to turn the tables on the poet's critics. Leigh Hunt observed that the "extreme" to which the "Revolutionists" of the "new" school went was calculated "to make the readers of poetry disgusted with originality and adhere with contempt and resentment to their magazine common-places."[54] Yet there is also a sense in which their contact with the Lake poets provided the occasions on which these commonplaces were to be refreshed and multifariously redeployed.

Wordsworth's characterization as self-parodic brought his poetry into alignment with the perspective being adopted by his critics; but, with very few exceptions, this parodic criticism insisted that, being staid or simple, the poet was himself unconscious of the parody he displayed: *The Simpliciad* ended by noting his "solemn buffoonery" (p. 47n.); the *Eclectic Review* took even his *Waggoner* as proof "that as he is himself devoid of any talent for humour, so he is, through a singular simplicity of mind, insuspectible of the ludicrous" (*Eclectic Review* 12 [July 1819][55]). That Wordsworth lacked a sense of the ridiculous enabled it to be assumed on his behalf, just as his poetry routinely got treated as though it were itself the "doggrel rhime" his critics

and parodists supplied (*Simpliciad,* line 129). This transference to the parodist's script of the power to amuse has had lasting effects in the criticism of
Wordsworth and of "Romanticism" more generally. And yet the possibility
of such a transference can ultimately be traced to Wordsworth himself.
Steven Jones has noted recently that "the many parodies" of *Peter Bell*
"brought out its own latent satiric tendencies," while at the same time "the
seeds of absurdity are planted in the text as part of its dialectical potential—
then are resisted or displaced."[56] Paul D. Sheats has finely observed that
"The Thorn" presents both "a trap, baited with a remarkably offensive 'pro-
saism'," and evidence of "a larger strategy of confrontation that the poet conceived as immediately satiric but ultimately edifying."[57] The potential for
laughter is excited, but also unaccountably diverted. The peculiarity of the
case is connected with its leaning toward the very things that formerly pro-
voked a parodic response: when Carey overheard Namby Pamby, it was,
"Now methinks I hear him say, / Boys and girls come out to play! / Moon
do's shine as bright as day" (Macdonald, p. 27); when Wordsworth quotes
Johnny Foy, his "very words" are "'The cocks did crow to-whoo, to-whoo, /
And the sun did shine so cold.'" What was self-evidently ludicrous to the
Scriblerian set is transformed into a tale told by an "idiot" signifying, not
nothing, but on the contrary the luminous expressiveness that lies in revers-
ing the normal order of things, or in momentary exemptions from the logic
that deprives ordinary life of its fullness. And that, apparently, is Wordsworth's way of having his joke and eating it, too.

Notes

1. James K. Chandler, "The Pope Controversy: Romantic Poets and the English Canon," *Critical Inquiry* 10 (1984): 481–87; William Hazlitt, "On Dryden and Pope," in *Lectures on the English Poets,* intro. by Catherine
   Macdonald Maclean ([1910] London: Dent, 1959), hereafter cited parenthetically in the text; Matthew Arnold, "The Study of Poetry," in *Essays in
   Criticism. Second Series* (London: Macmillan and Co., 1895).
2. Robert J. Griffin, *Wordsworth's Pope: A Study in Literary Historiography*
   (Cambridge: Cambridge University Press, 1995), chapt. 1; hereafter cited
   parenthetically in the text.
3. *Byron's Letters and Journals,* ed. Leslie A. Marchand, 13 vols. (London: John
   Murray, 1973–1982), V, 265 (September 15, 1817); hereafter cited as *BLJ.*
4. *Jeffrey's Criticism: A Selection,* ed. Peter F. Morgan (Edinburgh: Scottish Academic Press, 1983), 45, 52.
5. Jerome J. McGann, *The Beauty of Inflections: Literary Investigations in Historical Method and Theory* (Oxford: Clarendon Press, 1985), 307.
6. Claude Rawson astutely detects class at work: "Shelley and Byron are the
   two major Romantic poets who are closest to the Augustan 'aristocratic'

sensibility" in *Satire and Sentiment 1660–1830* (Cambridge: Cambridge University Press, 1994), 102.

7. Coleridge, *Table Talk*, in *The Table Talk and Omniana of Samuel Taylor Coleridge* (Oxford: Oxford University Press, 1917), 189 (July 21, 1832).

8. *The Letters of William and Dorothy Wordsworth, The Early Years 1787–1805*, ed. Ernest de Selincourt, 2nd edn., rev., Chester L. Shaver (Oxford: Clarendon Press, 1967), 169 (March 21, 1796); hereafter cited in the text as *EY*.

9. *Barron Field's Memoirs of Wordsworth*, ed. Geoffrey Little (Sydney: Sydney University Press, 1975), 37n.43.

10. Gary Dyer, *British Satire and the Politics of Style, 1789–1832* (Cambridge: Cambridge University Press, 1997), 17.

11. Coleridge, *Biographia Literaria*, ed. James Engell and W. Jackson Bate (London and Princeton, N.J.: Routledge & Kegan Paul and Princeton University Press, 1983), II, 9; hereafter cited parenthetically in the text as *BL*.

12. Richard Mant (anon.), *The Simpliciad; A Satirico-Didactic Poem* (1808), facsim. ed. Jonathan Wordsworth (Oxford: Woodstock Books, 1991).

13. *Pace* Nathaniel Teich, "Wordsworth's Reception and Copleston's *Advice* to Romantic Reviewers," *The Wordsworth Circle* 6 (Autumn 1975): 280–82 (280); and *Romantic Parodies, 1797–1831*, ed. David A. Kent and D. R. Ewen (London and Toronto: Associated University Presses, 1992), 54, the *British Critic* was not hostile: on the contrary, its review of Mant's *Poems* expressed "the warmest praise" and its Preface saw him as a "credit to the Wartonian School" (vol. 28 [November 1806], 559–60, xv.

14. Edward Copleston, *Advice to a Young Reviewer*, in *Romantic Parodies*, 54; and see Teich, 280–81

15. *BLJ*, III, 213.

16. Published in *The Satirist*, 1809, and attributed to its editor, George Manners; see *Romantic Parodies*, 62–67.

17. See Arthur H. Beavan, *James and Horace Smith* (London: Hurst and Blackett, 1899), 104–105, 109–10.

18. Dwight Macdonald, ed., *Parodies: An Anthology from Chaucer to Beerbohm—and After* (London: Faber and Faber, 1960), 79–80; *DNB*.

19. N. Stephen Bauer, "Early Burlesques and Parodies of Wordsworth," *JEGP* 74 (1975): 553–69 (556–57).

20. Simon Dentith, *Parody*, New Critical Idiom series (London and New York: Routledge, 2000), 110–11; and see Dyer, 16–17.

21. Dryden, "A Discourse concerning the Original and Progress of Satire," in *Essays of John Dryden*, ed. W. P. Ker, 2 vols., second edn. ([1900] Oxford: Clarendon Press, 1926), II, 105. Wordsworth's rhymes were a recurrent source of complaint: cf. *Annual Review* 6 (1808): 527: "Forced, imperfect, and double rhymes abounding to an offensive and sometimes ludicrous degree."

22. Reynolds' device produces what Oliver Elton describes as "a mosaic-parody" of *Lyrical Ballads* in *A Survey of English Literature, 1780–1830*, 2 vols. (London, 1912), I, 293.

23. *The Letters of John Keats,* ed. Hyder Edward Rollins, 2 vols. (Cambridge: Cambridge University Press, 1958), I, 151–52.

24. Dyer, 88.

25. Peacock, *Sir Proteus* ii (st.12), in *The Works of Thomas Love Peacock* (Halliford Edition), ed. H. F. B. Brett-Smith and C. E. Jones, 10 vols. (London: Constable & Co., 1924–1934), II, 290.

26. Peacock, *Melincourt,* chaps. 28, 39, in *Works,* II, 301, 398.

27. The continued currency of the term is suggested by Coleridge, who in 1793 made light of a piece of poetic "Gallantry" ("As late each Flower") by classing it "of the namby pamby Genus" (*Collected Letters of Samuel Taylor Coleridge,* ed. E. L. Griggs, 6 vols. [Oxford, 1956–1971], I, 57–58.

28. See M. G. Segar, ed., *The Poems of Ambrose Philips* (Oxford: Basil Blackwell, 1937, xxiii, xxxviii, xliv-xlv.

29. *Works of Addison,* VI, 696.

30. Dwight Macdonald, ed., *Parodies: An Anthology from Chaucer to Beerbohm—and After,* 25, hereafter cited parenthetically in the text; and see Segar, 182.

31. As Byron would be well aware, it was the criticism of Pope's Pastorals for their lack of the "simplicity" associated with "Pastoral Philips" that caused Pope to send an essay to the *Guardian* in which the simple Philips was ridiculed by means of ironic praise.

32. Reynolds' publishers, Taylor and Hessey, named his poem a "burlesque imitation of the 'Idiot Boy'" (quoted Leonidas M. Jones, *The Life of John Hamilton Reynolds* [Hanover and London: University Press of New England, 1984], 174; for possible disingenuousness, see 175).

33. *The Life of John Hamilton Reynolds,* 176. Reynolds's praise of Wordsworth's "excellencies" (p. 174) is found in his journalism from 1816: see *Selected Prose of John Hamilton Reynolds,* ed. Leonidas M. Jones (Cambridge, MA: Harvard University Press, 1966), 62, 70–75, 79.

34. *Monthly Review* 89 (August 1819): 420, hereafter cited as *MR;* as the reviewer facetiously observes, "This infantine pamphlet is dedicated to Robert Southey, Esq. *P.L.* or Poet Laureate, by William Wordsworth, Esq. *L.P.* or Lake Poet" (419).

35. N. Stephen Bauer's checklist of forty-seven burlesques and parodies starts in 1801 and ends in 1836 (567–69); of these, "only fifteen [appeared] before 1819" and the increase "parallels the progress of Wordsworth's reputation, which was not firmly established until around 1820. Yet [almost] all [. . .] mock poems that Wordsworth had written in 1802 or earlier" (566).

36. Which is not to say that "Augustan" principles were invariably or universally applied: for the view that Jeffrey represented a "see-saw" between old and new, see Thomas Crawford, *The Edinburgh Review and Romantic Poetry* (Aukland: Aukland University College, 1955); but for evidence of a sea-change around 1816, see Leigh Hunt's *Examiner* for December 1: "We were delighted to see the departure of the old school acknowledged in the number of the *Edinburgh Review* just published, a candour much more generous

and spirited, inasmuch as that work has hitherto been the greatest surviving ornament of the same school in prose and criticism."

37. Jeffrey's use of typography has been observed by Robert Daniel, "Jeffrey and Wordsworth: The Shape of Persecution," *Sewanee Review* 50 (1942): 195–213 (208); see also *The Simpliciad*'s presentation of its "Authorities."

38. Leigh Hunt, *The Feast of the Poets* (1814), facsim. ed. Jonathan Wordsworth (Oxford: Woodstock Books, 1989), 12.

39. See Swaen, A. E. H., "Peter Bell," *Anglia* 35 (1923): 136–84 (142).

40. *The Autobiography of Leigh Hunt,* ed. J. E. Morpurgo (London: Cresset Press, 1949), 233.

41. However, Hunt's *Autobiography* bemoans his neglect by "the Whig critics" and the *Edinburgh*'s failure to notice *The Feast* in particular (chapter 12; 227–28). Jeffrey did at last recognize Hunt in a review of *Rimini,* which, though mixed, took pleasure in it as a product of "the antient school" (*Edinburgh Review [ER]* 26 [June 1816], 477).

42. So Keats called it in his review for *The Examiner* (cited in Swaen, 158)

43. Susanna Centlivre, *A Bold Stroke for a Wife,* ed. Thalia Stathas (London: Edward Arnold, 1969), xxii–xxiii.

44. *Lyric Odes,* IX, 1785, reissued in 1816. A Simon Pure also authors a satirical tale called *Hops! Hops!! Hops!!!* (London, 1813).

45. Taylor and Hessey's reply to Coleridge's letter of protest, quoted, Leonidas M. Jones, *Life,* 174. Cf. Keats's professed sorrow "that an appreciator of Wordsworth should show so much temper at this really provoking name of Peter Bell" (1819 journal-letter, quoted, Swaen, 141; his review of Reynolds, which differs slightly, is reprinted Swaen, 158–59).

46. *Bold Stroke,* 4, from the dedication to Philip, Duke and Marquis of Wharton (who had Whig ancestry, but had supported the Pretender) and referring to the 1610 murder of Henry IV of France by a fanatical Catholic, and the loss of Henry's hard-won tolerance for Huguenots under Louis XIV.

47. E. V. Lucas, ed., *The Letters of Charles Lamb to which are added those of his sister Mary Lamb,* 3 vols. (London: J. M. Dent and Methuen, 1935), II, 241.

48. The Wordsworth circle duly rose to the bait: Coleridge is said to have pronounced the poem to be the work of Lamb, though as Lucas points out his letter to the publishers about "a base breach of trust" suggests otherwise. Lamb, meanwhile, told Wordsworth he guessed it to be another effort by "one of the sneering brothers—the vile Smiths—but I have heard no name mentioned" (Lucas, *Letters of Charles Lamb,* II, 243, 241).

49. George L. Marsh, "The *Peter Bell* Parodies of 1819," *Modern Philology* 40 (1943): 267–74 (274); Leonidas M. Jones, *Life,* 176.

50. It has since been attributed to J. G. Lockhart; see Jack Benoit Gohn, "Who Wrote *Benjamin the Waggoner?* An Inquiry," *The Wordsworth Circle* 8 (Winter 1977): 69–74 (69).

51. Marilyn Gaull, "Romantic Humor: The Horse of Knowledge and the Learned Pig," *Mosaic* 9 (1976): 43–64 (43).

52. See J. G. Riewald, "Parody as Criticism," *Neophilologus* 50 (1966): 125–48; and E. V. Knox, quoted Mrs. Herbert Richardson, *Parody,* The English Association Pamphlet no. 92 (August 1935), 6.

53. Robert Mortenson, "'The Nose-Drop': A Parody of Wordsworth," *The Wordsworth Circle* 3 (Summer 1971): 91–100 (92).

54. Quoted in Dyer, 23.

55. Smith, 300ff.

56. Steven Jones, *Satire and Romanticism* (New York: Palgrave, 2000), 32.

57. Paul D. Sheats, "''Tis Three Feet Long and Two Feet Wide': Wordsworth's 'Thorn' and the Politics of Bathos," *The Wordsworth Circle* 22 (Spring 1991): 92–100 (93–94).

Chapter 5 ∾

Jane Austen's *Northanger Abbey:* Self-reflexive Satire and Biopoetics

Karl Kroeber

Biopoetics, an offshoot of sociobiology, is not primarily concerned with environmentalism or "nature writing," because it aims to discover how art may contribute to co-evolutionary processes by which cultural and biological forces have interacted to make human beings the unusual creatures that they are.[1] Although many empirical sociobiological studies and much of its theorizing has been subjected to damaging critical analyses,[2] the basic concept of co-evolution has proved viable and, in fact, is increasingly a locus of interdisciplinary discussions more mutually enriching for both humanists and biological scientists than most eco-criticism. A key interdisciplinary focal point is evolutionary psychology, which seeks to identify specific linkages between genetics and culture. Evolutionary psychologists try to define with some precision the psychic systems of information processing that enable human behavior to modify the effects of purely biological evolution.[3] In this commentary on the satiric self-reflexivity of Jane Austen's *Northanger Abbey* I illustrate how humanists might use their special expertise at evaluating the special human behavior that produces works of literature to increase understanding of how cultural history can modify our biological heritage.

Literary critics study artifacts constructed by language. Human language is the only biological information-communicating system that has arisen to supplement the genetic information mechanism, which for most of the history of life on earth was the unique power driving evolution. A special product of evolution, human language differs from so-called animal "languages" because it is syntactical, which permits us both to understand and to create an infinite number of original sentences immediately meaningful to others. Syntactical language is also superior to the repertoire of signals that most animals possess because it permits the retention, modification, and *retransmission* of information—when writing supplements memory, even across vast spans of time. The linguistic artifact with which this essay is concerned, Jane Austen's *Northanger Abbey,* was first written down some six genetic generations ago. Language above all else allows culture to affect genetic evolution, makes possible co-evolution. Literary scholars by experience and training should be better equipped than anyone else to analyze and evaluate the linguistic artifacts that (as is signaled by their endurance, their capacity to be endlessly re-transmitted) embody this potency of human psychic processes to reorient even the forces of physical evolution.

Syntactic communication, not being confined to reference to whole events (as is the blue-jay shrieking, warning of the appearance of a predator), allows preservation and re-transmission of information about the *uniqueness* of each and every event—not just about happenings that are unexpected and unusual but also (and much more importantly) about the unique character of customary and commonplace occurrences. Detailed, systematically constructed narratives that report and evaluate ordinary and often repeated human experiences are probably a major means by which culture affects biological evolution. "Fictional" narratives, from orally recited myths to contemporary printed novels, seem likely to be the most important "thought experiments" that can modify those psychic processes through which culture modulates effects upon humankind of biological history.[4]

I

I choose *Northanger Abbey* to exemplify this potency of fictional narrative because I (like many thousands of readers over the past two centuries) thoroughly enjoy the novel. Pleasure as the mental self-reward of psychic exertion has for too long been disregarded in our criticism.[5] Furthermore, the satiric attack of Austen's novel on abuses in and of eighteenth-century English Gothic fiction offers relatively clear understanding of her purposes. Every satire opposes some specific social attitude or activity, some historically particularized human behavior. Because the explicit intention of satire is plainer than in other literary forms, it provides the most solid basis for identifying more implicit functions of a text. This advantage was seized upon in one of the earliest and best "biopoetic" essays, Alvin Kernan's account of satire as a means for controlling impulses of violence toward members of our own species, a control we need to develop because, unlike most other dangerous animals, human beings are not genetically preprogrammed to resist such impulses.[6] Kernan works, however, at a high level of abstraction. He discusses satire in general and impulses to violence in general, with the result that, while I believe he is generally right, his approach can show only how satire encourages humans to make their cultures resist unmodifiable effects of our genetic heritage. The concept of co-evolution, however, tempts us toward the more daring hypothesis that it may be possible for certain kinds of cultured activity (such as writing satires) to alter what appear to be immutable genetic determinants of our behavior.

To test this hypothesis we must enter more deeply into what an evolutionary psychologist would regard as behavioral specifics, taking account, for example, of different effects of different kinds of satire. *Northanger Abbey* in fact exemplifies what Steven Jones describes as the dominant form taken by satire in the Romantic period, distinctive in being relational and resistive to sharp definition, both because it mingles with other modes and because its condemnatory thrust is "local, specific, and relational," so that critical self-reflexivity is decisive to both its "performance and reception."[7] Satiric fiction tends toward self-reflexivity because narrative discourse exploits language's capacity for productive feedback, and for "internal expansion and differentiation without external leverage," its "self-opening" potentialities.[8] An elegant illustration of these is provided by Henry and Elinor Tilney's discussion of the picturesque to the edification of Catherine Morland.[9]

> They were viewing the country with the eyes of persons accustomed to drawing, and decided on its capability of being formed into pictures, with all the eagerness of real taste. Here Catherine was quite lost. She knew nothing of drawing—nothing of taste:—and she listened to them with an attention which brought her little profit, for they talked in phrases which conveyed scarcely any idea to her. The little which she could understand however appeared to contradict the very few notions she had entertained on the matter before. It seemed as if a good view were no longer to be taken from the top of a high hill, and that a clear blue sky was no longer proof of a fine day. She was heartily ashamed of her ignorance. (1, Chapter 14, 110)

These sentences force readers to reassess their original judgment, as "real taste" turns out absurdly to deny that "a clear blue sky" is "proof of a fine day." The admirable Tilneys—so definitively superior to the Thorpes—here display how they have been infected by a faddish jargon, which we recognize that Catherine would be better off to stay clear of, as she would be better off resisting the influence of Radcliffian Gothicism. But, instead, Catherine is ashamed of her ignorance of this false knowledge, shame that is immediately subject to authorial condemnation from a different angle entirely.

A misplaced shame. Where people wish to attach, they should always be ignorant. To come with a well-informed mind is to come with an inability of
administering to the vanity of others, which a sensible person would always
wish to avoid. A woman especially, if she have the misfortune of knowing any
thing, should conceal it as well as she can. (1,14, 114)

The satiric target, however, at once shifts from Catherine back again to
Henry to expose his conventional male prejudices. Yet immediately female
authors are gathered back into the critique, so that when Austen swings back
to the courtship of Henry and Catherine with a judgment equally unflatter-
ing to both, she encourages us to laugh even at her own practice so far as it
appears to take them seriously.

The advantages of natural folly in a beautiful girl have been already set forth
by the capital pen of a sister author;—and to her treatment of the subject I
will only add in justice to men, that though to the larger and more trifling
part of the sex, imbecility in females is a great enhancement of their personal
charms, there is a portion of them too reasonable and too well informed
themselves to desire anything more in a woman than ignorance. But Catherine did not know her own advantages—did not know that a good-looking
girl, with an affectionate heart and a very ignorant mind, cannot fail of at-
tracting a clever young man, unless circumstances are particularly untoward.
In the present instance, she confessed and lamented her want of knowledge;
declared that she would give any thing in the world to be able to draw; a lecture on picturesque immediately followed, in which his instructions were so
clear that she soon began to see beauty in every thing admired by him, and
her attention was so earnest, that he became perfectly satisfied of her having
a great deal of natural taste. (1,14, 115)

Nobody writes better than Jane Austen, but all superior fiction offers its
readers analogous dynamics of self-reflexive psychological activity in the
process of reading. Austen's light-hearted but deep-striking satire makes it
relatively easy to perceive the linguistic manipulations by which all fictional
narration affects the reader's mind by compelling it to assess the *systems* by
which it comprehends and comes to judgments.[10] This is why literary art is
so valuable for analyzing what evolutionary psychologists call our "information processing mechanisms." The core of these mechanisms involves
human beings' intense self-awareness, which means in essence a capacity for
autonomously modifying how these mechanisms operate. The productive
self-reflexivity stimulated by literary narrative offers probably the best insight into how language, by interconnecting social behavior and individual
psychic activity, gives humans power to adjust the functioning of their biological inheritance as social animals.

The self-reflexivity of narrative satire appears vividly in Austen's exposure of the foolishness of picturesque jargon, because this satire's efficacy derives from the construction of her novel according to some essential principles of the picturesque aesthetic. Thus *Northanger Abbey* demonstrates how a properly trained observer may detect interesting and affecting qualities within material customarily regarded as so banal as to be unworthy of careful attention. In satirizing Gothic fiction, *Northanger Abbey* downgrades sublimely extraordinary subject-matter by enabling us to attend with unfaltering delight to the mundane non-adventures of a most ordinary young woman in the most commonplace of situations and settings. Jane Austen, after all, was writing *Northanger Abbey* about the time Wordsworth was perfecting his Preface to *Lyrical Ballads,* with its condemnations of the popular thirst for outrageous stimulation. By involving herself deeply in the problematics of picturesqueness, Austen invited her readers into a complicated evaluation of attitudes and aspirations of contemporary social significance—as Thomas Pfau recently has impressively demonstrated.[11]

Pfau shows that the "Picturesque" aesthetic was much more than a transient fad. It sought, indeed, to demonstrate rewards for intensified self-reflexivity about human beings' interrelations with their immediate physical environment, and thus was a precursor of important environmentalist ideas. And, however much this aesthetic may have influenced professionals (the focus of Pfau's study), it at least as powerfully affected amateurs, both artists and connoisseurs, like Henry and Elinor Tilney. From the late 1760s, increasing numbers of amateur painters of both sexes flooded out over Britain sketching, drawing, watercoloring parts of their native landscape. The picturesque is the first how-to-do-it aesthetic, directed toward assisting the beginner's practice, rather than training her judgment in evaluating revered masterpieces. Even the neoclassic Alexander Cozen's pedagogical device of creating landscapes by beginning with an inkblot was developed to facilitate the work of beginners.[12] For those who, like Henry Tilney, either lacked talent or judiciously perceived the limitations of their skill (for the underlying principle of picturesqueness is that anybody can do it), picturesqueness usefully taught one how to *see*—see not the over-varnished old masters in great houses but the actual landscapes of the British countryside.

The picturesque, moreover, became a patriotic, nationalistic aesthetic, founded on a quite conscious assertion that Britain, although without the sublime Alpine landscapes or the classical beauty of Mediterranean scenery, possessed different but equivalently rewarding natural features worthy of viewing and sketching.[13] Instead of the Grand Tour of foreign countries by a few aristocrats, multitudes of gentry-class lovers of the picturesque became tourists in their native land, moving shorter distances and more quickly, and focusing their attention less on what was stable, either in a landscape or architectural grandeur, than evanescent variations in light and shade in natural prospects or temporal corrosions of architecture, therefore taking delight as much in peasant huts as in castles. The charm they sought was in ever-shifting visual experiences of the irregular and uncertain rather than the unchangingly spectacular and awe-inspiring.[14]

Edmund Burke has long been recognized as an inadvertent inspirer of the picturesque. His influential *Philosophical Enquiry into the Sublime and the Beautiful* of 1757 was constructed around the binary opposition of his title, which reflected what for him were the fundamental driving forces in all humankind: desire for self-preservation and desire for self-propagation. For Burke, however, the intense experience of either beauty or sublimity, especially the latter, was rare, did not persist, and, being fundamentally a-temporal, did not undergo modulations. Burke's sublime experience is epiphanic. In contrast, picturesque experience was stimulated by more commonplace, continuous, non-instantaneous experiences, tending toward Wordsworth's view that "the human mind is capable of being excited without the application of gross and violent stimulants." The picturesque found reward in the mild surprises of continuities of transformation, including those of the perceiver, as when a traveler advanced on a curving mountain road offering continuously shifting vistas, or a low-lying mist gradually dissipated to reveal features of a landscape it had shrouded.

The picturesque was thus a precursor of aesthetic ideas that developed among the Romantics into defamiliarization as articulated by Coleridge and Shelley, and even anticipated some twentieth-century concerns with feedback processes. More immediately, the picturesque focused attention on the value of upsetting established preconceptions, what Wordsworth condemned as the worst enemies of our enjoyment. Jane Austen seized on the ironic contradiction in fanciers of the picturesque like the Tilneys because they in fact reduce it to a preconceived system, and that error helped to dramatize why the education of Catherine Morland is valuable for readers of her simple story. Catherine's difficulties arise, of course, not from her ignorance, but her false knowledge, her preconceptions—notably those derived from reading Gothic fiction in the company of Isabella Thorpe. So Austen's critique of the Gothic is severe but always double-edged, because *Northanger Abbey* defends the novel form as an exemplary means for freeing us from crippling assumptions that novels may themselves foster. That novels can do harm is testimony to the power they possess. It is not accidental that Austen's most celebrated praise of the genre in which she writes succinctly articulates the special virtues of her own artistry.

> There seems almost a general wish of decrying the capacity and undervaluing the labour of the novelist, and the slighting of performances which have only genius,

wit, and taste to recommend them. . . . [Works] in which the greatest powers of the mind are displayed, in which the most thorough knowledge of human nature, the happiest delineation of its varieties, the liveliest effusions of wit and humour are conveyed in the best chosen language. (1, Chapter 5, 37–38)

Henry Tilney is both a professed admirer as well as a parodic imitator of Ann Radcliffe, but the author's ridicule of his sensibility denies us any simple view of pleasure in or fear of literary Gothicism. Henry represents attitudes superior to those of Catherine's other wooer, John Thorpe, who in espousing masculine contempt for novels by women inadvertently reveals the mindlessness of his addiction to the Gothic sensationalism of female writers. Thorpe is a walking encyclopedia of false knowledge, which is put to use more actively and revealingly by his sister Isabella. Isabella, one of Austen's most brilliant inventions, is a very modern young woman in exemplifying cutting-edge conventionality. With the addition of a few dozen instances of "you know" and "like" to her speech she would fit perfectly into most teenage conversations in a contemporary shopping mall. Isabella is very knowing; she knows all about up-to-the-minute styles of dress, speech, thought, money, and sex. She is in consequence always mistaken. Constantly insisting on the absoluteness of her judgments and on her firmness of conviction even as she shifts with every smallest breeze, Isabella is incapable of learning anything because she thinks she knows everything. She is necessarily false, a creature of artifice so shallow that one hesitates to honor her with the epithet of hypocrite. Yet she exemplifies a profoundly dangerous tendency in Austen's (and our own) society, as is proved by how her cutting-edge conventionality highlights the same qualities empowered by gender, social position, and wealth in General Tilney. Like virtually all of Austen's most despicable characters, the General's faults are most significantly displayed in his exaggeration of conventional good manners, transforming behavior intended to foster ease and geniality into oppressive performances that prevent the reciprocal interchanges that are the rewarding pleasure of sociability.

> . . . she was far from being at ease; nor could the incessant attentions of the General himself entirely reassure her. Nay, perverse as it seemed, she doubted whether she might not have felt less, had she been less attended to. His anxiety for her comfort—his constant solicitations that she would eat, and his often expressed fears of her seeing nothing to her taste—though never in her life before had she beheld half such variety on a breakfast-table—made it impossible for her to forget for a moment that she was a visitor.
>
> (2, Chapter 5, 154)

It is appropriate that General Tilney's false knowledge about Catherine's financial situation is derived from a witless cad like John Thorpe, but the appropriateness is scarcely complimentary to the existent social power structure, the system to which behavior is supposed to conform. As Catherine's parents rightly judge, General Tilney's behavior toward their daughter disqualifies his pretensions to being either a responsible father or an authentic gentleman (2, 14, 234).

The force of their judgment, however, is easily overlooked, because they make no exaggerated display of it. In fact, they do not find the peculiarity of his behavior as worthy of extended consideration. Their unpretentious good sense dramatically contrasts with the General's vainglorious ostentation and keeps them free from any taint of self-righteousness. Their coolness, though it may border on culpable indifference, in fact contrasts starkly with the savagery of recent literary critics' condemnations of the General. Austen in no way justifies the General, but she prevents her condemnation from simplifying into self-righteous absoluteness, thereby permitting us to appreciate how the Morlands' "good" attitude, if not encouraging the General's "bad" behavior, is part of a social situation that enables him to persist in deplorable conduct. She makes us admire the Morlands' good sense but enables us to recognize that good sense may impede needed social reformations.

Austen here exemplifies how, in diverse fashions, superior novels activate and make possible an "education" of "information processing systems" of considerable importance to ways in which cultures may influence our biological heritage. Austen's fictive education of Catherine Morland presents her readers with an opportunity to engage themselves in a learning process. Through a narrative self-reflexivity she encourages skepticism, first, about our assurance that we need little education in understanding what is good and bad for human beings in the ordinary conduct of life and, second, that we can easily estimate exactly the consequences of particular behavior. One cannot read the story of Catherine Morland with genuine attention without being continually forced into assessments requiring subsequent reassessments of causes of motives for actions, as well as of the complexity of consequences, practical and moral, arising from commonplace and conventional behavior. Our entanglement in the processes of judging our own judgments of the characters' behavior draws us into learning about how and why we behave as we do. It is reasonable to suppose that this reading *experience*—which includes consideration of ethical issues but is probably most potent if not expressive of a formalized ethical system—may have practical consequences affecting how we subsequently "process information" about our relations with other people.

I am, of course, here tiptoeing in the footprints of Horace and his followers—the pleasure of literature lies in learning from it. I only urge that we take the old saw more seriously, and consider the idea of evolutionary psychologists that systems by which we mentally order and put into action information offer a new way (albeit an enormously complicated one) of specifying exactly how we learn from literature—and how, therefore, literary art may be important to co-evolution, to helping make us more fully human. Good fiction presents us an opportunity to learn in both subtle and original ways about our capabilities for *learning,* capabilities that surely are valuable in enabling culture to modify biological inheritance.

Northanger Abbey, like all of Austen's novels, is very much about learning (this seems to me one reason for their popularity). Like any experienced teacher, Austen knows that the worst enemy of learning is didacticism. Learning is in its essence a process of self-development. Ignorance offers the possibility of self-transformation. "I have learned to love a hyacinth," Catherine tells Henry Tilney. His response to this announcement is significant: "You have gained a new source of enjoyment, and it is well to have as many holds on happiness as possible. . . . though the love of a hyacinth may be rather domestic, who can tell, the sentiment once raised, but you may in time come to love a rose. . . . the mere habit of loving is the thing; . . ." (2, 7, 174).

The concept of learning to love underlies all of Austen's courtship novels, which tell us that authentic love is not instinctive, instantaneous, intuitive, but an attachment rationally and imaginatively developed, though it properly begins in sensual attraction. Darcy learns to value Elizabeth's capacity for enriching his inner life, but he is first attracted by her eyes. Even in *Persuasion,* a turning point is William Elliott's openly admiring Anne's face and figure without recognizing her, thereby triggering Captain Wentworth's jealousy. In the present case Catherine's love is for a common flower. We tend, unthinkingly, to regard love as a generic mode of feeling, but Austen discriminates. Loving a hyacinth may *lead* to loving a rose, and perhaps there is a distinctive quality to loving flowers. Learning how to love this way may encourage other kinds of love, but that remains only a possibility. Learning to love a flower is different from learning to love music, or people. Some very affectionate people have never learned to love any flower. Learning to love is a specific process, not a general one—just as learning algebra is a specific process, quite different from learning to be a good parent. Yet development of one kind of capacity in a living organism is likely to have ramifying effects: one suspects Catherine's growing love for Henry may have fostered her love for a hyacinth.

Because *Northanger Abbey* not only is about learning but also enables its readers to learn, it must be in complex ways intensely self-reflexive, even in the realm of the emotions. Austen making fun of herself, as when she observes in her penultimate chapter that the "tell-tale compression of the pages" alerts readers that "we are hastening together to perfect felicity," entertains us with a slapstick form of the self-reflexiveness that more subtly and continuously challenges her own storytelling. Doubts raised about Henry as exemplary hero are by most contemporary critics emphasized ferociously, but whatever the degree to which Henry betrays the role of hero, his failures are principally important in their interaction with self-testing ambiguities running everywhere through every level of the novel: we end, for example, in some doubt as how to assess the value of Austen's prime satiric target, Gothic fiction.[15] And of course on the level of minute verbal detail the dynamism of Austen's simple-seeming prose encourages endless rereadings—because the language of the narrative carries with limpidly nuanced ease possibilities of imagining qualifications, and even reversals, of what is overtly articulated throughout this picturesquely anti-picturesque story. Everywhere there are verbal self-involutions more nuanced but just as provocative as the overtones of self-ridicule in the novel's final sentence, "whether the tendency of this work is altogether to recommend parental tyranny, or reward filial disobedience."

From *Northanger Abbey* we may learn how easy it is to misuse imagination. It is not merely appropriate but even necessary, therefore, that Austen include her own imaginative working in what she scrutinizes critically. She would not be so effective at helping us to recognize how we encourage ourselves to deform our imaginations were her text not so unsparingly self-challenging. To learn how best to exercise our psychic potencies in social life, we need not abstract rules but what environmental psychologists call domain-specific systems, sharply focused behavior patternings that encourage flexibility through ongoing self-assessments that facilitate continuous readjustments. The power to make fun, to take pleasure in absurdities in a responsible way, is possible only if one does not exclude oneself from participation in what is perceived as absurd. The self-righteous are never fun-loving. Integral to the enjoyment of absurdities is recognition that, because few if any of our judgments can be definitive, proactively evaluative and reevaluative responses are continually required of us. Living, at least for self-conscious creatures, *is* learning: not learning in general, but rather learning a variety of often connected but always intensely specific skills of interaction with diverse portions of our environment.

Henry Tilney suggests by using Isabella's idiom what Catherine may feel after her friend's display of utter selfishness and stupidity.

> You feel, I suppose, that, in losing Isabella, you lose half of yourself: you feel a void in your heart which nothing else can occupy. Society is becoming irksome; and as for the amusements to which you were wont to share at Bath, the very idea of them without her is abhorrent. . . . You feel that you have no longer any friend to whom you can speak with unreserve; on whose regard you can place dependence; or whose counsel, in any difficulty, you could rely on. You feel all this?"

To his irony, "after a few moments' reflection," Catherine replies, "No . . . I do not—ought I?" She goes on to observe, "I do not feel so very, very much afflicted as one would have thought," to which Henry responds, "You feel, as you always do, what is most to the credit of human nature.—Such feelings ought to be investigated, that they may know themselves" (2,10, 207). Henry's observation is particularly striking, not only because like so much else in the novel it alerts us to a use of language that brings that usage into question, but also because it allows the somewhat "afflicted" Catherine's limitations to escape absolute condemnation even though they are not glossed over. No name is given to her feelings that are "most to the credit of human nature," because these are always particular feelings appropriate to a specific situation involving unique individuals. Yet feelings "to the credit of human nature" are identified as discernible. Henry proposes, furthermore, that these creditable feelings *ought* to be investigated so that they *may* know themselves. In a changing human society in a changing world there can be no definitive classification of such feelings; the investigations must be ever ongoing as the self-knowledge obtained will be continuously open to modification. The self-knowledge sought is not a set of principles but development of patterns of awareness useful for orienting specific behavior in inevitably unique situations—patterns perpetually open to self-readjustment for processing unpredictable information into newly efficacious behavior.

Literary art, I suggest Jane Austen is telling us, is a primary site for learning from and about such discoveries—which is why one should be cautious of some fiction, such as the Gothic. Austen demonstrates above all else that so far as novels allow us to learn, they instruct by example. One learns from example by attending to specific, usually intensely specific, behavior. The primary condition of such learning, furthermore, is awareness of the difference between oneself and the one who exemplifies. This is why learning by example is the most active form of learning. It is not mere imitation, because it is built upon recognition that exemplar and learner are not identical and, in the case of complex behavior, one must expect to face situations that in some ways will be unpredictable. Skills learned through exemplarity are valuable because they are intrinsically adaptable to changing circumstances.

The Gothic novel, in Jane Austen's view (at least for the midland counties of England in 1800), offers a poor example, whereas *Northanger Abbey,* because in satirizing the Gothic it satirizes itself (what the Radcliffian Gothic cannot do), is a superior exemplar. The most important feature of the novel's exemplarity is its condemnation of the misuse of the peculiarly human powers of imagination and language, and in this it lucidly illustrates at least one "evolutionary function" of literary art. We don't know when oral storytelling originated, but it seems safe to say that it has existed for perhaps only fifty to a hundred thousand years, emerging long after the establishment of all the major features of human biological evolution. But the effects of the evolutionary process that resulted in humans attaining the ability through language to create cultures meant that we have been able radically to alter the environment in which we live. In so doing we have assured that in some ways we will be maladapted to the new conditions for which we are responsible, since they will differ from those Pleistocene ones in which our hunting-and-gathering ancestors so successfully evolved. Literary art is a primary means by which we can explore our behavior in ways that permit us to identify actual or potential maladaptations. A satiric fiction such as *Northanger Abbey* offers an obvious illustration, but even seemingly more "positive" and celebratory works arise out of the peculiarly human possibility of awareness of having become, or having the potential to become, poorly adapted to new conditions of living we have ourselves created.

Human self-consciousness, the consciousness of being conscious, by definition opens a separation between the individual and her environmental circumstances: our self-consciousness gives us the ability to conceive of oneself and one's surroundings as different from what they in fact are. And of course such conception makes possible at least attempts to change one's behavior or the environment or both. Literary art is not the only way to addresses such difficulties/possibilities, present or potential, but, especially because it teaches primarily by example, it is a mode superbly fitted to enable us to grapple with the subtlest and most complex forms of our achieved maladaptations, which, of course, we regard as triumphs of culture. The satire of *Northanger Abbey* beautifully displays how in superior literature the awareness of consciousness may become embodied in a form of representation that exemplifies changes in thought and feeling that could improve our lives. In this novel the author's capacity for a playfulness that produces self-criticism in all her critiques carries our imaginations not toward abstract ethical principles but, instead, toward a practical psychic flexibility that enables us to *enjoy* grappling with difficulties that the evolution of our species has made inevitable for us. Reading *Northanger Abbey,* we experience the intense pleasures of resisting the hegemony of false knowledge every society necessarily fosters. Through Austen's witty self-referencings we may enjoy the artificiality of the novel, its overtly fictive character, which allows us a satisfying play of our awareness upon itself, a play requisite if self-conscious beings are to succeed in an environment that is ever-changing, not least through their engagements with it.

Notes

1. Lawrence Buell, *The Environmental Imagination* (Cambridge, MA: Harvard University Press, 1995), provides a comprehensive overview and source of

references for environmentally oriented commentaries; he prefers the term "environmental prose" to the more common "nature writing," since he is principally concerned with American traditions and especially with the work of Thoreau (see p. 426n.16).

2. A devastating but still unanswered critique of the empirical shortcomings of sociobiology is S. L. Washburn, "Animal Behavior and Social Anthropology," in *Sociobiology and Human Nature,* ed. Michael S. Gregory et al. (San Francisco: Josey Bass, 1978), 53–74. The same volume includes philosophical critiques by Marjorie Grene, "Sociobiology and the Human Mind," 213–24, and J. B. Schneewind, "Sociobiology, Social Policy, and Nirvana," 225–39. See also Paul Ziff, "Art and Sociobiology," *Mind* 90 (1981): 505–20.

3. Excellent introductions to the principles of environmental psychology are provided by John Tooby and Leda Cosmides, "Evolutionary Psychology and the Generation of Culture," *Ethology and Sociobiology* 10 (1989): 29–49, and the same joint authors' earlier "From Evolution to Behavior: Evolutionary Psychology as the Missing Link," in *The Latest and Best Essays in Evolution and Optimality,* ed. John Dupress (Cambridge, MA: MIT Press, 1987), 277–306.

4. Even before the rise of sociobiology Morse Peckham argued cogently, first in his book *Man's Rage for Chaos* (1965) and subsequently in a variety of essays, for instance, "Philosophy and Art as Models of Behavior" in his *Romanticism and Ideology* (Greenwood, FL: Penkeville Press, 1983), 187–201, that art is counter-adaptive: art resists "channeled" behavioral patterning, offering instead disorientation and thereby training in non-automatic, non-genetically inherited response systems.

5. An important exception is Frederick Turner—see for example his "Sociobiology of Beauty" in *Sociobiology and the Arts,* ed. J. B. Berdaux and Brett Cooke (Amsterdam: Rodophi, 1999), 63–82, which builds upon Turner's *Beauty: The Value of Values* (Charlottesville: University of Virginia Press, 1991). The Berdaux-Brett collection offers a good introduction to the variety of current work in the field of biopoetics.

6. Alvin B. Kernan, "Aggression and Satire: Art Considered as a Form of Biological Adaptation," in *Literary Theory and Structure: Essays in Honor of William K. Wimsatt,* ed. Frank Brady, John Palmer, Martin Price (New Haven, CT: Yale University Press, 1973), 115–29.

7. Steven Jones, *Satire and Romanticism* (New York: Palgrave/St. Martin's Press, 2000), 9.

8. Koen DePryck, *Knowledge, Evolution, and Paradox* (Albany: New York State University Press, 1999), 103. DePryck continues on the same page to observe that language is a system that can exist without claim to any "absolute origin," and can refer to "any given level of complexity, since its internal open-endedness will make it possible to construct that same complexity within its own structure. . . . we are able . . . to stretch the reality of our language way beyond the complexity of our physical, chemical, biological, and even cultural environment."

9. All citations from *Northanger Abbey* are from the Oxford Illustrated Edition, edited by R. W. Chapman, third edn. (London: Oxford University Press, 1933), and appear parenthetically in the text; since readers now use a variety of paperback editions, I cite by chapter number (with volume).

10. In thus evaluating how one evaluates, the reader's processing of the fictional text operates much in the manner described by Wolfgang Iser but more self-reflexively than he recognizes. See his influential "The Reading Process: A Phenomenological Approach" in *The Implied Reader* (Baltimore: John Hopkins Press, 1978), 274–94.

11. Thomas Pfau, *Wordsworth's Profession* (Stanford: Stanford University Press, 1997).

12. See the valuable essay by Charles A. Cramer, "Alexander Cozens' *New Method:* The Blot and General Nature," *Art Bulletin* 64 (1997): 112–22. Among the wealth of studies of the picturesque, beyond Pfau's both deep and wide-ranging book, one should notice the excellent summarizing and evaluative essay of Dabney Townsend, "The Picturesque," *The Journal of Aesthetics and Art Criticism* 55:4 (1997): 365–76, which includes references to most of the major earlier studies, such as those of Christopher Hussey, John Barrell, and John Dixon Hunt.

13. "Picturesque touring was suitable to the pockets and moral sensibilities of the middle classes. . . . Britain became for the middle classes what the Continent had been for the wealthy." Ann Bermingham, "The Picturesque and Ready-to-Wear Femininity," in *The Politics of the Picturesque,* ed. Stephen Copley and Peter Garside (Cambridge: Cambridge University Press, 1994), 86. Horace Walpole, of course, was the most vigorous propagandist for appreciation of the attractiveness of what he celebrated as the "homely and familiar" aspects of English landscape: see for example his interesting but generally overlooked "On Modern Gardening," which was available to Austen in the three-volume edition of Walpole's works published in 1798 by G. G. Robinson in London, vol. II, 519–45.

14. As Townsend observes, the picturesque approach is always in terms of "looking from some point of view, wandering, or traveling through, etc." (371) Ronald Paulson, recognizing that the development of John Gilpin's aesthetics of the picturesque began in the 1740s, draws attention to how it follows Hogarth's adaptation of Addison's concept of the "novel," and identifies essential features of picturesque aesthetics as deriving from Hogarth's ideas of the Beautiful/Novel and his serpentine Line of Beauty. See *The Beautiful, Novel, and Strange: Aesthetics and Heterodoxy* (Baltimore: The Johns Hopkins Press, 1996), esp. chapt. 9, 225–42.

15. Few contemporary commentators on *Northanger Abbey* imitate Austen's critical self-reflexivity, not only savaging Henry Tilney but even suggesting that General Tilney actually murdered his wife. Thus Barbara Seeber, *General Consent in Jane Austen* (Montreal and Kingston: McGill-Queens University Press, 2000), claims that the "only 'proof' of the general's innocence" depends

on the dubious testimony of Henry, and in the light of "overwhelming evidence in the text of the general's capacity for violence," readers must believe Catherine's dark suspicions may be justified (p. 123). In this view Catherine's parents must appear as utterly irresponsible, and the Tilney children as either fools or hypocrites. Worse, such a reading effaces *Northanger Abbey's* connections with significant intellectual contexts of the late eighteenth century. Some of these are traced out by Peter Knox-Shaw in "*Northanger Abbey* and the Liberal Historians," *Essays in Criticism* 44 (1998): 319–42. Knox-Shaw demonstrates close parallelisms between Austen's novel and the work of liberal historians following Hume, including interest in mundane domestic improvements (such as General Tilney takes pride in). Omission of attention to these practical realities both the historians and Austen identify as a key weakness in "Gothic" historicism, illustrated when Catherine notices the absurdity that in Mrs. Radcliffe's works "abbeys and castles in which, though certainly larger than Northanger, all the dirty work of the house was to be done by two pair of female hands at the utmost" (2, 8, 184). The reflexive consciousness that I have highlighted in Austen's text, in fact, is closely associated with changing attitudes and foci of self-awareness less visible but equally important in other modes of discourse of her time.

Relevant to this issue is *Northanger Abbey's* curious publication history. It was the first of Austen's novels to be purchased by a publisher in 1803, who then, however, did not print it, and the ms. was bought back by the Austens years later, but was not finally published until after Jane Austen's death. *Northanger Abbey* seems to mark the *end* of Austen's early novel-writing phase; there appears persuasive evidence that early versions of both *Sense and Sensibility* and *Pride and Prejudice* existed before the ms. of *Northanger Abbey* was sold. This would make the third of Austen's major novels appropriately self-critical in parodying eighteenth-century Gothic fiction, because the last three complete novels she wrote differ so radically from those originally composed more than a decade and a half earlier. *Mansfield Park* of 1814, then, is Austen's first truly "nineteenth-century" novel; along with Scott's *Waverley,* published in the same year, it is a harbinger of novelistic innovations of style and theme that distinguish "nineteenth-century" fiction.

This view justifies critics who for half a century have quoted approvingly Lionel Trilling's observation that *Mansfield Park* appears to be a deliberate reversal of the central qualities and purposes of *Pride and Prejudice,* Fanny Price being a heroine opposite to Elizabeth Bennett in almost every way. But there have been few remarks on how, in turn, the second of Austen's "nineteenth-century" novels, *Emma,* offers a "handsome, clever, and rich" protagonist as an inversion of Fanny Price, and how *Persuasion's* heroine to an extraordinary degree stands in opposition to both Emma and Fanny, just as this last novel's emphasis on professionalism signals the profundity of Austen's final counter-turn against her earlier social judgments on society.

The self-reflexivity I have described *within Northanger Abbey* as being a characteristic of most excellent fiction would make it reasonable to identify some such "self-correcting" quality in the sequence of Jane Austen's novelistic compositions, and I suspect, equivalent revisionary practices are to be found in the sequence of novels of most eminent writers of fiction.

Chapter 6 ∼

Satirical Birds and Natural Bugs: J. Harris' Chapbooks and the Aesthetic of Children's Literature

Donelle R. Ruwe

> Come take up your Hats, and away let us haste,
> To the Butterfly's Ball and the Grasshopper's Feast
> The Trumpeter Gad-Fly has summoned the crew,
> And the Revels are now only waiting for you.
> On the Smooth-Shaven Grass by the side of a Wood,
> [Beneath a broad oak which for ages had stood,][1]
> See the Children of earth and the tenants of Air,
> To an evening's amusement together repair.
> And there came the Beetle so blind and so black,
> Who carried the Emmet, his friend on his back.
> And there came the Gnat, and the Dragon-Fly too,
> And all their relations, Green, Orange, and Blue . . .
>
> —William Roscoe, *The Butterfly's Ball and*
> *the Grasshopper's Feast* 1807, pp. 1–4

In 1806, a short, twenty-six-line poem by the botanist, historian, and politician William Roscoe appeared in the *Gentleman's Magazine* and the *Ladies Monthly Museum*. *The Butterfly's Ball and the Grasshopper's Feast* was a smashing success—it was set to music for the royal family, William

Mulready illustrated it for the publisher John Harris, and Harris used it to launch a series of cheaply produced, illustrated juvenile books. It sold more than 20,000 copies in the first year at the advertised price of "one shilling plain, and eighteen-pence coloured." The poem begins with a speaker inviting children to attend a Butterfly's Ball. Among the invited insects are a blind, black beetle who carries an emmet on his back, snails, hornets, wasps, and a bee who supplies honey for the feast. To make a full-length chapbook of Roscoe's poem, Harris printed no more than four lines of verse per page, with Mulready's illustrations beneath. The minimal text, the tiny pocket size, and the whimsical illustrations identify the chapbook as early children's literature. Mulready's illustrations feature humans with attached animal parts, such as a young boy with an enormous grasshopper on his head.[2] The female snail carries her shell on her head but seems to be collapsing under its weight (see figure 6.1). One could argue that a woman carrying a winding baggage (the shell) on her head, a black beetle carrying others on his back, and a reference to domestic honey (rather than imported sugar) suggest anti-slavery sentiments.[3] Certainly Roscoe was an active abolitionist who published *The Wrongs of Africa* in 1788.

Analysis of *The Butterfly's Ball,* however, has always been dehistoricized. The poem is presented as a seminal work that liberates children's literature from "pedagogical constraints" and ushers in the happily-ever-after golden age of imaginative children's literature, which is produced by notable Victorian men such as Lewis Carroll.[4] Over and over again, Roscoe's text is given the hero's role in this patriarchal rescue fantasy about the beleaguered state of early children's literature. Such narratives ignore basic facts. First, imaginative children's poetry existed before Roscoe's poem. Most notable is Sarah Martin's 1805 *The Comic Adventures of Old Mother Hubbard and her Dog,* published by John Harris and advertised on the back of *The Butterfly's Ball's* first chapbook edition. *Old Mother Hubbard* was mistaken for political satire, suggesting that the division between children's satire and imaginative verse was not yet fully in place.[5] Second, *The Butterfly's Ball* was originally published not as a child's chapbook but in adult miscellanies and magazines.

What Roscoe's text does do astoundingly well is to conform to and promote the Romantic ideology of the child. Unlike Martin's comical text, *The Butterfly's Ball* is recognizably Wordsworthian. What could be more Romantic than a young boy who takes up his hat, leaves the house, and enters a natural world that is, through the power of his imagination, full of animate, sentient creatures? Even the chapbook's frontispiece asserts its pro-nature and anti-domesticity stance: a group of children leave home through an opened door beyond which the natural world beckons in the form of a beautiful tree, mushroom, and butterfly. As with Huckleberry Finn and Rousseau's Émile, these children learn through escaping feminine influence

And the Snail, with her horns peeping out of her fhell.

Came, fatigu'd with the diftance the length of an ell.

Figure 6.1. William Mulready's illustrations to the 1807 Butterfly's Ball *feature Regency figures with bug and insect parts. (All illustrations in this chapter courtesy of the Department of Special Collections, Charles E. Young Research Library, UCLA.)*

and returning to nature. In commenting on this phenomenon, Mitzi Myers and William McCarthy contend that the ongoing dichotomizing in children's literature between imagination and didacticism, or nature and socialization, is an "ongoing reinscription of Wordsworth's myth of the 'natural' boy, the Boy of Winander, tutored directly by wild Nature . . . and gloriously independent of formal instruction by socializing agents such as actual mothers."[6] Authors who instruct children are aligned with an oppressive hegemony in contrast to an ongoing celebration of texts considered imaginative, playful, innocent, and delightful.

Roscoe's text achieves canonicity, I suggest, because it falls on the winning side of three mutually reinforcing binary constructions of literary history:

masculine versus feminine writing traditions (gender); adult versus children's writing traditions (genre); and Romantic versus eighteenth-century aesthetic traditions (periodization). It is not surprising that various narratives of literary history have favored early-nineteenth-century texts that fit masculine, adult-oriented, and Romantic aesthetic traditions. What is surprising, however, is the relative importance that these three different binary ideologies have in determining the ultimate canonicity of a particular text. I will argue, in effect, that when these binary constructions of gender, genre, and period are brought to bear upon the same group of literary texts, gender and genre cancel each other out and what matters most, ultimately, is Romantic aesthetics. Of course, Romantic aesthetics is always already gendered and has its own relationship to the cult of the child. However, in literature actually written for child readers, the gender of the author, while still significant, becomes less important than the text's performance of Romantic aesthetics and the Romantic ideology of the child. In other words, gender is a less powerful indicator of canonicity within children's literature than is the Romantic ideology's antipathy to satire and its concomitant belief in the natural and innocent (non-satirical) child. Indeed, Romanticism's suppression of satire is perhaps nowhere as fierce as in its condemnation of politicized children's texts, a condemnation that crosses gender lines and is expressed by both men and women, conservatives and radicals.

In order to investigate how Romantic and gendered ideological assumptions have determined the selection of canonical children's poems, I examine the reception history of a series of illustrated children's chapbooks printed by the London publisher John Harris in 1807–09. I focus on three chapbooks from this series: a fantasy poem by William Roscoe (*The Butterfly's Ball and the Grasshopper's Feast*), which exemplifies the Romantic ideology of the child; a satirical parody of Roscoe's poem by Catherine Ann Dorset (*The Peacock "At Home": A Sequel to the Butterfly's Ball*), a seminal work that inspired thirty years of similar parodies; and an anonymous chapbook, *The Council of Dogs,* which is both political and satirical. As I move from William Roscoe's poem, to Catherine Ann Dorset's, to the anonymous *Council of Dogs,* I ask a series of questions inspired by the following irony: Roscoe's poem has retained a canonical status in the field of children's literature and Romanticism *even though* the form of Dorset's poem was more influential in its day.

Because *The Butterfly's Ball* is, as I will show, often falsely praised for being the first fantastic rather than didactic work of children's poetry, it is a pivotal text in my analysis, for its reception history reveals how the Romantic ideology has shaped children's poetry. Like other critics working in this area, I question our use of problematic Romantic ideological assumptions in constructing children's literary history: that imagination is superior to reason; that childhood is an ahistorical time of innocence and joy; that nature is superior to society; that poetry by men is better than poetry by women; and that the history of children's literature is unified and progressive.[7] By re-historicizing *The Butterfly's Ball* within the context of early satirical children's verse, I demonstrate how our celebration of Roscoe's escapist fantasy has blinded us to the very real political protests and social work found in other contemporaneous animal poems.

I

The Butterfly's Ball first appeared in a local miscellany sometime before July 1805. This version, which contained some alterations made without Roscoe's knowledge, was sent by Lady Elizabeth Spencer, daughter of the Fourth Duke of Marlborough, to the composer George Thomas Smart. She asked him to set the poem to music for the daughters of George III. This setting was printed by May 20, 1806. Meanwhile, Roscoe learned of the commission, sent Smart a corrected copy of the verses, and added a few extra lines "on the real incident mentd. in the first verse wch if you think can be set to music are much at your service" (Roscoe, rpt. in Hurst). The earlier, corrupt version had already been printed in *The Lady's Monthly Museum* and *The Gentleman's Magazine* in 1806, and John Harris had used *The Gentleman's Magazine* version as a children's chapbook in 1807. In 1808, Harris published a new and revised edition, with new and less engaging illustrations from a lesser artist than Mulready.

The text and illustrations of the *Butterfly's Ball*, revised between the poem's various editions, increasingly enhance the poem's participation in the Romantic ideology of childhood. The 1807 and 1808 chapbook editions depict two prototypical Romantic scenes of childhood: the first, that of the adult observer who admires from afar the special qualities of childhood's imaginary worlds; and the second, that of the child, who is able to join freely with nature and become one with it. The 1808 version, the first clearly printed with Roscoe's permission, adds four extra quatrains about animals and, significantly, two additional lines in the opening and closing quatrains. These lines refer to Roscoe's son:

> Come take up your hats, & away let us haste
> To the Butterfly's ball, & the Grasshopper's feast;
> *So said little Robert, and pacing along,*
> *His merry Companions came forth in a Throng.* (emphasis added)

The couplet about Robert is repeated with a slight variation as the final lines of the poem. In the earlier version, the narrator openly commands children to enjoy an insect ball, an overt expression of the adult's desire for children to play in an imaginative, natural world. In the 1808 version, however, the adult's desire is disguised: it is projected onto the children themselves and presented as their own desire. By embedding the child as narrator, "so said little Robert," the adult's voice disappears, and the poem becomes a child's monologue. The game is now Robert's idea, and he invites the other children to join him. The revised illustrations, like Roscoe's textual revisions, enhance the emphasis on childhood imagination and erase the traces of adult desire. In the 1807 chapbook, the illustrations feature adult figures in fashionable Regency clothing with only a suggestion of their insect counterparts, such as a woman wearing a snail's shell on her head. In the 1808 edition's new illustrations, the adult figures are gone, and only animals in a natural environment are portrayed.

Roscoe's poem, besides being a prototypical Romantic poem of childhood, also participates in the aesthetics of the miniature: nostalgia, control, and tableau. *The Butterfly's Ball* is a textual doll house: miniature furniture (tables made from mushrooms), miniature clothing (a wasp's brown and yellow "jacket"), and miniature dolls (insects) at a miniature party. Indeed, as Susan Stewart contends, miniature worlds are essentially tableaux in which the observer is transcendent, larger and more powerful than the miniature; miniatures open up interior worlds with their own sense of time, private fantasy, and play: they are a "stage on which we project . . . a deliberately framed series of *actions*."[8]

The tableau's characteristic mode, that of obsessive control over what is essentially a highly stylized, static, and artificial recreation of a visual scene, affirms the power of the looker, the subject who transcends and controls. The narrator of the 1807 chapbook condescends to the children, telling them not only how to dress ("Come take up your Hats"), but also, explicitly, to look: "*See* the Children of earth and the tenants of Air" (emphasis mine). The illustrations, one per page, enhance the poem's visual nature and contribute the sense of seeing rather than moving. The politics of miniaturization also participate in the politics of gender—what is miniaturized, referred to by diminutives, is the feminine and the child. But importantly, such tableaus "fix" childhood, keeping the child forever innocent, forever apart from adulthood as a private special place without time and without movement. Further, the poem is a nostalgic representation of childhood play, for "little Robert" would have been eighteen years old in 1808.

Children's poetry has historically been associated with magic and music, the smallness and prettiness of children, and rural settings.[9] This tradition, combined with the Romantic ideology of the child, with its veritable worshiping of the child as natural, innocent, and imaginative, catapulted *The Butterfly's Ball* into literary history. Whether it was a perfect

expression of a preexisting Romantic ideology of the child or whether it fa-
cilitated the incorporation of this ideology within children's poetry,
Roscoe's poem was destined for the canon. Throughout the Victorian era
and the twentieth century, it was constantly republished in various forms
from a fold-out diorama to a concert overture.[10] Roscoe's nondramatic
poem was even adapted for the stage, as a musical burlesque by Henry R.
Addison (author) and Alexander Lee (composer). It was staged throughout
1833 at the Adelphi Theatre under the title *The Butterfly's Ball; or, The
Jealous Moth,* and contained such memorable characters as Papillon, the
Butterfly Beau, a group of sensitive plants, and "Toddygrass, Daddy Long
Legs and a score of fluttering things." Its most glorious incarnation is a
1996 limited-edition, high-end art book with beautiful black and white
linoleum prints by the contemporary artist Vance Gerry. The book is promoted with the same old Manichaean canard, "the first bit of children's literature to break with the tradition of the moral tale." As always, praise of
The Butterfly's Ball repeats the anti-feminine and pro-Romantic binarism
of didacticism versus imagination.

II

> It is not often that we notice the publications of the Juvenile library; . . . But
> there is something so peculiar in the merit of these two Poems that we cannot
> deny ourselves the pleasure of distinguishing them, far above the class in
> which they appear. . . . the two Poems, before us, and particularly the second,
> . . . we consider as a specimen of playful wit conducted by genius, judgment,
> and taste, such as has not been seen since the publication of that, which in
> some points it resembles, the Bath Guide.[11]

When John Harris published *The Butterfly's Ball* in 1807, he included it in
a series of juvenile books beginning with four poems: Roscoe's *Butterfly's
Ball;* an anonymous parody of Roscoe's poem called *The Peacock "At Home":
A Sequel to the "Butterfly's Ball"* (later identified as by Catherine Ann Dorset);
and two other poems that mimic Dorset's format, *The Lion's Masquerade: A
Sequel to The Butterfly's Ball* and *The Elephant's Ball and Grand Fete Champetre: Intended as a Companion to Those Much Admired Pieces, The Butterfly's
Ball and The Peacock "At Home."*[12] Although *The Lion's Masquerade* and *The
Elephant's Ball* pay titular homage to Roscoe's poem, they in fact mimic not
Roscoe's but Dorset's format. Dorset took Roscoe's idea of anthropomorphized creatures having a social event, fleshed it out, added a subtle layer of
satire, and inspired thirty years of parodies and faithful imitations before disappearing from literary history. When Dorset's poem appeared under the
pseudonymous "By a Lady," it caused an immediate stir and was compared

favorably to its precursor, as in the above quoted review from *The British Critic,* for its humor, wit, use of natural imagery, and poetic beauty. Correspondents from *The Gentleman's Magazine* found it to be a "humorous, but unoffending satire upon the manners of the times, and of the Great," and reviewers for the *Critical Review* suggest that it "vastly transcended the original" and that the author's talents might be better spent in amusing men and women than in writing nonsense for children.[13]

The Peacock "At Home" is a narrative with the type of social satire found in Jane Austen's comedy of manners. Quick-paced, full of petty jealousies, a mix of low and high diction and social cant, it exemplifies Horatian satire. Its several hundred lines depict a Lord and Lady Peacock who, envying the success of the Butterfly's Ball, decide to host their own social event; thereafter, it depicts complicated social maneuverings behind the scenes and throughout the hosting of a high society social gathering—all made ludicrous by Dorset's clever linking of society types (the snob, the social climber) to types of birds.

The Peacock announces that he and the other birds shall not "Sit tamely at home, hum drum, with our Spouses, / While Crickets, and Butterflies, open their houses" (p. 4). He decides to host an "At Home" for Saint Valentine's Day, sends out invitations, and receives his answers by post. As the guests arrive, Dorset invents fashionable as well as ornithologically correct attire for each and describes each specie's mode and direction of travel. She details the events of the party (card games, dancing, and refreshments) (see figure 6.2) and gently mocks the pretensions of high society. For example, a group of "Birds past their prime":

> Look'd on, and remark'd, that the prudent and sage,
> Were quite overlook'd in this frivolous age,
> When Birds, scarce pen-feather'd, were brought to a rout,
> Forward Chits! from the egg-shell but newly come out;
> That in their youthful days, they ne'er witness'd such frisking,
> And how wrong! in the GREENFINCH to flirt with the SISKIN.
> So thought LADY MACKAW, and her Friend COCKATOO,
> And the RAVEN foretold that "no good could ensue!"
> They censur'd the BANTAM for strutting and crowing,
> In those vile pantaloons, which he fancied look'd knowing
> And a want of decorum caus'd many demurs,
> Against the GAME CHICKEN, for coming in spurs.

(pp. 12–13)

Dorset's primary mode is satiric wit, and her poem's style has more in common with the mock epics of Pope than the nostalgia of Roscoe. Unlike Roscoe's brief rhyme, *The Peacock "At Home"* is text heavy: it has 154 lines, three extensive botanical footnotes, but only six illustrations.[14]

"The Dowager Lady Toucan, first cut in."&c.
P.12.

Figure 6.2. In Catherine Ann Dorset's The Peacock "At Home," *elderly birds play cards at a society gathering while gossiping about the younger genderation.*

Dorset's pattern of witty poetry in triple meter, in which anthropomorphized animals jealously attempt to outdo other species, proved to be enormously popular and adaptable. Harris published at least seventeen chapbooks between 1807 and 1831 modeled after Dorset's poem. Numerous other publishers capitalized on its popularity and published at least thirty more, such as *The Fishes' Feast* (Tabbey), *The Farm Yard Quadrille, The Jack-Daw "At Home," The Peahen "At Home," The Horse's Levee, The Butterfly's Funeral,* and *The Butterfly's Birthday* (Roscoe). These follow the publishing format of Harris' Cabinet of Amusement and Instruction series and, in terms of content, follow the basic structure established by Dorset. Some of the Dorset-like poems are imperialist adventure stories such as *Lobster's Voyage to the Brazils;* some are pedagogical such as *Rose's Breakfast,* which provides the Linnean names for and characteristics of plant species attending a breakfast; and some are political statements, such as the Tory propagandistic *Lion's Parliament: Or the Beasts in Debate* and Harris' radical *Council of Dogs,* a bitter working-class diatribe against government oppression. Although it is not a direct parody of Dorset, one could add to this list a well-known parodic satire by William Hone and George Cruikshank, the title of which, *The Political Showman—At Home!* (1821), is clearly an allusion to Dorset.[15]

What made Dorset's poem so adaptable is hard to define. In part, her focus on social gatherings was appealing, her use of animal types and lists of characteristics was easily mimicked, and her wordiness and sense of social chit-chat seemed to welcome dialogue and invite others to participate in the game. Further, the focus on multiple plant or animal species capitalized on the Romantic era's craze for cataloging the natural world and intersected with a rise in the publishing of pedagogical children's books that used narrative frames to deliver lessons.[16] Dorset's basic pattern in the *Peacock "At Home"* consists of the following elements:

1. A species (animal, plant, or even constellations as in the case of the *Horses's Levee, or the Court of Pegasus*), has heard of the Butterfly's Ball and is jealous. This species decides to host a gathering to rival the ball. These gatherings are modeled after a range of high-society social events such as fetes, breakfasts, masquerades, concerts, and suppers.

2. A guest list is created; invitations are sent; and regrets and acceptances are received. The regrets are particularly witty and topical: some animals cannot come south during the winter, some are hibernating, some are delayed by Napoleon. During this section, the authors make catty comments about the bad habits of various species.

3. An extensive reception line details all of the guests who come to the event. The reception line provides additional opportunity for commentary, this time focusing on species-specific clothing and behaviors. In didactic chapbooks, this section is heavy reading, for the author uses the species list to convey science lessons about botanical classifications of flower types, for example, or about the specific habits and appearances of birds. In *The Lioness's Rout*, the entrance of the camel is accompanied by eight lines about the camel's habitat and water storage capacities.

4. The activities of the gathering are detailed (cards, dances, charades, plays, refreshments). The success of the gathering varies widely depending on the guest list. In *The Lobster's Voyage to the Brazils*, the lobster is caught and eaten by humans along the way. Sometimes the civilized veneer falls away, and the animals revert to animalistic behavior. In *The Court of the Beasts*, a tyrannical lion presides over a feast during which the carnivores brawl until "mangled heads, limbs, and carcasses cover'd the ground" (19).

5. The event finishes with closing speeches. Sometimes the author includes a moral. For example, after King Lion stops the violent brawl in *The Court of the Beasts,* he lectures about the ill effects of alcohol.

These small chapbooks contain approximately sixteen pages of text with six to ten full-page illustrations interspersed throughout. The names of the species are set off from the text in some way, sometimes written in all capital letters, sometimes italicized. The books are pocket-sized, as befits children's literature.

Harris' publishing house became so associated with the trend of publishing satires for children that it was condemned by the *London Magazine* in 1820. An essayist praised Tabart's collection of fairy tales (overlooking this firm's knock-off chapbooks modeled after Harris' books) and attacked the "poisonous" chapbooks of Harris and son: "When the scandals of the drawing room become the sports of the nursery; when fathers and mothers present their children with caricatures of their own foibles and ridiculous pretensions, there only wants the government to assist the debasement of manners, by some such public spectacle of infamy and ignominy, in elevated station, as has been now exhibited in the Upper House of Parliament, to render the future destiny of the nation pretty nearly certain." The critic then attacks the chapbook authors directly, "'you have no children, butchers!',", and links the writers to the authors who "bring out the political caricatures, and personal lampoons of the day" (p. 180). The logic and language of chivalry underpins this review, for protecting children's natural innocence from corruption, not unlike protecting the purity of women, is linked to the fate of the nation. By 1820, then, the line between innocence and politics in children's literature is clearly drawn, and the fate of the nation and the child hangs in the balance.

III

It should not be surprising that satire and children's literature were once connected, for satire's "horizon of reception is often multilayered: some in the audience hear and do not understand, and only a select few are ever fully in the know."[17] All children's literature is arguably cross-written for a double audience, adult and child. However, in the more overtly political of these children's chapbooks, the strength of the satire seems to work in inverse proportion to the strength of the work as children's literature. The double nature of satire, in which signals are to be interpreted by one reader as a criticism of another, can be effectively cross-written for the adult and child audience within the less violent, conversational modes of Horatian satire, but as soon as the politics in these chapbooks becomes more grim, more obvious, more angry, in a word, more Juvenalian, the element of cross-writing for the child falls away.

To demonstrate my point, I will turn now to *The Council of Dogs* from the same series as *The Butterfly's Ball* and *The Peacock "At Home."* Published by Harris in 1808, the first, explosive year of the Dorset imitations, *The Council of Dogs* follows Dorset's format, but its satire as well as its illustrations are much darker. Unlike the other, whimsical illustrations in J. Harris' Dorset-style chapbooks that intermix human and animal parts, *The Council of Dogs's* pictures might as well be British dog-breeding prints: dogs are displayed in naturalist settings engaged in outdoor dog activities such as running, hunting, or sniffing in holes. These are standard adult illustrations, not illustrations created to appeal to children. The text of the poem begins in the same amusing fashion as Dorset's poem and its imitators: after announcing that the dogs feel overlooked in all the excitement over the Butterfly and Peacock gatherings, various dog types appear, each of which makes partisan soapbox speeches about the superiority of a particular dog breed over another. The poem, however, moves away from Dorset's pattern as the content becomes increasingly dark. Eventually, all sense of the child-as-reader disappears, and the poem becomes an overt protest of the dog tax and a covert call to unionizing.

The poem begins with the President Sheepdog's address to the convention of dogs. He declares that dogs must claim their own share of "poetical fame," for they have been neglected by poets who write of butterflies and peacocks (p. 3). The animals who choose not to attend are given appropriate, politically relevant excuses: "All pleaded the times; some could not get passports, / Some feared BONAPARTE, some were stopt by their own courts" (p. 4).

During the roll call, each dog has his say and presents the case for his breed's superiority. The Fox-Hound, for example, brags of hunting. The Poacher's Dog describes his secret activities with his master. The Spaniel brags of his ancestor's close association with King Charles and his Queen. When the Turnspit claims to have done some "good turns" in his day (8), the Scotch Terrier proclaims that he is an obsolete manual laborer who has been replaced by "Smoak-jacks, and Rumfords" (9). Contemporary readers would have recognized the parallels between the Turnspit's situation and that of the British laborers displaced by machines. When the Barbet speaks, he presents the image of a proud pet of the upper class (see figure 6.3), and his be-ruffled and overly cultured appearance suggest that the upperclass, like their dogs, is effete:

> . . . a dapper BARBET. so blithe and so smart,
> With his ruffles, and ruff, all shorn with such art,

"But a dapper Barbet, so blithe and so smart."   p.10.

Figure 6.3. Illustrations of The Council of Dogs, *as in this scene depicting the dancing Barbet, are more realistic and less fanastic than in other J. Harris chapbooks for children.*

Tript forward, and said his tricks he would play—
He tumbled,—fetch'd ball,—and down for dead lay,—
Then started alive to defend GEORGE THE THIRD
While, in pleasure loud barking, their plaudits were heard.

(p. 10)

The Barbet performs for the favor of the upper class—he performs tricks, plays dead, defends the king, and is much praised for his show. But readers soon realize that his performance is no more than pandering to one's master, for the tone of the poem shifts sharply in the final two pages. From the midst of the dog pack comes a starving, enraged mixed-breed cur. Although other curs and mongrels have attended the gathering (eight curs even dance a quadrille for the company's entertainment), the presence of this cur immediately antagonizes the council:

On the sudden a howling went round
From each TERRIER and MASTIFF and POINTER and HOUND,
For, full in the midst of the council, a CUR

(Whose presence no member had noticed before)
Uprose to address them; blood-red was his eye,
His carcase [sic] was fleshless, and shrill was his cry,
His knees were all bent, as with weakness he shook,
And death and starvation scowled in his look.—
"You may talk of Parnassus and Poets," he cried,
"Of their scorn, and neglect, may complain in your pride,
But that is all vanity, folly, conceit,
The disgust of the pamper'd, the pride of the great;
Look at me; I am starved—In yon hamlet I dwelt
And contented for years no distresses I felt,
Till the TAX, that my master had no means to pay,
From the comforts of home drove me famished away;
'Tis for *life* I contend—
. . . . .
Revenge, then, Revenge"—Exhausted he sunk,—
And back from the sight in horror they shrunk.

(pp. 14–15)

It is hard to interpret the stance of the poet. Is it abject horror of the un-
washed, underfed, and violent under class? A rejection of the scapegoated
cur, who seems to bear curses and disease and is described as physically disgusting? Are the lines intended to inspire sympathy or fear? The poem never
clarifies how the reader should respond to the cur and the other dogs. The
dogs physically shrink back in horror, but they do not argue with or attack
the cur. This lack of retaliation and back-biting is a notable shift from the
early pattern in which different dogs would challenge each other's claims.
After the cur speaks the unspeakable, the other dogs are silenced. The closing speech by the President Sheepdog does not respond directly to the cur.
Rather, he closes the council with a mixture of admonitions and possibly
threats:

A silence ensued—Thus the president spoke,
"This Council, my friends, I wished to convoke
Our rights to assert, but though each dog pretends
To valour, or beauty, or skill, yet my friends
If we look for success, much on union depends;
Let no separate claims then this union betray,
For remember the promise, *each dog has his day.*—
Tis our aggregate worth must our merits decide,
Our patience, sagacity, faithfulness tried;
We then shall deserve, if we don't obtain fame,
And the Poets, not we, incur the just blame;
This perhaps too may cause our arch-foe to relent,

And move to compassion the hard hearted D* * *;
If so, my companions, the good that may follow,
Is better than all we can get from APOLLO."

(pp. 15–16)

Although the pro-union sentiment is clear, so too is the sense of damage control and containment. The Sheepdog, a breed noted for loyalty, urges passivity and suffering rather than violence. At the same time, the children's verse successfully performs in print what the gagging acts had made illegal in reality: public, political speech making and the gathering of a crowd.

The "hard hearted D ***" to whom the poem refers is almost surely John Dent, a Member of Parliament who was famous for having successfully proposed a dog tax in 1796. He introduced the measure with such an alarming tirade against dogs, which was joyously seized on by the opposition wits, that he was ever after known as Dog Dent (Thorne, p. 587).[18] Dent was a fairly conservative M. P. who voted to suppress seditious societies, and he opposed allowing Dissenters to hold militia commissions without taking the sacrament. As an M.P. from Lancaster, a district heavily dependent on the slave trade, he persistently opposed all attempts to abolish or curtail slave trading.[19]

The Council of Dog's references to Dent, though topical and political, are not its main point—after all, this poem is published twelve years after the instigation of the dog tax. What does drive this poem is middle- and upper-class anxiety about an increasingly threatening working class. Rural dog gatherings were associated with unruly working-class gatherings, such as animal fights and bear- and bull-baiting. Animal control laws were one of many legal measures to circumscribe and contain the lives of the poor and protect the privilege of the rich.[20] As Harriet Ritvo notes, the dog licensing act was intended to control unregulated dogs that roamed the city streets. Since the dog owner (not the dog) was required to carry the license, it ultimately regulated owners. The compelling force behind the 1796 dog tax was not to generate revenue, but to discourage the rural poor from owning poaching dogs. It is significant that one of the animals who speaks in the dog's council is a Poacher's Dog. Further (as Harriet Ritvo suggests), when dog shows began in 1859, they were dedicated to controlling dog breeds and stopping indiscriminate dog cross-breeding. These dog shows created model breed specimens and discouraged mongrels.

The uneasy politics of *The Council of Dogs* can be contrasted to a straightforwardly propagandistic, patriotic chapbook published in the same year, 1808, by Harris' rival firm, J. B. Batchelor.[21] *The Lion's Parliament,* like *The Council of Dogs,* uses animals to make coded references to public political figures. In the parliament, for example, the Speaker of the House of Commons is Fox (though Charles James Fox had died in 1806, his animal name was clearly too rich a coincidence for the chapbook writer to pass up). After learning that the Tiger might attempt to take over the throne, the Admiral Crocodile, a Nelson reference, promises that his monarch will still rule the sea, and that he will attack "should the *Frogs* on the ocean advance." Its illustrations are beautifully realized, presenting apotheosized human-like animals, in parliamentary wigs and robes, and behaving with all ceremony.

IV

The mental qualities imputed to childhood are those befitting a solitary creative genius who in isolation from human society is able to form unitary visions of a world instinct with meaning. Within the Romantic discourse of essential childhood, the mind of the child is set up as a sanctuary or bank vault of valuable but socially-endangered psychological powers: idealism, holism, vision, animism, faith, and isolated self-sufficiency.[22]

Judith Plotz notes that Wordsworth and Coleridge, for whom "holism and idealism are crucial to the essentializing discourse of childhood," present childhood as tied to animism; they see the child's perception of the universe as instinct with life, and see that the child regards objects as living and endowed with will (pp. 18–19). The children of *The Butterfly's Ball* regard nature with just such wonder, and Roscoe's work became canonical. The sparse lines and fantastical images of the *Butterfly's Ball* are static and nonpermeable. It resists change to such an extent that the poem, as a whole, can be transported from one setting to another without changing its contours. Roscoe's poem suits the New Critical tendency to find perfect poems that satisfy the demand for poetic autonomy and self-referentiality. It is inward-looking, simple, and it presents childhood as enclosed special time. By contrast, Dorset and the author of *The Council of Dogs* are writing about society only slightly disguised as nature. Their poems do not fit the Romantic ideology of the innocent child. As satire, they are topical, local, and contextual. Their wordiness and flow of names and places with quick, humorous rhymes is more associated with eighteenth-century "wit." They are by traditional definition non-Romantic.

In closing, I return to my opening conjectures about what the reception of these texts reveals about our historiography of children's literature and Romantic poetics. I began my research as a feminist Romanticist working with children's poetry. I expected to find that Dorset's gender was the ultimate cause of her noncanonical status. I discovered instead that although Dorset published anonymously, neither her anonymity nor her femininity detracted from the praise that her book received. Her poem was widely admired, endlessly imitated, and generally considered better than Roscoe's. It was republished throughout the century in various formats: from game boards to ornithological pedagogical texts.[23] Dorset even capitalized on its success by naming her own poetry collection *The Peacock "At Home" and Other Poems.*[24] In 1816, the ever entrepreneurial Harris published a laudatory sequel, *The Peacock and the Parrot, on Their Tour in Search of the Author of* The Peacock "At Home," in which the bird species, desiring to praise the author of the poem, go on a long journey in search of her home and identity. Further, gender bias cannot explain the fate of poems such as *The Council of Dogs.*

Although gender does not appear to have been a deciding factor in the early reception of these texts, gender does affect their later reception, primarily through the stranglehold of the Romantic ideology of the innocent child of nature. And here is where the disjunction between the disciplines of Romanticism and of children's literature is most apparent and most damaging. Since the 1983 publication of Jerome McGann's *The Romantic Ideology,* Romanticists have been busy critiquing the ways in which Romantic aesthetics has worked to exclude texts not fitting its ideology—from Gothic novels to sentimental poetry to texts by women and writers of the working class. By contrast, the field of children's literature, which recognizes its indebtedness to Romantic aesthetics, has not yet analyzed the effects of the exclusionary politics of Romanticism on the inclusion and exclusion of texts from its canons.[25]

Finally, consider the children's texts of the Taylor family, for they published Roscoe-like poetry, Dorset imitations, and full-fledged satire for children. Jane Taylor authored one of the most loved children's poems in history, "The Star" ("Twinkle, Twinkle, Little Star"), which was published in Ann, Jane, and Isaac Taylor's and Adelaide O'Keefe's *Rhymes for the Nursery* (1806). Jane's sister Ann Taylor was not immune to the Butterfly's Ball craze, for she published a chapbook in the mode of Dorset's *The Peacock "At Home"*: *Wedding Among the Flowers* is a poetic tour de force along the lines of Erasmus Darwin's *The Love of the Plants.* It is not, however, very readable for anybody but historians interested in the field of early botanical curiosities. The poem is so lengthy and full of ornate descriptions of plants, that Darton and Harvey reduced the font size of the print in order to make the poem fit the sixteen-page chapbook format. Finally, Ann, Isaac, and Jane Taylor published *Signor Topsy Turvey's Wonderful Magic Lantern* in 1810, a collection of comic-satiric poems that reverse the order of men and beasts. The Dorset-like *Wedding Among The Flowers* went through only one edition. The satire *Signor Topsy Turvey* was published only twice in the Romantic era, once in England and once in America. By contrast, "Twinkle, Twinkle, Little Star" has never been out of print. Like Roscoe's *The Butterfly's Ball*, it contains the elements of child-hood imagination, wonder, animus attributed to nature, and simple direct images.[26] In the end, then, it would appear that the author's explicit gender matters less than the ability to participate in the implicitly gendered, anti-satiric, Romantic ideology of the child.

Notes

1. The excerpt of William Roscoe, *The Butterfly's Ball and the Grasshopper's Feast*, is taken from the 1807 edition published by J. Harris (London). The sixth line was added in the 1808 edition.

2. The Mulready illustrations I discuss are from the first Harris edition (1807). A revised edition in 1808 contained less attractive illustrations (by a different illustrator) featuring animal pictures. For a full history of the publication of these two versions as well as the first magazine publications of the poem, see Clive Hurst's discussion of the early texts of *The Butterfly's Ball*, "'From a Great Distance': The Early Texts of *The Butterfly's Ball*," *The Bodleian Library Record* 13.5 (1990): 415–22. The full 1808 text and illustrations are accessible at the University of Toronto Library website: Representative Poetry On-Line, <*http://www.library.utoronto.ca/utel/poems/roscoe1.html*>.

3. The politics of *The Butterfly's Ball* remain unclear. Its first appearance was in *The Gentleman's Magazine*, a conservative journal stridently opposed to the 1790s campaign for political reform (see Paul Keen, *The Crisis of Literature in the 1790s: Print Culture and the Public Sphere* [Cambridge: Cambridge University Press, 1999], 10). Yet John Harris' chapbook series included radical and satirical writings. See Nanora Sweet, "Lorenzo's Liverpool and 'Corrine's' Coppet: The Italiantate Salon and Romantic Education," in *Lessons of Romanticism: A Critical Companion*, ed. Thomas Pfau and Robert F. Gleckner (Durham, NC: Duke University Press, 1998), 244–60, on Roscoe's importance to the political, literary, and cultural vitality of Liverpool.

4. Michael Scott Joseph, "William Roscoe: 1753–1831," in *Dictionary of Literary Biography*, ed. Meena Khorana (Detroit: Gale, 1996), 234–38. Alan Richardson suggests that John Harris had a pivotal role in creating this new understanding of children's literature: his earlier *Old Mother Hubbard* in addition to the *Butterfly's Ball* and the *Peacock "At Home"* established the tradition of light verse for children (*Literature, Education, and Romanticism: Reading as Social Practice, 1800–1832* [Cambridge: Cambridge University Press, 1994]).

5. For specific information about Martin's work and its relationship to satire, see Marcus Wood, *Radical Satire and Print Culture, 1790–1822* (Oxford: Clarendon Press, 1994), pp. 222–23.

6. William McCarthy, "Mother of all Discourses: Anna Barbauld's *Lessons for Children*," *Princeton Library Chronicle* 60.2 (Winter 1999):196–219 (199). Jaqueline Rose, *The Case of Peter Pan: The Impossibility of Children's Fiction*

(Philadelphia: University of Pennsylvania Press, 1984), links the emphasis on nature in children's literature to Rousseau as well as Locke: childhood is set up by adults as a primitive state in which nature can be recovered, and traditional educational and social institutions deform the child's unity with nature (pp. 44–45). Mitzi Myers has written extensively on female pedagogues and the "gendered codes" of children's literature; see "Little Girls Lost; Rewriting Romantic Childhood, Righting Gender and Genre," in *Teaching Children's Literature: Issues, Pedagogy, Resources,* ed. Glenn Edward Sadler (New York: MLA, 1992), 131–42; and "Of Mice and Mothers: Mrs. Barbauld's 'New Walk' and Gendered Codes in Children's Literature," in *Feminine Principles and Women's Experience in American Composition and Rhetoric,* ed. Louise Wetherbee Phelps and Janet Emig (Pittsburgh: University of Pittsburgh Press, 1995), 225–88. For discussion of gender bias in the construction of literary histories of children's periodicals and Bibles, see Donelle Ruwe, "Guarding the British Bible from Rousseau: Sarah Trimmer, William Godwin, and the Pedagogical Periodical," *Children's Literature* 29, Ed. Elizabeth Lennox Keyser and Julie Pfeiffer (New Haven, CT: Yale University Press. 2001), 1–17.

7. Alan Richardson, for example, has attributed the formal creation of an "official" children's literature to the Romantic era's gradual separating out a literature of imagination and innocence from the uncensored chapbooks of the eighteenth century. Richardson builds on the earlier work of Jacqueline Rose's *The Case for Peter Pan,* which argues that it is adult readers who desire the innocent child in order to restore their own innocence and to affirm their roles as protectors of the innocent. Judith Plotz, *Romanticism and the Vocation of Childhood* (New York: Palgrave, 2001), has suggested that the canonical Romantics had so much at stake in their belief in the imaginative, innocent child that they crippled their own chosen exemplar, Hartley Coleridge, who was never able to mature beyond his special status as the child of wonder.

8. Susan Stewart, *On Longing: Narratives of the Miniature, the Gigantic, the Souvenir, the Collection* (Baltimore: Johns Hopkins University Press, 1984), 54.

9. See Morag Styles, *From the Garden to the Street: An Introduction to 300 Years of Poetry for Children* (London: Cassell, 1998), for specific information about the history of children's poetry since the early 1700s.

10. *The Butterfly's Ball* was published as a diorama and pirated and expanded for publication in American and British children's magazines such as *March's Penny Library.* In 1857, it was rewritten as a prose narrative and set to music; in the fin de siècle, it inspired a concert overture by the British composer Frederick Hymen Cowen.

11. Review of the *Butterfly's Ball* and *The Peacock "At Home,"* in *The British Critic* (1807).

12. At various times *The Elephant's Ball, The Lion's Masquerade,* and *The Lioness's Route* (1808) have been attributed to Dorset. However, I have not been able to determine how this attribution came about; the chapbooks were all published

anonymously, the poetic skill and style varies widely, and *The Lioness's Route* was published by R. Tabart, a rival firm of Harris'. Further, although Dorset republished *The Peacock "At Home"* as well as other children's poetry in her collection, *The Peacock "At Home" And Other Poems* (1809), she did not include any of the above poems. The misattribution of authorship of children's books is a persistent problem for scholars. For example, the current Chadwyck-Healy database has been sloppy enough to list Charlotte Smith, Dorset's sister, as the author of *The Peacock "At Home" And Other Poems.* I thank Stuart Curran for drawing to my attention this error by Chadwyck-Healy.

13. These quotations from *The Gentleman's Magazine* and *Critical Review* are taken from Marjorie Moon's *John Harris's Books for Youth, 1801–1843* (Folkestone, Kent: Dawson, 1992), 43.

14. See Mary V. Jackson, *Engines of Instruction, Mischief, and Magic: Children's Literature in England from its Beginnings to 1839* (Lincoln: University of Nebraska Press, 1989), esp. 208–213, for specific discussion of Dorset's poem as mock epic. When Dorset republished the poem in her own collection of works, she expanded the footnotes after the style of Erasmus Darwin's botanical poetry. Perhaps she was attempting to make the poem more appealing to adult readers, or perhaps the format of a poetry collection provided greater scope for intellectuality than was available in the circumscribed length of a chapbook.

15. See Marcus Wood, *Radical Satire and Print Culture,* 170–79, on Hone and Cruikshank and their connection to early children's literature. Katie Trumpener, "Visits to the Juvenile Library: Bookselling, Advertising and the Making of Child Readers," Plenary Address, North American Society for the Study of Romanticism conf., University of Washington, Seattle, August 16, 2001, points to the marketing politics of early children's literature, suggesting that the derivative writing and promotion of children's books within children's books is essential to the early establishment of a specific field of children's publishing. Those children's publishers such as William Godwin who chose to solicit work from only prestigious writers were unable to compete. Marjorie Moon's many annotated catalogues of the books produced by Romantic era children's publishers are invaluable resources to any scholar of early children's work.

16. Dorset's first published poetry appeared in one such children's work, her sister Charlotte Smith's *Conversations Introducing Poetry, Chiefly on Subjects of Natural History,* which embedded poems about nature and pedagogical lessons within a story about a mother taking rural walks with her two children. For additional information on Smith's and Dorset's poetry and use of conversational dialogues, see Donelle Ruwe, "Charlotte Smith's Sublime: Feminine Botany, and *Beachy Head,*" *Prism(s)* 7 (1999): 117–31.

17. Steven E. Jones, *Shelley's Satire: Violence, Exhortation, and Authority* (Dekalb: Northern Illinois University Press, 1994), 7.

18. Dent represented Lancaster from 1790 to 1812 and Poole from 1818 to 1826, and he was part of George Canning's inner circle. Dent envisaged the dog tax as being appropriated for the relief of the poor, but it passed only

after Pitt reintroduced the bill as a revenue earning measure. Political commentary as well as letters and notes of friends consistently compared Dent to dogs. In 1802 he introduced a bill to abolish bull-baiting and was accused of a "fanatical cry of the dogs of Hudibras against lewd pastimes" (R. G. Thorne, *The House of Commons 1790–1820,* 1986, vol. III, 588). His speeches were described as "barking" or "howling." When he changed his mind after turning down a baronetcy, George Canning wrote, "How could I guess the Dog's wish to be Sir Dogby, when he so positively denied it? Has Mrs. Dog changed her mind?" (Thorne, 590).

19. As a banker by profession, Dent was most heavily engaged in matters involving the regulation of finance and trade and in the economic improvement of the country and the poor. For example, he called for a total prohibition of hair powder in 1795 so that soldiers, whose servants (he felt) stole vast quantities of flour, would not endanger the food supply. He also pushed through an enquiry into abuses of franking by the Members of Parliament.

20. Harriet Ritvo's *The Animal Estate: The English and Other Creatures in the Victorian Age* (Cambridge, MA: Harvard University Press, 1987), provides an extended analysis of the history of dog control laws, rabies, and dog shows. In the Romantic era, the increasing number of dog fanciers led to a craze for dog books, beginning with Sydenham Edwards' *Cynographia Britannica,* which was issued in parts between 1800 and 1805. Thomas Bewick's *General History of Quadrupeds* (intended for youths but a bestseller with adults) devotes thirteen pages to horses and thirty-nine to dogs. *The Naturalist's Library* had thirteen volumes on quadrupeds, of which two volumes were on dogs alone. Christine Kenyon Jones has discussed the Romantic understanding of animals, as influenced by Locke and Rousseau, and how that use influences children's books, which encourage children to be kind to animals, in *Kindred Brutes: Animals in Romantic Period Writing* (Aldershot, UK: Ashgate, 2001).

21. *The Council of Dogs* might also be compared to the satirical chapbook *The Council of Hogs: a Descriptive Poem, Containing a Patriotic Oration to the Swinish Multitude,* which is listed in Gary Dyer's bibliography of Romantic-era satires in *British Satire and the Politics of Style* (Cambridge: Cambridge University Press, 1997).

22. Judith Plotz, *Romanticism and the Vocation of Childhood,* 13; hereafter cited in the text.

23. For example, an 1835 board game of *The Peacock "At Home"* contains full-color illustrated birds on its cards, fold-out playing board, and a box. The game board is so striking that the Osborne Collection of Early Children's Books uses a full-color photographic display of the game board and all its pieces on its glossy advertisement and informational brochure.

24. The gimmick of searching for the anonymous author was a little stale in that Dorset's authorship was widely recognized by then and a footnote within the text gives her identity away. In any case, it allowed Harris to promote both Roscoe's and Dorset's books; the back cover lists the 27th edition of *The Peacock "At Home."*

25. Although children's literature includes among its producers many important women writers, history has favored texts written by "major" (male) authors, even when the value of the work as literature for children is questionable. Blake, for example, is always included in children's anthologies though he is not historically a children's author but uses the forms of children's texts to produce books for adult readers. Morag Styles, in her history of children's poetry, notes that anthologists select poems written mainly by men for other adults, and that the ratio of male to female authors is one to twenty (*From the Garden to the Street,* p. 195). Further, children's poetry anthologists usually assume that reading children's poetry is an apprenticeship in which children are being prepared to read adult texts; therefore, the "best" children's poems are produced by prestigious, canonical male authors, for these poems are most effective in helping children to appreciate the great works of canonical poets.

26. On Jane Taylor, See Stuart Curran in the next chapter (chapter 7) of the present volume.

Children's chapbooks cited

Addison, Henry R. [author] and Alexander Lee [composer]. *The Butterfly's Ball; Or, the jealous Moth.* Adelphi Theatre 1806–1900. Calendar for 1833–1834. Jan. 7, 2002. <*http://www.emich.edu/public/english/adelphi_calendar/m33d.html*>.

B. J. L. *Butterfly's Funeral: Intended as a Sequel to* The Butterfly's Ball And the Grasshopper's Feast *by Mr. Roscoe.* London: John Wallis. 1808.

Comus. *The Butterfly's Ball and the Grasshopper's Feast by Comus, author of The Three Little Kittens.* London: Thomas Nelson and Sons. 1857.

The Council of Dogs. London: J. Harris, 1808.

The Council of Hogs, a Descriptive Poem, Containing a Patriotic Oration to the Swinish Multitude. London: Hatchard. 1809.

The Court of the Beasts. London: Darton and Harvey. 1808.

Dorset, Catherine Ann. *The Peacock "At Home" and other Poems.* London: John Murray. 1809.

———. *The Peacock "At Home": A Sequel to The Butterfly's Ball.* London: J. Harris. 1807.

The Eagle's Masquerade. (By Tom Tit). 2nd Edition. London: J. Mawman, Poultry. 1808.

The Elephant's Ball, and the Grand Fete Champetre: Intended as a Companion to Those Much Admired Pieces, The Butterfly's Ball and The Peacock "At Home." London: J. Harris. 1807.

The Farm Yard Quadrille. Uxbridge: William Lake for W. Darton. 1825.

The Horse's Levee, Or the Court of Pegasus, Intended as a Companion to the Butterfly's Ball and The Peacock "At Home." *London: J. Harris. 1808.*

The Jack-Daw "At Home." (By A Young Lady of rank). London: Didier and Talbot. 1808.

The Lion's Masquerade: A Sequel to The Peacock "At Home." (By a Lady). London: J. Harris. 1807.

The Lion's Parliament, or the Beasts in Debate. London: J. B. Batchelor. 1808.

The Lioness's Rout: Being a Sequel to The Butterfly's Ball, The Grasshopper's Feast, and the Peacock "At Home." (By a Lady). London: R. Tabart. 1808.

Lobster's Voyage to the Brazils. London: J. Harris. 1808.

The Peahen at Home, or the Swan's Bridal Day. London: J. L. Marks, ca. 1840.

The Peacock and the Parrot, on Their Tour in Search of the Author of The Peacock "At Home." J. Harris, 1816.

Roscoe, William. *The Butterfly's Ball and the Grasshopper's Feast.* Illustrated by Vance Gerry. Pasadena: Weather Bird Press. 1996.

——. *The Butterfly's Ball and the Grasshopper's Feast.* London: J. Harris. 1806.

——. *The Butterfly's Ball and the Grasshopper's Feast.* London: J. Harris. 1807.

——. *The Butterfly's Ball and the Grasshopper's Feast.* 1883. Representative Poetry On-Line. University of Toronto Library. 1998. <*http://www.library.utoronto.ca/ utel/rp/poems/roscoe1.html*>.

The Butterfly's Birth-Day, St. Valentine's Day, and Madame Whale's Ball: Poems to Instruct and Amuse the Rising Generation. J. Harris. 1808.

Rose's Breakfast. London: J. Harris. 1808.

Tabbey, A. *A Fishes' Feast, with a Mermaid's Song, Dedicated to the Author of the* Peacock at Home, *with a Poetical Address. To Which is Added the Ape's Concert.* London: R. Spencer and T. Hughes. 1808.

Taylor, Ann. *The Wedding Among the Flowers, by One of the Authors of* Original Poems, Rhymes for the Nursery. London: Darton and Harvey. 1808.

Chapter 7 ∼

Jane Taylor's Satire on Satire

Stuart Curran

In an age in which it is widely felt that poetry no longer occupies a prominent position in the hierarchies of art or even literature, Jane Taylor, by a
nice paradox, has returned to a central station among the poets of the
British Romantic age. In truth, she never actually left it. For generations, as
the unacknowledged author of the single most popular poem of the age, her
enduring evocation of a Romantic ideal, called "The Star" but commonly
known from its first line as "Twinkle, twinkle, little star," she has been trea-
sured literally by millions across the entire English-speaking world. That
poem, at last, has been duly acknowledged and has taken its place in at least
one major anthology of the period where, in another paradox, it is probably
passed over with wry bemusement by those who think they ought to have
long outgrown its influence and who instead take their pleasures from her
other major contribution to the literature of the Romantic age.[1] Though her
output is small, she is the only woman poet of the period to be classified as a
satirist, and, in possession of a style of striking originality, she seems at once
culturally significant and anomalous. But, as a further extension of these
paradoxes, it is highly likely that Jane Taylor did not view herself or construe
her poetic mission within the terms of satire as it is traditionally understood.
Like another great satirist of the age, Byron, although from a distinctly different vantage, she undermines the premises on which satire, particularly that
of the eighteenth century, constructed its edifice.

Her principal volume of verse, *Essays in Rhyme, on Morals and Manners*
(1816), containing twelve poems, would certainly seem to most readers to
possess the habiliments of satire.[2] The central position is occupied by
"Recreation," a poem that, from its title on, is composed of consummate

doubles entendres that reinforce the double performance it relates, as "Miss B." retails the malicious gossip she and her mother had picked up from their neighbor "Mrs. G." to an unknown hearer, whom we can anticipate will recycle it in yet another form down the line of her acquaintance. Through a masterful use of italic print, Taylor even manages to convey a simultaneous double perspective that captures the pervasive hypocrisy that links all the speakers in this poem.

> At first, we all were somewhat dry;
> Mamma felt cold, and so did I:
> Indeed, that room, sit where you will,
> Has draught enough to turn a mill.
> 'I hope you're warm,' says Mrs. G.
> 'O, quite so,' says mamma, *says she;*
> 'I'll take my shawl off by and by.'—
> 'This room is always warm,' *says I.*

(pp. 108–109)

This passage, as uncomplicated as it might seem, may be used to introduce the characteristics that make Taylor's voice so distinctive. First of all, she lodges her verse within a vernacular rhetoric, recreating authentic middle-class voices whom we overhear in colloquy, perhaps in pained recognition of how much we share their timbres. Even in poems whose purposes are more formal than "Recreation," Taylor never strays from this determined plain style. Yet, within its simple confines she can achieve surprisingly heightened and even deeply moving effects. The second figure in "A Pair," the rude mechanic eking out a bare subsistence in the midst of urban squalor, for instance, is represented by an unexpected Miltonic attenuation of line that mirrors the unvaried patterns of his existence:

> There stands the bench at which his life is spent,
> Worn, groov'd, and bor'd, and worm-devour'd, and bent.

(p. 135)

The conclusion of this poem skillfully embodies its contrast between the healthy existence of country life and the mechanic's claustrophobic confinement through a progression of clauses that spill over each other and across adjoining lines until suddenly they collide with the perfectly measured, insistent caesuras of his quotidian life.

> —At length the taper fades, and distant cry
> Of early sweep bespeaks the morning nigh;
> Slowly it breaks,—and that rejoicing ray

That wakes the healthful country into day,
Tips the green hills, slants o'er the level plain,
Reddens the pool, and stream, and cottage pane,
And field, and garden, park, and stately hall,—
Now darts obliquely on his wretched wall.
He knows the wonted signal; shuts his book,
Slowly consigns it to its dusty nook;
Looks out awhile, with fixt and absent stare,
On crowded roofs, seen through the foggy air;
Stirs up the embers, takes his sickly draught,
Sighs at his fortunes, and resumes his craft.

(pp. 138–39)

Along with a style designed to represent a realistic world to readers who are conceived to be without pretension to rise above their own middle-class roots, Taylor employs a continual store of witty and domestic proverbial expressions. Reverting to "Recreation," we can see its effect in the colloquial hyperbole of the cadence "that room, sit where you will, / Has draught enough to turn a mill." The first portrait of "A Pair," that of a wealthy but wholly undistinguished young man, begins by typifying him as "like one pea among a peck" (p. 129). The grocer and his wife, the initial subjects of the introductory poem, "Prejudice," are said to apply themselves assiduously to their business: "Hard was the toil, the profits slow to count, / And yet the mole-hill was at last a mount" (p. 2). In the Romantic period, we are long accustomed to the notion of poetry written in what Wordsworth called "the real language of men," but it comes as something of a surprise to confront in so undiluted and direct a form the real language of women. It sounds far more naturally homely than any of the monosyllabically reduced diction we honor in *Lyrical Ballads.*

Gary Dyer is right to call our attention to how unconventional to satire in this age is such an insistently vernacular voice.[3] Where one does encounter strongly deflated rhetoric, as in Thomas Moore's "Fudge Family" poems, its vernacular debasement is generally itself the subject of satire. In Jane Taylor's *Essays in Rhyme,* in contrast, the plain style reverts to its source in the stylistic revolution that, fostered by the establishment of the Royal Society in the years after the Restoration, came to distinguish the unmannered, transparent prose of the latter third of the seventeenth century. Taylor's verse is intended to serve as an agency without pretension to art or barriers to comprehension by any literate person speaking standard English. Its use of homely sayings, its conversational tonalities, and its expressive pith are all aspects of its underlying sense of assured purpose. Taylor's distinctive style has all the hallmarks of the Dissenting middle-class culture in which the Taylors of Ongar were rooted, and it is meant to be read and comprehended with a felt ideological force.[4] The most common verse form of the *Essays in Rhyme* is the pentameter couplet made standard for prescriptive verse through the long eighteenth century, and, as we have seen in a setting like the conclusion of "A Pair," Jane Taylor employs it with great skill. But to compare her style with that customary to satire by prominent male voices of the Romantic age, from William Gifford and Thomas James Mathias in the 1790s to George Daniel and Charles Colton in the Regency, is to realize how markedly "un-heroic" is her verse, and her mindset, in comparison.

The traditional satire of masculine culture also, in general, occupies a public realm centered in questions of literary taste. In *The Baviad* and *Mæviad* Gifford focused his indictment on decadent Della Cruscan poetry as a means of attacking a more general cultural debasement of his elitist literary ideal, and this double thrust then offered Mathias a model from which, in *Pursuits of Literature,* he launched a generalized misogynist assault on the encroachments of women writers on high culture. Fifteen years later Daniel, in *The Modern Dunciad,* and Colton, in *Hypocrisy,* with less vitriol and greater wit, essentially follow the same prescription of literary criticism as a lens for cultural proscription. Colton's title is itself suggestive of the moral arena in which Jane Taylor focuses her entire attention, but it is highly indicative of how entrenched is this generic model that Colton, always identified on his title pages as an Anglican cleric, never seizes the opportunities provided by his ostensible subject to move beyond the vantage point offered by contemporary literature and confront actual hypocrisy of mind, of the kind, perhaps, to be found among his own congregation. Taylor, in contrast, makes only one specific literary reference in her entire volume, and she does so, it would appear, as a means of differentiating her entire focus from the merely literary, as she observes in "Experience" that the "female stranger" who has come to a remote village to live out her remaining years, "although her whole array / Bespoke neglect, indifference, and decay," is "not 'crazy Kate,' nor 'crazy Jane'," but rather "A common-care-worn person, that was all" (p. 56). This reference, in turn, suggests both a literary heritage and a cultural affinity. Crazy Kate is a famous "portrait" realized in just twenty-two lines in Cowper's *Task,* book I. The title of the poem in which she is cited, "Experience," like all the early verses of *Essays in Rhyme* ("Prejudice," Egotism," etc.) as well as the generic rubric of "essays" in which the volume is cast, is reminiscent of the titles of the long verse essays that compose most of Cowper's earlier volume, *Poems,* published three years before *The Task,* in 1782 (e.g., "Truth," "Expostulation," Hope," "Charity"). Although wit is certainly not the retiring Cowper's forte, the moral foundation of his major verse exactly suits the temper of Taylor's mind.

The same may be said for his retirement from public space. As Taylor is not interested in literary criticism per se and remains steadfastly unconcerned with high culture and aristocratic tastes, her focus is not on the public realm but rather on the domestic establishment as an index of broadly held private values. The intensity of the focus is made forcefully clear by the paired last poems of her volume, which over their progress increasingly eschew her characteristic wittiness of expression for Cowper's meditative sobriety, "The World in the House," "The World in the Heart." Laying strong claim to our recognition of her as a significant forerunner of nineteenth-century realism, Taylor continually directs her sharp eye to the nuances of domestic materiality. In the opening sequence of the first poem, "Prejudice," the portrait of the retired grocer (now the mayor) and his wife, there is not a detail that does not reveal their inner characteristics.

> In yonder red-brick mansion, tight and square,
> Just at the town's commencement, lives the mayor.
> Some yards of shining gravel, fenc'd with box,
> Lead to the painted portal—where one knocks:
> There, in the left-hand parlour, all in state,
> Sit he and she, on either side the grate.
> But though their goods and chattels, sound and new,
> Bespeak the owners *very well to do,*
> His worship's wig and morning suit betray
> Slight indications of an humbler day.
>
> (p. 1)

Although Taylor thus begins the volume by physically reducing this elderly couple of *nouveaux riches* to the status of andirons, she quickly shifts her attention to the nature of the wife as adjunct to her husband, and her lack of independent spirit is pursued with a rhetoric that at first we might think unmerciful.

> Her thoughts, unused to take a longer flight
> Than from the left-hand counter to the right,
> With little change, are vacillating still,
> Between his worship's glory and the till. . . .
>
> (p. 4)

> Were but her brain dissected, it would show
> Her stiff opinions fastened in a row,
> Rang'd duly, side by side, without a gap,
> Much like the plaiting on her Sunday cap.
>
> (p. 5)

Yet, the very next lines suggest quickly how Jane Taylor refuses the easy self-indulgences, exactly those in which she has just demonstrated her skills, that characterize the satiric arbiter.

It is not worth our while, but if it were,
We all could undertake to laugh at her.

(p. 5)

Indeed, through a very slight nuance earlier in the portrait, Taylor has already indicated that she wants to understand the grocer's wife within a perspective that transcends the merely satirical.

You might, perhaps, with reasons new and pat,
Have made Columbus think the world was flat;
There might be times of energy worn out,
When his own theory would Sir Isaac doubt;
But not the powers of argument combin'd,
Could make this dear good woman change her mind . . .

(p. 5)

The adjectives of the last line slip in with such facility that we scarcely note the tonal alteration they bring, but in retrospect it is almost startling. Accustomed to the excesses of satirical portraits that reduce people to the status of things, indeed, already lulled into this mental framework by the introductory lines emphasizing the complicity of the grocer and his wife in assuming a condition indistinguishable from the commodities they purvey, we are suddenly forced to acknowledge our common humanity with those to whose otherness we are tempted to condescend. It requires only that gentle intrusion of "dear good" to remind us of the salt-of-the-earth, middle-class values—industry, perseverance, thrift, civic responsibility, spousal devotion—we might find ourselves sharing with this woman.

As Taylor develops the excursive trajectory of "Prejudice," she compounds the tonal shift initiated here. Changing her vantage point from the narrow confines in which the grocer and his wife have immured their existence, Taylor turns to the perspective of the well-educated and cultured upon the world lying within their purview.

Those minds that stand from all mankind aloof,
To smile at folly, or dispense reproof;
Enlarged, excursive, reason soars away,
And breaks the shackles that confine its sway:
Their keen, dissecting, penetrating view,
Searches poor human nature through and through;
But while they notice all the forms absurd,
That prejudice assumes among the herd,

And every nicer variation see,
Theirs lies in thinking that themselves are free.

(pp. 7–8)

That it takes Taylor rather a length of verse to insinuate that a cultural elite
has its own blindnesses may suggest that those preceding lines house a larger
purpose, and this clearly seems to entail interrogating the attitude of mind
by which a self-styled elite would insulate itself from the common humanity shared with those constituting a category it finds absurd. "To smile at
folly, or dispense reproof," to pride oneself on being "keen, dissecting, penetrating," is, Taylor intimates, the very premise on which prejudice paradoxically casts its foundations. The specific language grounds the earlier
subjunctive hypothesis about the grocer's wife: "Were but her brain dis-
sected." It is not this writer's purpose merely to "dissect" and therefore se-
curely and even severely judge and dismiss, but rather to comprehend a
condition of mind rife at all levels of her culture.

In truth, it is also Jane Taylor's purpose in this initial poem strongly to
counter a skeptical detachment that would characterize religious devotion as
fanaticism, but that she does so in terms applicable to satire also suggests
how she is endeavoring from the first to reposition the stance her readers
might expect to assume from the rhetorical and generic means she employs.

. . . should the Christian code from all the rest
Be singled out, and own'd to be the best,
The same keen shafts of ridicule are bent
Against its spirit, and its true intent.

(p. 11)

Satire is specifically identified with an attitude of mind that, in Bunyan's vision in *Pilgrim's Progress,* stood foremost to bar the progress of the individual soul to its salvation: "The Christian's aims and motives, simple, grand, /
The wisest worldlings cannot understand" (p. 11). And, in general, Jane
Taylor casts these aims within a broad latitudinarianism, conducting much
of the later argument in "Prejudice" against religious sectarianism itself, in
which, not surprisingly, Taylor discerns the same roots of self-righteousness
she identifies with the spirit of satire. The "truly philosophical mind" pur-
sues an undogmatic end.

. . . this, with simple aim,
He follows, caring little for the name;
Not with the poor intent to make her stand
And wave his party's ensign in her hand,

Mocking his neighbour's pitiful mistake;
But for her own invaluable sake.

(p. 33)

As the argument is constructed here, it has only one logical implication, which is that God alone possesses the necessary purity for self-righteousness: "There is an eye that marks the ways of men, / With strict, impartial, analyzing ken" (p. 40), but God's perspective as Creator disallows the step humans take when they presume themselves to become "impartial" and "analytical": rather God's "unembarrass'd, just survey" is conducted "with compassion for our feeble powers" (p. 40). This same compassion, emulated in plain piety by God's servant, is what distinguishes the "dear good" modification that reassimilates the grocer's wife to a human community.

A willed separation from this community is the burden of all the opening poems of Taylor's *Essays in Rhyme:* "Prejudice," "Experience," "Egotism," "Poetry and Reality," in their turn, all enlarge upon common ground, inviting us to read them as successive repositionings of the reader's perspective. As prejudice insinuates a false judgmental interdiction at various points in the social constitution, so the erosions of experience may isolate and barricade a personality, and the continual self-regard of egotism further reinforces that withdrawal from a commonality of interests. What the reader of these successive poems is likely to be unprepared for is the surprising addition of lyric poetry, in the fourth of them, "Poetry and Reality," to the list of common threats to human solidarity. It may well be that this poem, which so directly pits one commitment of the author against an equally powerful one, should be read self-reflexively as an indication of why Taylor, after the great success of *Essays in Rhyme,* designed no further verse for publication. But there is a simpler way of comprehending the apparent self-questioning dynamic of this poem, one that would link its admonitions against poetic self-indulgence to those we have earlier begun to discern against the spirit and the means of satire. Lyric poetry, as it is conceived in "Poetry and Reality," is sanctioned highly within the hierarchies of value accorded art by society. In Taylor's poem that sanction reinforces poetry not just as an alternative to religion, but as an alternative to true fellowship as well. From the way in which she situates her poem, it appears that Jane Taylor has Thomas Gray principally in mind in this portrait of a solitary poet who haunts picturesque churchyards and reveres churches for their architecture, windows, and ceremony instead of their potentiality for spiritual access. But insofar as Gray adumbrated the prototype of alienated poet immersed in his own subjectivity to be reconfigured by successive generations of British lyricists, Taylor's target could be any number of her contemporary poets, even ostensibly religious figures like Coleridge. Moreover, in her sardonic depiction of the typical lyrical poet, she certainly has an eye for the themes and genres that distinguish mainstream Romanticism, from its attention to human interaction with nature and landscape to its concerns with mutability, even to the common forms of its expression.

> . . . let him slumber in luxurious ease,
> Beneath the umbrage of his idol trees,
> Pluck a wild daisy, moralise on that,
> And drop a tear for an expiring gnat,
> Watch the light clouds o'er distant hills that pass,
> Or write a sonnet to a blade of grass.
>
> (p. 92)

Having thus observed the dialectical patterning that provides the progressive momentum for the *Essays in Rhyme,* we may expect that the poem succeeding "Poetry and Reality" would move to adjust this final portrait. "Aims at Happiness" begins with yet another self-absorbed youth, one Felix who has "projected many a fair essay, / To make life fritter pleasantly away" (p. 94). Jane Taylor details his various frivolous dissipations, tracing him at last to a sea-coast holiday and a catalog of types to be found in that milieu. Among them is the obverse of the lyricist of the preceding poem: "He, nature's genuine lover, casts his eye, / Lit up with intellect, on sea and sky" (p. 99). As Taylor elucidates this man's character, her readers may feel that, one hundred pages into a volume deliberately characterized by negative examples, they have at last encountered the perspective she would valorize.

> He goes unnotic'd by the motley race;
> But not so they—he has an eye to trace
> The lines of character in every face.
> His, not the broad, unmeaning, vacant stare;
> He does but turn to study nature there:—
> The eye of suffering ventures not to meet,
> The even arch with hopeless dulness fraught,
> The wandering eye, bespeaking distant thought,
> The languid smile, that strives to smooth in vain
> Features contracted by incessant pain;
> —Nor his, the cold, severe, sarcastic quest,
> A pure philanthropy has warm'd his breast;
> And many a generous sigh from thence will steal,
> For woes and vices that he cannot heal.
>
> (pp. 99–100)

The slow adjustment of perspective seems at this point complete: the portrait is clearly intended as a mirror of the author, representing a vantage at once unblinking and compassionate.

Yet, at the same time, a later reader might well wonder if such a portrait is not a little self-serving, placed at this juncture in the volume to absolve Jane Taylor from the charge that she herself, with her skill at penetrating deception, might be the first to level, which is that, when all is said and done, she relishes the savagery to which satire is prone and wields its scalpel with a surgeon's deft facility and a self-evident pride in her accomplishment. Certainly, she leaves her bored Felix no closer to satisfaction in his aims at happiness than before, and, as with the grocer's wife of "Prejudice" and the backbiting gossips of "Recreation," he is seemingly incapable of reform.

> The lessons taught at Disappointment's knee,
> Some dunces cannot learn, no more could he.
>
> (p. 102)

From this viewpoint Taylor would not be the first satirist to wish to have her cake and eat it too, by claiming a socially positive effect to issue from caustically detached negativity.

That she must have been conscious of this possible reaction is suggested by the fact that, except for the representation of the grocer's wife (and there, as we have seen, she deliberately adjusts the lens through which we focus the picture), Jane Taylor buries her caustic portraits in the center of her volume, using them as illustrations of the endemic social ills her poems, in their gradual accumulation, seek to identify and represent within a totalized perspective. Hers is an exceedingly delicate balancing act, allowing her at once to taxonomize these ills through traditional satiric means while denying that she is adopting the posture or even the attitude of the traditional satirist.

Her last two poems, virtually devoid of her brilliant wit, seem intended to bring her perspective into sharply delineated focus, starting with their titles: "The World in the House," "The World in the Heart." The first of these poems ends by once again reverting to its author's double stance:

> Oh, for a soul magnanimous, to know
> Poor world, thy littleness, and let thee go!
> Not with a gloomy, proud, ascetic mind,
> That loves thee still, and only hates mankind;
> Reverse the line, and that my temper be,
> —To love mankind, and pour contempt on thee!
>
> (p. 154)

A satire that embodies misanthropy (or, as in the case of Mathias, a generalized misogyny) is incompatible with the mission of an evangelical Christian, in Taylor's view. In its self-righteous pride, traditional satire actually practices what it inveighs against. Its strictures are punitive rather than reformative, leading to scapegoating rather than social inclusion, and are predicated on damnation rather than redemption as their end. Literary satire is no different from one broadly directed against social problems in this regard: they both assume the premise of a worldly measurement of good and ill and by their assumption of a standard of social hegemony take original sin as their starting point. Against that essential depravity satire raises the Law.

In the last poem, "The World in the Heart," Jane Taylor directly interrogates what she sees as the dead-end that will result from such a stance, in a lengthy citation of the mental barriers that stand in the way of a true redemption, each introduced as a "what if" clause conducting us further into the cul-de-sac. One of these seems to touch the essence of her rejection of the inherent ethos of satire.

> What, if in strange defiance of that rule,
> Made not in Moses', but the Gospel school,
> Shining as clearly as the light of Heaven,
> 'They who forgive not, shall not be forgiven,'
> We live in anger, hatred, envy, strife,
> Still firmly hoping for eternal life. . . .
>
> (pp. 167–68)

True reform cannot be brought about through the means of an attitude that cannot issue in reform.

Yet, if that is the case, why write this volume of poems? Why, in turn, should a public take so seriously this moralist, who has up to now been known largely for agreeably educating children, as to sell out three editions in two years? The actual character of the *Essays in Rhyme,* if we revert to it, can answer these questions. In some sense, Jane Taylor in these poems is not really interested in reforming specific departures from an acceptable standard of behavior. That she can have no effect on the grocer's wife or Felix or Miss B. and Mrs. G. she takes for granted—none of them seems capable of reading a book, anyway—which is why in these cases she so reminds one of Jane Austen, who would have no art if the world were devoid of the likes of Lady Catherine de Burgh and Mr. and Mrs. Elton. What animates the *Essays in Rhyme* is not prescription or proscription but rather its revelation of the conditions forging the modern world. The grocer and his wife, through their long tutelage at the counter, have become like the things they sold; Felix accumulates things and places that are centers for thing-ness in a futile attempt to satisfy a desire that has higher, if misunderstood, ends; the gossips' analytical prowess only needs to be turned inside-out to become like the author's; the rude mechanic of "A Pair" resists the crushing weight of necessity that would reduce him to the condition of a mere "hand" at his bench by poring over and over again the algebra text that opens a perspective out of not just his close confinement but the world as material construction. Wherever the reader sets gaze in this volume are threads to the larger patterns of a world of mere commodities first delineated by Pope in *The Dunciad.* But the difference is salient. Pope's desire is to reform that world. Jane Taylor's concern is with restoring an interior spirituality that will deny the world its power over the human condition. That she does this through the paradoxical means of an acute stylistic realism anticipates, like so much of her volume, a later generation in Britain, when evangelical missionaries established their centers of activity in the midst of urban slums. The way in which Taylor invokes realism to give authority to the spiritual is symmetrical with her uses of genre. Within the endemic secularity of the Romantic period, Jane Taylor stands as a unique religious voice using satirical means to undo the very essence of satire.

Notes

1. "Twinkle, twinkle, little star," in all its verses, can be found in *British Literature: 1780–1830,* ed. Anne Mellor and Richard Matlack (Fort Worth: Harcourt Brace, 1996), 839.

2. Throughout my treatment of this volume, since it has not been reprinted in any modern form, I am quoting and cite parenthetically from the second edition slightly revised by the author and published by Taylor and Hessey in 1816 (the year before they published John Keats's first volume of verse). For those with subscriber access to the Brown University Women Writers Project, the same edition is available electronically at *<http://www.wwp. brown.edu/wwphome.html>.* The fourth edition of 1840 reproduces in a newly set version this same pagination: it can be found online from the website of "British Women Romantic Poets, 1789–1832: An Electronic Collection of Texts from the Shields Library, U. California, Davis," available without charge to the user at http://www.lib.ucdavis.edu/English/BWRP/Works/#T.

3. Gary Dyer, *British Satire and the Politics of Style, 1789–1832* (Cambridge: Cambridge University Press, 1997), 154–55.

4. An excellent account of the members and activities of this remarkably industrious family can be found in Lenore Davidoff and Catherine Hall, *Family Fortunes: Men and Women of the English Middle-Class, 1780–1850* (Chicago: University of Chicago Press, 1991), 59–69, *et passim.*

Chapter 8 ~

Intercepted Letters, Men of Information: Moore's *Twopenny Post-Bag* and *Fudge Family in Paris*

Gary Dyer

In March 1813, Thomas Moore's satirical *Intercepted Letters: or, the Twopenny Post-Bag* was published. Moore's name appeared nowhere in the book, which according to the title page was the work of "Thomas Brown the Younger." "Brown"'s preface spelled out the book's premise:

> The Bag, from which the following Letters are selected, was dropped by a Twopenny Postman about two months since, and picked up by an emissary of the Society for the S—pp—ss—n of V—e, who, supposing it might materially assist the private researches of that Institution, immediately took it to his employers and was rewarded handsomely for his trouble. Such a treasury of secrets was worth a whole host of informers; and, accordingly, like the Cupids of the poet (if I may use so profane a simile) who "fell at odds about the sweet-bag of a bee," those venerable Suppressors almost fought with each other for the honour and delight of first ransacking the Post-Bag. Unluckily, however, it turned out upon examination, that the discoveries of profligacy which it enabled them to make, lay chiefly in those upper regions of society, which their well-bred regulations forbid them to molest or meddle with.—In consequence, they gained but very few victims by their prize, and, after lying for a week or two under Mr. H—TCH—D's counter, the Bag, with its violated contents, was sold for a trifle to a friend of mine. (pp. xi-x)

The Society for the Suppression of Vice had taken upon themselves the task of improving the morality and deportment of the lower classes, with the help of supporters like publisher John Hatchard ("Mr. H—TCH—D"). The eight letters contained in *The Twopenny Post-Bag* supposedly were composed by the Prince Regent, his daughter Princess Charlotte, his private secretary Colonel John McMahon, the Countess Dowager of Cork, the anti-Catholic M. P. Patrick Duigenan, the publishing house Lackington, one Colonel Thomas, and a fictitious Persian visitor to London named Abdallah. (Part of the joke is that the Regent or Princess Charlotte would use a courier, not the London twopenny post.) The Society's spying is really voyeurism, as they eagerly anticipate more secrets than their network of informers could ever gather. The bag was intercepted inadvertently ("dropped"), not by design, but the Society does pay its alert "emissary" for his work. Although there is plentiful evidence of profligate behavior in the bag, the Society aims only at the misbehavior of the lower orders, not the misbehavior found at the Prince's parties at Carlton House. "Brown"'s acquisition of these letters composed by illustrious people is a parody of the Society's surveillance. More important, it is a parody of government surveillance. Brown/Moore's sarcasm is heavy when he calls the Society's investigations "private researches"; though it was a private body, its prosecutions of blasphemy, obscenity, and other offenses supplemented the efforts of the government. Indeed, their snooping is a handy way of alluding to the government's snooping.

Moore's book has usually been referred to, in his day and ours, as *The Twopenny Post-Bag*, but my aim is to show how its primary title is significant: these letters have been *intercepted*, and their interception points to the critique of government information-gathering central to both this book and Moore's next book-length exercise in what he termed the "lighter" style of satire, *The Fudge Family in Paris* (1818).[1] These books are topical satires, confronting immediate political issues, and the world had changed between 1813 and 1818: Napoleon was defeated, various European kings were restored, and the continental Holy Alliance was established; the British economy declined, and discontent led to popular movements in favor of parliamentary reform. Yet the books have more in common than their "lighter" style: the "intercepted letter" device they share reflects their concern with issues of government surveillance. The government routinely intercepted both domestic and foreign mail to ferret out sedition and treason, to obtain secrets that were "worth a whole host of informers"; *The Twopenny Post-Bag* reverses things, envisioning what would happen if the Prince Regent's letters were seized and handed over to a Whig poet.[2] In *The Fudge Family in Paris*, "Thomas Brown the Younger" makes public the confidential letters written by four fictitious Irish visitors to post-Napoleonic France. Brown's strategy is to publish certain communications among royalty, the ministry, and their hirelings, so that his readers can spy on those who normally do the spying. This is not as unthinkable as it may appear: as David Worrall has pointed out, "Britain 1790–1820 was a spy culture. Even the surveillers were surveilled."[3]

The fictional interceptions are one of the ways *The Twopenny Post-Bag* and *The Fudge Family in Paris* allude to surveillance and encryption. The government's mail-readers can represent its methods of scrutiny (spies, informers), including those trained on verse satires in newspapers or books. Moore thereby evokes the challenges he and others faced writing satire in an era of government persecution. As we will see, the 1817 circular letter by Lord Sidmouth, which contained instructions for the nation's magistrates, specifically mentioned using informers to identify seditious writings.[4] Moreover, legally the prosecution of sedition or blasphemy involved a kind of informer, insofar as the most common kind of prosecution was termed "an *ex officio* information."

The Fudge Family in Paris spies on the spies even more directly than *The Twopenny Post-Bag*. Unlike Moore's earlier book, *The Fudge Family in Paris* tells a story, and the story concerns not real illustrious personages but fictitious ones. Whereas the eight "intercepted letters" in *The Twopenny Post-Bag* involve eight different writers and eight different recipients, the twelve letters in *The Fudge Family* are the work of four fictitious visitors to France: Philip Fudge, his son Bob, his daughter Biddy, and their third cousin, Phelim Connor, an Irish Catholic patriot who serves as Bob's tutor. The thematic unity of this book is more subtle than that of *The Twopenny Post-Bag*, most of which deals directly with the Prince's political desertion of the Whigs in 1812 and the related issue of Catholic claims. Biddy's and Bob's letters are dedicated to describing

> . . . the endless delights
> Of this Eden of milliners, monkeys, and sights—
> This dear busy place, where there's nothing transacting
> But dressing and dinnering, dancing and acting [. . .] (p. 39)

Yet even their letters illuminate the larger political issues on which Phelim Connor and their father Phil focus. In the 1790s Phillip Fudge was a radical who informed on his allies; now he helps supervise the network of informants sponsored by the home secretary, Lord Sidmouth. Brown, however, happily turns the tables on this turncoat by publishing his letters.

Intercepted correspondence is in general a handy device for a satirist, but in 1813 or 1818 the opening of mail was no benign topic but rather a common practice that had to worry people critical of the government—including Moore. This device had special resonance when there was so much government surveillance, domestic as well as foreign, and when that surveillance often involved intercepting mail. Several "intercepted letter" satires appeared in Britain between 1807 and 1821, perhaps more than at any time since the seventeenth century, and most allude to the government's spying on their political opponents. (Several of these works were inspired directly by *Twopenny Post-Bag* or *The Fudge Family in Paris.*) The home secretary and the foreign secretary had the legal right to order mail secretly intercepted;[5] this privilege was sometimes exercised by other members of the cabinet. In the later eighteenth century, interceptions within Britain helped the government deal with such troublesome men as Lord George Gordon, Thomas Paine, John Horne Tooke, John Wilkes, and the Prince's friend Charles James Fox (Ellis, pp. 71–72). The interception of letters written in cipher to Lord Edward Fitzgerald played a role in the case against three United Irishmen,[6] and the correspondence of Moore's friend Robert Emmet was ordered intercepted in 1803.[7] Although Moore in 1813 could not know the precise extent of British government interception of domestic and overseas mail—not even parliament knew that—his connections among the elite certainly were such that he would know interception was common.[8] He was aware that in general the post was not a secure medium of communication. From 1806 to 1811 Moore sent letters by way of his friend Edward Connor in the War Office of Dublin Castle in order to avoid postage charges (see *Letters* I, 109, 114, 131, 132, 144, 171, 193), but sometimes a British government office was too risky. His August 17, 1811, letter to Lady Donegal contained a joke concerning the king's madness, and in concluding Moore observed, "I would enclose this through the War Office, but the paper is too *thin* for stranger eyes" (I, 156).

In *The Twopenny Post-Bag,* the Countess Dowager of Cork's letter to a friend describes the difficulties of having the Prince Regent and his mistress, Lady Hertford ("the Marchesa"), at the same gathering:

> But, my dear Lady————! can't you hit on some notion,
> At least for one night to set London in motion?—
> As to having the R—G—T—*that* show is gone by—
> Besides, I've remark'd that (between you and I)
> The MARCHESA and he, inconvenient in more ways,
> Have taken much lately to whispering in door-ways;
> Which—consid'ring, you know, dear, the *size* of the two—
> Makes a block that one's company *cannot* get through,
> And a house such as mine is, with door-ways so small,
> Has no room for such cumbersome love-work at all!—(p. 22)

The phrase "between you and I" reminds us that we are spying, thanks to this mail-bag's interception—seeing while remaining unseen ourselves. For readers who were aware that Brown was Moore, part of the pleasure was knowing that until recently he had been able to observe the Prince up close; as the protégé of the Regent's longtime advisor Lord Moira, Moore knew what went on when the Prince was among his close friends. When Moore's humor is most cutting (and most apt to provoke libel charges), he gives us the sense we know something we are not supposed to know. The Prince writes to Lord Yarmouth about the dinner the night before given by Yarmouth's father, Lord Hertford:

> Our next round of toasts was a fancy quite new,
> For we drank—and you'll own 'twas benevolent too—
> To those well-meaning husbands, cits, parsons, or peers,
> Whom we've, any time, honour'd by kissing their dears:
> This museum of wittols was comical rather;
> Old H——T gave M——Y, and *I* gave ————. (pp. 14–15)

In all of Moore's writings, there is no instance when a long dash better serves the satirist's attack.

Most of the correspondence seized by authorities was copied and sent on its way, so the recipient never knew his or her mail had been violated. Yet intercepted mail sometimes became public if it formed the basis for criminal prosecution or if something was to be gained by revealing it. The genuine intercepted letters published in Britain in this period were mostly international correspondence seized because of the war with France, such as *Copies of Original Letters from the Army of General Bonaparte in Egypt, Intercepted by the Fleet under the Command of Admiral Lord Nelson* (1798).[9] *Copies of Original Letters Recently Written by Persons in Paris to Dr. Priestley in America, Taken on Board of a Neutral Vessel* (1798) made public letters by Helen Maria Williams and John Hurford Stone, whose reputations were thereby damaged. Obviously, published documents did not become private again. The editor of *Intercepted Correspondence from India, Containing the Marquis of Wellesley's Dispatches &c. in November 1803 and from then to October 1804* (London: 1805) condemns the practice of publishing intercepted letters, but then claims that since the French have already published these, he may as well bring them to the attention of British readers (pp. iii–iv).

Before *The Twopenny Post-Bag* it was not conventional in fictitious satirical collections of epistles to explain how the letters were gathered. For example, in the most famous such work prior to Moore, Christopher Anstey's *The New Bath Guide: or, Memoirs of the B——r——d Family* (London: 1766), the "editor" never mentions how he got hold of these letters.[10] Real-life interceptions did inspire fictional ones, however. In Maria Edgeworth's novel *Leonora* (1805), the ship carrying Olivia's letters addressed to her French confidant is taken by the British, and an official in the Foreign Office forwards them, with a slanted summary, to Mr. L——, the married man with whom she has had an affair. The official explains that "as *intercepted correspondence* is the order of the day, these, with all the despatches on board, were transmitted to our office to be examined, in hopes of making reprisals of state secrets"; however, "these papers contain only family secrets" (p. 421).[11] John Wilson Croker's anonymous prose satire *An Intercepted Letter from J----T----, Esq. Written at Canton, to His Friend in Dublin, Ireland* (1804) situates itself among wartime seizures of mail when the editor reminds the reader of the recent "capture of the Admiral Aplin, and of the publication of the letters found on board her," and then claims that J----T----'s letter has similar origins: "it is not so generally known, that the Althea, homeward-bound East Indiaman, has been also taken, and carried into the Mauritius, and that the French have translated and published the following correspondence, which she was conveying to these countries" (pp. iii/iv).[12]

Writing and publishing satire, particularly satire dealing with royalty or the government, meant fending off the threat of prosecution for seditious libel, and Moore's satires continually remind the reader of the chances they take. It is hard to say how close Moore or his publishers came to being prosecuted (the latter took a much greater risk, since the newspapers or books bore their names). On April 3, 1812, Moore wrote to his mother that "I shall take care and not write anything in the papers. Poor Hunt is *up* for his last article but one against the Prince" (*Letters* I, 186).[13] He quickly broke a promise he made only to reassure his mother, but she would be right to feel concern: Leigh Hunt had insulted the Regent in *The Examiner* of March 22, 1812, and eventually he and his brother John were convicted, imprisoned for two years, and fined five hundred pounds each. In *The Twopenny Post-Bag* Moore reminds his readers not only of the Hunts' fate but also of the Prince's role in prosecuting them: the Regent's letter to Yarmouth describes a dinner "in gay celebration / Of *my* brilliant triumph and H—nt's condemnation" (p. 13). One of his ministers, Lord Ellenborough, presided over the trial, and so the dinner also honors "his Lordship the J——e / For his Speech to the J—y" (p. 13). In May 1813, when Moore was about to visit Hunt in prison, their friend and political ally Lord Byron penned a verse epistle to Moore in which he prayed that "our political malice / May not get us lodgings within the same palace"; one example Byron cites of this political malice is the recently published *Twopenny Post-Bag*.[14]

Fear that his satires might be prosecuted was not Moore's only motive for the reticence they repeatedly display. In fact, the reticence becomes a theme of the work, a way of alluding to the pressures faced by authors of antigovernment satire. Even if Moore was fairly secure, others were not, and he assumes the defensive posture necessitated by the uncertainties of the situation. In this respect he is typical of his age. Satires in the Romantic period, much like satires in other periods, often dramatize their own need to fend off prosecution. For example, they not only use dashes within or in place of proper names but also point out this very strategy, turning it to their own satirical advantage.[15] The name "C———h" says less than "Castlereagh," yet says more. Consider how satirist N. T. H. Bayly describes reformist political rhetoric in his *Parliamentary Letters* (1818):

> Talk loud and long, and only just withdraw
> In time to shun the vigilance of law;
> And in each prudent pause it will appear
> That more is understood than meets the ear:
> Spare none in place,—or, if one man is spared,
> Show you would talk high treason,—*if you dared.* (p. 24)[16]

Moore specializes in the kind of indirection at which Bayly sneers. He wants to draw the reader's attention to the need for such prudent pauses and strategic dashes—he stresses *why* more must be understood than meets the ear.

Prudence is a key principle in Moore: Brown records in his preface to *The Twopenny Post-Bag* that he "did not think it prudent . . . to give too many Letters at first." In *The Fudge Family in Paris,* Brown has "thought it prudent to omit some parts of Mr. Phelim Connor's letter," as he tells us in a footnote. "He is evidently an intemperate young man, and has associated with his cousins, the Fudges, to very little purpose" (*Fudge Family,* p. 30n). As Biddy puts the matter, Connor "talks much of Athens, Rome, virtue, and stuff" (p. 9), and as a result of Brown's editing, Connor's jeremiad against the Continental monarchs and the British foreign minister looks like this:

> Instead of themes that touch the lyre with light,
> Instead of Greece, and her immortal fight
> For Liberty, which once awak'd my strings,
> Welcome the Grand Conspiracy of Kings,
> The High Legitimates, the Holy Band,
> Who, bolder ev'n than He of Sparta's land,
> Against whole millions, panting to be free,
> Would guard the pass of right-line tyranny!
> Instead of him, th' Athenian bard, whose blade
> Had stood the onset which his pen pourtray'd,
>   Welcome * * * * *
>   * * * * * *

And, 'stead of ARISTIDES—woe the day
Such names should mingle!—welcome C———GH!

Here break we off, at this unhallow'd name,
Like priests of old, when words ill-omen'd came.
My next shall tell thee, bitterly shall tell,
                              Thoughts that * * * *
                                 * * * * * *

Thoughts that—could patience hold—'twere wiser far
To leave still hid and burning where they are! (pp. 35–36)

Brown's lines of asterisks are not the only expurgation visible in this passage: here and throughout the book the conventional dashes have been inserted in names like that of Lord Castlereagh, the foreign secretary. Brown's censorship of Phelim's letter resembles the self-censorship traditionally exercised by satirists and printers. The reason Brown gives for trimming Connor's letters is not that what the tutor says is wrong, but merely that expurgation is "prudent" (30n); each of his epistles is "so full of unsafe matter-of-fact" that Brown is reminded of Fontenelle's maxim that "if he had his hand full of truths, he would open but one finger at a time" (p. 127n). Brown's editing protects Connor in other ways, too: whereas he gives the reader at least part of each name among the Fudges' correspondents, and one of Phil's letters even goes to an identifiable real person ("C———h"), Phelim Connor's recipient or recipients are named only as "———." Brown does not risk exposing Connor's friends in England or Ireland. This prudence only makes the satirist's target look worse, as though both Castlereagh's offenses and Moore's disgust transcend representation. Moore complained in his 1800 translation of Anacreon that the "substitution of asterisks [that] has been so much adopted in the popular interpretations of the Classics [. . .] serves but to bring whatever is exceptionable into notice";[17] the asterisks in Connor's letters bring into notice objectionable men.

The Fudge Family in Paris focuses on the government's use of spies and informers during the Regency. The British justice system in general depended on them, and had done so for a long time, since without an adequate police force, magistrates needed people to come forward to testify to crimes, and the law therefore authorized substantial rewards for those who turned king's evidence. As Iain McCalman points out, early-nineteenth-century English spies and informers "include casual observers of all classes, nosey clergymen, anonymous informers, professional shorthand writers, stolid police undercover men, self-appointed sensation seekers, needy, greedy or fearful radicals and their disgruntled relatives, and a few schizoid individuals with loyalties to both government employers and radical colleagues."[18] By

1818 the role of informers in prosecuting radical organizers for treason had become controversial, largely because of the abuses committed by the notorious John Castle (often called "Castles") and William Oliver.[19] Furthermore, the government that employed these men also searched for "information" on seditious satirical writings. Although Castlereagh's name appears in *The Fudge Family in Paris* more than any other actual person's, Moore indicated that the book's primary target was the other secretary of state, Sidmouth, who had earned this honor as "the author of the Circular, the patron of spies and informers, the father of the Green Bag" (letter to Lady Donegal, January 9, 1818, *Letters* I, 437). Moore seems to equate Sidmouth's sponsorship of Castle and Oliver with his 1817 circular letter authorizing magistrates to detain without trial publishers responsible for "sedition." Lord Grey argued in parliament that one effect of Sidmouth's circular would be to encourage "that most pestilent curse by which society can be afflicted, the whole tribe of common informers"; now "any thing they may choose to call a libel may henceforth be made the subject of a prosecution, and thus become, in the hands of the worst men, acting from the worst motives, an instrument of pecuniary extortion, or any other base purpose, they may have to serve."[20]

Phil Fudge is in part a caricature of Thomas Reynolds, the member of the United Irishmen who in 1798 supplied the government with details about the organization's plans, and went on to testify in the ensuing treason trials. Fudge's letters, Brown observes in his preface, reveal that he is

> . . . one of those gentlemen whose *Secret Services* in Ireland, under the mild ministry of my Lord C———GH, have been so amply and gratefully remunerated. Like his friend and associate, THOMAS REYNOLDS, Esq. he had retired upon the reward of his honest industry; but has lately been induced to appear again in active life, and superintend the training of that *Delatorian Cohort,* which Lord S—DM—TH, in his wisdom and benevolence, has organized. (pp. v-vi)

For his cooperation in 1798, Reynolds received £5,000 and a pension of £1,000 annually as "the reward of his honest industry" (Fitzpatrick, 302). He also lobbied for and received a number of government appointments: in 1810 he became packet master at Lisbon; in January 1817 he was offered the position of British consul in Iceland, for which he could live in Copenhagen. In April 1817 Reynolds abruptly came back to the public's attention when he resurfaced as a member of the grand jury that indicted Dr. James Watson, Arthur Thistlewood, John Hooper, and Thomas Preston on charges stemming from the Spa Fields uprising on December 2, 1816. In June 1817 Watson was tried and acquitted, leading the government to drop the charges against the others, and the reason for the acquittal was that the prosecution's most pertinent evidence came from the disreputable John Castle, who clearly had tried hard to encourage the treason to which he testified. Reynolds' role in the indictment of Watson and the others looked bad, even if it really was little more than coincidence: here was the most notorious government informer in living memory, a man doubly hateful in the eyes of an Irish republican like Moore, evaluating a case that depended on a government informer.[21] Castlereagh had to defend Reynolds in the House of Commons (the home secretary, Sidmouth, sat in the House of Lords), and Moore observes in a note that "Lord C.'s tribute to the character of his friend, Mr. Reynolds, will long be remembered with equal credit to both" (*Fudge Family,* p. 53n).[22] Reynolds took off for Copenhagen later in 1817, and the ministers were glad to be rid of him.[23] It is a sign of the infamy attached to Reynolds, Castle, and Oliver that Moore spells out their names, whereas his enemy Castlereagh is "C—stl-r-gh," "C—st——h," "C———gh," or "C———h."

Twenty years previous, Phil Fudge worked for Castlereagh when Castlereagh was chief secretary for Ireland; now he serves the government of which Castlereagh is de facto leader. Much as Reynolds seemed to reappear at Watson's trial in order to support the Home Office's domestic espionage, Fudge put his experience to work in schooling spies. Fudge proclaims his kinship with Reynolds in his letter to his brother, Tim Fudge:

> REYNOLDS and I—(you know TOM REYNOLDS—
>   Drinks his claret, keeps his chaise—
> Lucky the dog that first unkennels
>   Traitors and Luddites now-a-days;
> Or who can help to *bag* a few,
> When S—D——TH wants a death or two;)
> REYNOLDS and I, and some few more,
>   All men, like us, of *information,*
> Friends, whom his Lordship keeps in store,
>   As *under*-saviours of the nation—
> Have form'd a Club this season, where
> His Lordship sometimes takes the chair,
> And gives us many a bright oration
> In praise of our sublime vocation; . . . (pp. 52–53)

Phil Fudge wonders to himself if Sidmouth has "any decent kind of Plot" in the works:

>   . . . if not,
> Alas, alas, our ruin's fated;

All done up, and *spiflicated!*
Ministers and all their vassals,
Down from C—TL———GH to CASTLES,—
Unless we can kick up a riot,
Ne'er can hope for peace or quiet! (p. 107)

Fudge offers his critique of the most recent attempt to create treason that would justify repression:

What's to be done?—Spa-Fields was clever;
   But even *that* brought gibes and mockings,
Upon our heads—so, *mem.*—must never
   Keep ammunition in old stockings;
For fear some wag should in his curst head
Take it to say our force was *worsted.*
Mem. too—when SID. an army raises,
It must not be "incog." like *Bayes's:*
Nor must the General be a hobbling
Professor of the art of Cobbling;
Lest men, who perpetrate such puns,
   Should say, with Jacobinic grin,
He felt, from *soleing Wellingtons,*
   A *Wellington's* great *soul* within!
Nor must an old Apothecary
   Go take the Tower, for lack of pence,
With (what these wags would call, so merry)
   Physical force and *phial*-ence! (pp. 108–109)

Moore stresses how unthreatening the conspirators' actions really were—a cobbler like Preston, used to handling boots ("wellingtons"), imagines himself the general of a revolutionary army; an "old apothecary"—Watson—aims to seize the Tower of London. (Note that Phil's first rule of stage-managing rebellion is to be careful not to render yourself vulnerable to puns.) Moore here reiterates the defense made by Watson's attorneys, who argued that the revolutionaries' strategy described by the informer Castles was so silly that Castles must have invented it. Moore's view of Spa Fields is a Whig view: if there were a threat of revolution, the government would nonetheless be the preeminent threat to liberty, yet in fact the only fomenters of revolution are the ministry's agents. Fudge tells Castlereagh that the next such plot must be handled better:

John Bull, I grieve to say, is growing
So troublesomely sharp and knowing,

So wise—in short, so Jacobin—
'Tis monstrous hard to *take him in.* (p. 109)

The more "knowing" the British people, the harder to use knowledge/"information" to deceive them.

At the moment Phil's assignment is not to spy or to train spies, but to compose conservative propaganda: he is in Paris to write a travel book at the request of Lord Castlereagh, a book that

Will prove that all the world, at present,
Is in a state extremely pleasant:
That Europe—thanks to royal swords
   And bay'nets, and the Duke commanding—
Enjoys a peace which, like the Lord's,
   Passeth all human understanding [. . .]

                                (p. 14; see also p. 6)

Phil moves easily between secret activities, like radical organizing or supervising espionage, and public activities, like writing travel books meant to counteract Whiggish accounts like Lady Morgan's *France.* (In *The Twopenny Post-Bag* Colonel McMahon's letter to writer Francis Gould Leckie gave us a glimpse of the genesis of conservative propaganda [*Twopenny,* pp. 6–11].) The name "Fudge" (presumably the family's adopted "Protestant" name) suggests that Phil's job as either propagandist or informer is to manufacture facts in service of the government. The Fudges enjoy or aspire to lucrative careers as "men of information": Tim Fudge, a barrister who prosecutes sedition (64–65), merely works in a different branch of this system than his brother does.

Many writers of letters had to veil their meanings (seditious or otherwise), but because Phil is a supporter of the ministry he has less to worry about. He usually writes as though he cannot imagine that *his* letters might be intercepted, although sometimes he becomes circumspect. After describing Castlereagh's club of informers, Phil assures his brother that "we get on gaily," adding parenthetically, "I'll thank you not to mention / These things again" (p. 55). Of Castlereagh, he writes, "I know my chap, / And he knows *me* too— *verbum sap*" (p. 51). The Latin saying is "Verbum sapientibus sat est," "A word to the wise is sufficient."[24] Telling his brother Tim *you know what I mean,* Phil mimics the hinting to which he seldom resorts now that he has joined the winning team. In fact, the Fudges' letters are full of allusions to the secrecy they seemingly can afford to eschew: when Biddy Fudge divulges to her friend Dorothy that her father is in France to write propaganda, she comments, "mind, it's all *entre nous,* / But you know, love, I never keep secrets from you" (p. 6); Phelim Connor's being a "Papist" is also "entre nous" (p. 9)—like the

Countess of Cork's observation that what she tells her correspondent must stay "between you and I." Dorothy, in other words, is worthy of the Fudges' secrets, but she must not pass them on to someone else. The Fudges do not anticipate that their letters will be read by outsiders, and their feelings of security allow them to joke that they are curtailing what they wish to say.

Yet Moore suggests that an informer's life is never entirely secure. Phil's letter to Tim begins with him telling his brother:

> Yours of the 12th receiv'd just now—
> > Thanks for the hint, my trusty brother!
> 'Tis truly pleasing to see how
> > We, FUDGES, stand by one another.
> But never fear—I know my chap,
> And he knows *me* too—*verbum sap.* (p. 51)

His "chap," Lord Castlereagh, and he are in fact "kindred spirits" (p. 51). Tim's "hint" to Phil was apparently a warning that he should not trust Castlereagh, who will remember, for example, Phil's Jacobin writings of twenty-six years earlier. But Phil has no reason for concern:

> As to my Book in 91,
> > Call'd "Down with Kings, or Who'd have thought it?"
> Bless you, the Book's long dead and gone,—
> > Not ev'n th' Attorney-General bought it.
> And, though some few seditious tricks
> I play'd in 95 and 6,
> As you remind me in your letter,
> His Lordship likes me all the better;—
> We, proselytes, that come with news full,
> Are, as he says, so vastly useful! (p. 52)

Phil commends Tim on "the art / With which you play'd the patriot's part, / Till something good and snug should offer" (p. 63). Yet Tim still has not learned how "information" works: Phil's *Down with Kings, or Who'd Have Thought It?* would help him with the ministers, not hurt him. In writing to his brother, Phil goes into detail

> > Because I saw your nerves were shaken
> With anxious fears lest I should fail
> > In this new, *loyal,* course I've taken. (p. 61)

Moore may be indicating that Phil is overconfident. Tim Fudge perhaps warned his brother that Castlereagh and Sidmouth sent him to Paris because they want him out of the public eye. Moore may have known that Castlereagh and company in fact were embarrassed by Reynolds' presence on the Watson grand jury, and that they would love to get this perennial place-seeker out of their hair. This letter addressed to Tim apparently reveals what Phil writes when Castlereagh won't be reading. But, of course, Castlereagh as foreign secretary would have the power to intercept correspondence from abroad, and he can easily read Phil's letters to Tim. The possibility remains, of course, that Tim is bearing this possibility in mind, and his expressions of confidence in the foreign secretary are meant for the Foreign Office.

But Phil's vulnerability to surveillance is the *foundation* of *The Fudge Family in Paris*. In the preface, editor Brown writes that "In what manner the following Epistles came into my hands, it is not necessary for the public to know," so we never learn how he spies on the master spy. Perhaps this is not an accident like the seizure of the twopenny post-bag. Brown presumably does not want to identify his source, who then would become useless, whereas now this source can pass on more letters. In an era when the government, and particularly the Regent's household, were troubled with leaks to the more scurrilous press, a menace like Brown's would be intimidating. Because the twelve letters in *The Fudge Family in Paris* span a period of months, they obviously cannot come from one mail bag, and so their presence in the book must be the result of regular interception of correspondence. These letters come from overseas, unlike those in *Twopenny*, and they therefore would be easier for the government to intercept, and they would be more likely to be on the Foreign Office's lookout list. The reader can speculate: has the government made copies of these letters? Has an underling given them to Brown after some pecuniary persuasion?

If your letters are intercepted, people will distort them to their own ends. Brown's editing is not neutral, but involves translation. In the preface to *The Twopenny Post-Bag*, he explains how after his friend bought the "violated" sack of mail he transformed it into a collection of poems:

> It happened that I had been just then seized with an ambition [. . .] to publish something or other in the shape of a Book; and it occurred to me that, the present being such a letter-writing era, a few of these Twopenny Post Epistles, turned into easy verse, would be as light and popular a task as I could possibly select for such a commencement. (pp. x-xi)

Brown identifies himself as the one who translated the prose letters into easy verse, and this translation is no passive reproduction: the anapestic meter and absurd rhymes that are Brown's doing undercut the correspondents' intended meanings. The poetry in *The Twopenny Post-Bag* and *The Fudge Family in Paris* is "double-voiced," composed of an original, earnest text, and a second text that appropriates and comments on it. The two voices belong to two distinct speakers, the character who writes the epistle, and editor Brown. This is the case whether the letter-writer is real, like Lord Castlereagh, or fictitious, like Phil Fudge. Readers in 1813 would remember how a year earlier Moore parodied in similar fashion an actual letter, the letter to the Duke of York in which the Prince Regent announced he was retaining his father's Tory ministers rather than replacing them with the Whigs who had been his allies for thirty years. The Prince's letter was made public on February 20, 1812, and Moore's poetic version was circulated in privately printed copies in early March, before being printed by *The Examiner*.[25] Following closely the structure of the original epistle, Moore versified it in such as way as to underscore the Prince's hypocrisy. The Whigs could not join in a coalition with the current ministry without violating their commitments to such principles as Catholic Emancipation, yet, toward the end of his letter, the Regent suggested that he would invite some Whigs to join the ministry:

> [. . .] I cannot conclude without expressing the gratification I should feel, if some of those persons with whom the early habits of my public life were formed, would strengthen my hands, and constitute a part of my Government. With such support, and aided by a vigorous and united Administration, formed on the most liberal basis, I shall look with additional confidence to a prosperous issue of the most arduous contest in which Great Britain was ever engaged.[26]

Here is Moore's parody, from the version of the poem that appeared in *The Examiner* on March 8, 1812:

> 'Twould please me if those, whom I've humbugged so long
> With the notion (good men!) that I knew right from wrong,
> Would a few of them join me—mind, only a few—
> To let *too* much light on me never would do;
> But even Grey's brightness shan't make me afraid,
> While I've C—md—n and Eld—n to fly to for shade;
> Nor will Holland's clear intellect do us much harm,
> While there's W—stm—rel—nd near him to weaken the charm.
> As for Moira's high spirit, if aught can subdue it,
> Sure joining with H—rtf—d and Y—rm—th will do it!
> Between R—d—r and Wh—rt—n let Sheridan sit,
> And the fogs will soon quench even Sheridan's wit;
> And against all the pure public feeling that glows
> Ev'n in Whitbread himself, we've a host in G—rge R—se![27]

The Prince wrote: "I think it hardly necessary to call your recollection to the recent circumstances under which I assumed the Authority delegated to me by Parliament. At a moment of unexampled difficulty and danger, I was called upon to make a selection of persons to whom I should entrust the functions of the Executive Government" (p. 113). Moore's method is to reveal the capriciousness behind the Regent's formality, and one of the techniques that allows him to do this is the anapestic tetrameter couplets—not to mention bizarre metaphors like that comparing the law that limited the Prince's powers for the first year of the Regency to his father's straitjacket:

> I need not remind you how cursedly bad
> Our affairs were all looking, when Father went ***;
> A ****** ********* on him and restrictions on me,
> A more *limited* Monarchy could not well be.
> I was call'd upon then, in that moment of puzzle,
> To chuse my own Minister—just as they muzzle
> A playful young bear, and then mock his disaster,
> By bidding him chuse out his own dancing master.
>
> (Moore, "Letter," p. 158)

In *The Twopenny Post-Bag* Brown does not provide the original intercepted letters that he "turned into easy verse," but he presumably has transformed them much as Moore transformed the Regent's letter to his brother the Duke. Moore's success in parodying the Regent's real letter led him to invent letters to parody, and this time not formal letters that were intended to be read widely, like the Regent's, but informal, confidential letters.

In *The Twopenny Post-Bag* and *The Fudge Family in Paris* Moore demonstrates the unreliability of the interpretive techniques that might uncover sedition in actual private, "intercepted" correspondence. If these techniques are unreliable, it is even harder to argue that a satirical text like Moore's can be demonstrated to be seditious. Identifying a seditious utterance, or an obscene, treasonous, or blasphemous one, is dependent on methods that are never airtight. One of the items in the intercepted post-bag is a play, titled *The Book,* which has been rejected by the publisher Lackington ("delicacy" and "fellow-feeling" lead Brown to suppress the unfortunate author's name). *The Book* is a farce in which the "P——E R—G—T" discovers on the floor at Carlton House "some scribbled fragments of paper," and he "discovers the following unconnected words '*Wife neglected*'—'the *Book*'—'*Wrong mea-sures*'—'the *Queen*'—'*Mr. Lambert*'—'the R—G—T.'" This garbled message indicates to him there is "treason in my House!" (*Twopenny,* p. 103). The phrase "the Book" commonly meant a secret compendium of documents that were the result of the 1807 "Delicate Investigation" into the behavior of the Prince's estranged ("neglected") wife, Princess Caroline. The contents would be embarrassing to the Regent, and, after he retained his father's ministers in 1812, rumors circulated that his former allies among the Whigs would publish it.[28] The Regent apparently assumes that "Lambert" is John Lambert, printer of the Whig *Morning Chronicle,* where most of Moore's short political squibs appeared.

After much hysteria and melodrama, the scraps of paper turn out to be remnants of a note from the Prince's tailor to Colonel McMahon. The tailor's message read:

> Honor'd Colonel—my WIFE, who's the QUEEN of all slatterns,
> NEGLECTED to put up THE BOOK of new Patterns.
> She sent the WRONG MEASURES too—shamefully wrong—
> They're the same us'd for poor MR. LAMBERT, when young;
> But, bless you! they wouldn't go half round the R—G—T—
> So, hope you'll excuse your's, till death, most obedient. (p. 111)

Fortunately the tailor still possesses the missing parts of the note, so it can be reconstructed and thereby prove his innocence. The Regent is on the lookout for allusions to his "neglected wife," and so he puts together the two words "wife" and "neglected" even though they appear on separate fragments.

The Book can be interpreted as illustrating both how easy it is to read a text as seditious when it isn't, and how a seditious text can be explained away as innocent when this becomes necessary. The Regent has intercepted this communication, and he faces the same impediment as any of his ministry's spies or mail-readers: the context that guides interpretation is faulty. "Lambert" turns out to be not John Lambert but Daniel Lambert (1770–1809), who weighed over 700 pounds (see Moore, *Letters* I, 169 and note), and a statement about the Regent's personal life turns out to be a statement about his waist-size. Tailors are in the business of using such information, so he can be excused for observing that the Regent's diameter is more than twice Mr. Lambert's. When we take into account Moore's satiric purpose, however, the tailor's note is not so innocuous, given how the Regent's obesity had long been used to represent his failings, personal and political. Indeed, *The Book* includes a long scene on the subject of two brothers who have been imprisoned (see *Twopenny,* pp. 107–108), and the Hunts now resided in Cold Bath Fields Prison for an article that memorably directed the reader's attention to the Prince's corpulence. It is unclear who is responsible for capitalizing the words in the tailor's note that offended the Regent, yet if the tailor did it, then the note indeed seems to hint at a coded message.

So, while the government promotes treason in order to justify repression, real offenses may only slip through their fingers. Whereas there is little or no real rebellion, there is sedition—Moore knows that what he attempts in his satires would, frankly, fit the legal definition. The ultimate view of "information" in *The Twopenny Post-Bag* and *The Fudge Family in Paris* seems to be skepticism. If you spy, you render yourself vulnerable to being spied on; indeed, even those who exploit your information will never trust you. More important, spying is crippled by uncertainties that trouble interpretation generally. By making unreliable the identification of epistolary sedition, Moore makes it harder to claim that a satire like his can be proven to be seditious.

Notes

1. [Thomas Moore] Thomas Brown the Younger, ed., *The Fudge Family in Paris* (London: Longman, Hurst, Rees, Orme, and Brown, 1818); and *Intercepted Letters; or, The Twopenny Post-Bag. To Which are Added, Trifles Reprinted*, 3d edn. (London: J. Carr, 1813); all quotations from these texts. *The Poetical Works of Thomas Moore, Collected by Himself*, 10 vols. (London: Longman, Orme, Brown, Green, and Longmans, 1841), III, vi; hereafter cited in the text. The fullest accounts of *The Twopenny Post-Bag* and *The Fudge Family in Paris* are in Gary Dyer, *British Satire and the Politics of Syle, 1789–1832* (Cambridge: Cambridge University Press, 1997), 80–84; and Jeffery W. Vail, *The Literary Relationship of Lord Byron and Thomas Moore* (Baltimore: Johns Hopkins University Press, 2000), chap. 2.
2. The concept behind *The Twopenny Post-Bag* was not Moore's invention. In November 1812, Moore wrote that "to give a bond of union" to his new book of satirical poems, he adopted "Hook's idea of the Twopenny Post-Bag, which tells in Rhyme amusingly . . ." (*The Letters of Thomas Moore*. Ed. Wilfrid S. Dowden, 2 vols. [Oxford: Clarendon Press, 1964], I, 219). Dowden's index identifies this "Hook" not as satirist Theodore Hook but as one Thomas Hook (II, 968). Moore's pseudonym pays tribute to Thomas Brown (1663–1704), one of seventeenth-century England's most prolific authors of topical verse satire (see Dyer, *British Satire*, p. 83). *The Twopenny Post-Bag* also contained nineteen "trifles reprinted," which were most of Moore's political squibs from the preceding year, and for the fourteenth edition, published in 1814, he added six more.
3. David Worrall, *Radical Culture: Discourse, Resistance, and Surveillance, 1790–1820* (Detroit: Wayne State University Press, 1992), 7.
4. William Wickwar, *The Struggle for the Freedom of the Press, 1819–1832* (London: Allen & Unwin, 1928), 39.
5. Kenneth Ellis, *The Post Office in the Eighteenth Century: A Study in Administrative History* (London: Oxford University Press, 1958), 62–63; hereafter cited in the text.
6. W. J. Fitzpatrick, *Secret Service Under Pitt* (London: Longman, 1892), 31.
7. See Roger Wells, *Insurrection: The British Experience, 1795–1803* (Gloucester: Alan Sutton, 1983), 35.
8. Moore was well placed to know how things were done in the Foreign Office: his friend Lord Strangford was a British diplomat, and in a September 1805

letter Moore wrote to Strangford, then in Lisbon, that he was "sorry to find that you are not employed in anything better than cyphers and dispatches" (*Letters of Thomas Moore,* I, 90).

9. On the genuine "intercepted letter" in the seventeenth century, see Annabel Patterson, *Censorship and Interpretation: The Conditions of Writing and Reading in Early Modern England* (Madison: University of Wisconsin Press, 1984), 216–17.

10. The Advertisement at the beginning of *The Groans of the Talents; or, Private Sentiments on Public Occurrences. In Six Epistles from Certain Ex-Ministers to Their Colleagues, Most Wonderfully Intercepted* (London: Tipper and Richards, 1807), which Jeffery Vail has rightly called the closest model for *The Twopenny Post-Bag* (Vail, p. 51), proclaims that "THE Public will easily perceive that we obtained possession of the following INTERCEPTED Epistles by no dishonorable means" ([p. iii]), but it is unclear how this is supposed to be perceived.

11. Maria Edgeworth, *Leonora* in *Tales and Novels,* 10 vols. (London: Routledge, 1893), 8: 243–423. On this scene, see Nicola J. Watson, *Revolution and the Form of the British Novel 1790–1825: Intercepted Letters, Interrupted Seductions* (Oxford: Clarendon Press, 1994), pp. 79–82.

12. "Intercepted letters" satires modeled on Moore's *Twopenny Post-Bag* and *Fudge Family* account for how their letters were collected, and, again, part of the joke is that the role of "accident" and "fortune" in this process seems far removed from what one would expect from surveillance. See "H. H." [John Agg], *The General Post Bag; or News! Foreign and Domestic To Which is Added, La Bagatelle* (London: J. Johnston, 1814), 14–15; "Peter Quince, the Younger, ed." [William Henry Halpin], *The Cheltenham Mail-Bag* (1820), iv; "Harry Nimrod," *The Fudge Family in Washington* (1820), 3; [William Russell Macdonald,] *The Dublin Mail* (1821), iii–iv; and "Leigh Cliffe" [George Jones], *The Protocol* (1820), vii–x. *The Protocol* bears the significant subtitle "Selections From the Contents of a Red Box, Found in the Neighborhood of St. James's Square."

13. For the date of this letter see Robert Brainard Pearsall, "Chronological Annotations to 250 Letters of Thomas Moore," *Papers of the Bibliographical Society of America* 63 (1969): 105–17 (107).

14. *Lord Byron: The Complete Poetical Works,* ed. Jerome J. McGann, 7 vols. (Oxford: Clarendon Press, 1980–93), III, 88, lines 9–10. Given the impediments the authorities would face demonstrating who really authored anonymous squibs, the central question is not why Moore was never prosecuted but why none of his publishers was prosecuted. John Hunt went to prison along with his co-publisher Leigh, even though it was the latter who wrote the seditious piece. A man with uncertain finances like Moore had to regret that he would never again find favor with those in power, but by the time he published *The Twopenny Post-Bag* he had waved farewell to preferment. He began writing the new poems for this book at about the time he realized that Lord Moira, newly appointed governor general of Bengal, had

no position to give him, and when Moira confirmed these suspicions, Moore asked his longtime sponsor not to "take the trouble of applying for me to the patronage of Ministers, as I would rather struggle on as I was than take anything that would have the effect of tying up my tongue under such a system as the present" (letter to Lady Donegal, December 8, 1812, *Letters* I, 235; for date, see Pearsall, 109).

15. See Dyer, *British Satire,* chap. 3.

16. Q in the Corner, [N. T. H. Bayly] *Parliamentary Letters, and Other Poems* (London: Baldwin, Cradock, and Joy, 1818).

17. Moore, *Odes of Anacreon* (London: John Stockdale, 1800), 76n.

18. Iain McCalman, *Radical Underworld: Prophets, Revolutionaries, and Pornographers in London, 1795–1840* (Cambridge: Cambridge University Press, 1988), 3.

19. On the use of spies and informers against subversion in Britain in the 1790s, see Clive Emsley, "The Home Office and Its Sources of Information and Investigation 1791–1801," *English Historical Review* 94 (1979): 532–61. On the role they played in the aftermath of the Napoleonic Wars, see E. P. Thompson, *The Making of the English Working Class* (New York: Pantheon, 1963), 484–94; and Worrall, chaps. 4 and 6. On Castle and Spa Fields, see Thompson, 632–36; McCalman, 106–12; and Worrall, 97–113. On Oliver, see J. L. Hammond and Barbara Hammond., *The Skilled Labourer: 1760–1832* (London: Longmans, Green, 1919), chap. 12; Thompson, 649–69; and Craig Calhoun, *The Question of Class Struggle: Social Foundations of Popular Radicalism during the Industrial Revolution* (Chicago: University of Chicago Press, 1982), 79–83. Thompson identifies two categories of informers against radical political organizations: "first, those who had fallen foul of authority in some way, and who purchased their immunity from prosecution (or secured their release from gaol) by taking up the trade" (Castle and Oliver fall into this class); second, "turncoats who, having been active reformers, became spies to save their own skins or for money; or, more simply, of casual mercenary volunteers attempting to sell information by the 'piece'" (Thompson, 489–90).

20. *The Speech of Earl Grey, in the House of Lords, May 12, 1817, on Lord Sidmouth's Circular* (London: Ridgways, 1817), 74–75.

21. For Moore's view of Reynolds' activities in the 1790s, see his *Life and Death of Lord Edward Fitzgerald* (1831), particularly II, 12–16, 39–47. Jeffery Vail points out that a character in Moore's *Lalla Rookh* (1817) is probably modeled on Reynolds (Vail, 127–28).

22. Moore presumably means Castlereagh's comments in the Commons on June 16, 1817 (see *The Political History of T. Reynolds, Esq. Containing An Account of His Transactions with the Rebellion in Ireland . . .* [London: Hay and Turner, 1817], 16). See also William Hazlitt's essays titled "On the Spy System," which appeared in the *Morning Chronicle* on June 30 and July 15, 1817; in *The Complete Works of William Hazlitt,* ed. P. P. Howe, 21 vols. (London: J. M. Dent and Sons, 1930–34), VII, 208–14.

23. Years later Reynolds' son noted, much as Moore would, that "The same persons who held the reins of Government in Ireland in 1798 were in 1817 in similar situations in England," but he complained that "instead of shielding my father, as they were in honour bound to do, against the shafts of his and their own slanderers, with one or two noble exceptions, they seemed glad to find that they could shake him off, or make him their political scapegoat." Thomas Reynolds [Jr.], *The Life of Thomas Reynolds, Esq. Formerly of Kildea Castle, in the County of Kildare,* 2 vols. (London: Henry Hooper, 1839), I, vi.

24. See Gary Dyer, "Thieves, Boxers, Sodomites, Poets: Being Flash to Byron's *Don Juan,*" *PMLA* 116.3 (May 2001): 562–78, on the connotations of the term "knowing" and the phrase "verbum sapientibus sat est" in this period.

25. On the composition, circulation, and publication of this poem, see Moore, *Letters* I, 177; *The Journal of Thomas Moore,* ed. Wilfred S. Dowden, 6 vols. (Newark: University of Delaware Press, 1983), II, 500–501; *Poetical Works* III, xi-xiii; and Vail, pp. 210–211 n17. In the *Examiner* the poem was titled "Letter from ——— to ———"; in *The Twopenny Post-Bag* it is "Parody of a Celebrated Letter" (*Twopenny,* pp. 46–53).

26. George IV, "Letter of the Prince Regent" [to the Duke of York], *The Examiner* no. 217 (February 23, 1812), 113–14.

27. Moore, "Letter from———to———," *The Examiner* no. 219 (March 8, 1812): 157–58 (158).

28. For material on "the book," see *A Catalogue of Political and Personal Satires in the British Museum,* ed. Frederic G. Stephens and M. Dorothy George, 11 vols. (London: British Museum, 1870-1954), entry 11990 (1813); George IV, *The Letters of King George IV, 1812–1830,* ed. A. Aspinall, 3 vols. (Cambridge: Cambridge University Press, 1938), I, 151n4, 176–77, 189–90; II, 364–65, 375.

Chapter 9 ~

Verbal Jujitsu:
William Hone and the
Tactics of Satirical Conflict

Kyle Grimes

As the present volume amply demonstrates, early-nineteenth-century satirical writing has recently become a prominent area of study for Romanticists. Works like Marcus Wood's *Radical Satire and Print Culture, 1790–1822* (1994) and Gary Dyer's *British Satire and the Politics of Style* (1997), with its splendid bibliography, have highlighted the varieties and the sheer quantity of satirical writing produced during the Romantic period.[1] Steven Jones' more recent *Satire and Romanticism* (2000) has expanded on this foundation, arguing that satirical writing can be thought of as a kind of generic Other against which the more canonical works of British Romanticism defined themselves or came to be defined.[2] Jones argues, in effect, that satire is often what Romanticism is not—hence, an understanding of one necessarily involves some grasp on the other. Thanks to these lines of historical and critical inquiry now focusing attention on the genre, satire is coming to be seen not so much as a leftover generic residue from a neoclassical eighteenth-century aesthetic as an essential contemporary background for the definition and differentiation of a distinctly Romantic writing.

This is an interesting and provocative line of inquiry into the generic history of Romantic-period writing, but a historical and theoretical problem emerges as the argument develops. The problem involves the central definition (or definitions) of such a broad literary type as satire. The traditional view, of course, has satire as a kind of "belated" form whose usually conservative ideological orientation is toward literary history (especially classical literary history), received formal models, and received cultural norms. Hence, satire has tended to be described in terms of conventional genre— Menippean, Juvenalian, Horatian, etc.—and, like all relatively clearly de- fined genres, such identifications involve implicit comparative relationships with past literature and are in an important sense formalist. Granted, more recent criticism has tended to emphasize the historically contingent, dialog- ical structure of satirical writing, but, regardless of how historically topical the satire might be, a Juvenalian satire (for example) is definable as such be- cause it takes up a distinctive, identifiable, and conventional attitude toward its subject and it is written in a particular and recognizable discursive form. Romantic literature, to fill in the other term of the opposition, is marked by originality, sincerity (to borrow the venerable Lionel Trilling's term), emo- tional intensity, and often an implicit utopian politics. As such, Romantic writing does not share the fundamentally conservative historical orientation of eighteenth-century satire. This is not to say, of course, that Romantic writing ignores received generic models—obviously it does not—but it puts them to rather different purposes. As this argument has it, Romantic writ- ing points toward some aesthetic, ideological, or even spiritual ideal that is yet to be realized—toward "something ever more about to be" or toward some future "finer tone" of more perfect repetition—rather than toward some ideal that has already been and that now requires the chastening preservative of satire.

These conventional ways of thinking about satire are limiting, mislead- ing, and sometimes flatly inaccurate in an early-nineteenth-century con- text. Indeed, Jones refrains from the conventional neoclassical terminology for exactly this reason, as "larger-than-history generic labels," preferring in- stead "more pragmatic modal positions taken by specific authors and works vis-à-vis other authors and works" (p. 9). And both Dyer and Wood focus much of their analysis on works that simply do not fit the generic molds. It will be more accurate, therefore, to bracket the traditional terminology for the moment and to consider some of most significant Romantic period satire as constituting a fundamentally new form of the genre. This writing is parasitic, derivative, opportunistic, or parodic and might at least provi- sionally be more appropriately called something like "hacker satire." For- mally, hacker satire may (or may not) fit into one of the conventional generic categories, but practically it is definable by the role it plays in very immediate and historically specific discursive power struggles. It is certainly not written with the preservation of some classical models or assumed cul- tural norms in mind, but rather as a material and intentionally disruptive intervention into the public discourses of the day. It exploits both the tac- tical ingenuity of the satirist/publisher and the technologies of print and distribution that can respond quickly and massively to momentary and fleeting opportunities in the public sphere. The kind of texts I have in mind here are, in effect, early instances of the actively, often joyfully rebellious ethic of contemporary computer hackers—they find the fissures in the apparently seamless surface of the dominant cultural discourse and they exploit those fissures to make their presence felt within the centers of social, political, and economic power—sometimes, though not always, with malicious intent. It is this kind of satirical writing, this "hacker satire," that in my view is the distinctive and emergent form of the genre during the Romantic period. And, if I might state my thesis bluntly here at the outset, it is this mode of satirical writing that effectively transforms the genre from a fundamentally literary, classically inspired, and conservative form of public writing into the more markedly dialogical forms that since the early nineteenth century have tended to be associated with widely and quickly distributed print journalism, with the socioeconomic panoramas of Victorian multiplot novels, and now with the decentralized but ubiquitous discourse of the Internet and the World Wide Web.

I can explain and describe this emergent satirical mode most clearly with the help of a few concrete examples drawn from the work of William Hone. With these examples in mind it will be possible later to consider more fully the generic and literary-historical implications of hacker satire. Before moving immediately to that stage of the argument, however, Hone himself will perhaps need a brief introduction.

William Hone (1780–1842), a prominent late-Romantic satirist and publisher, was arguably the best-selling writer in England in 1819 and 1820, the years that are now more famous among literary scholars as the dates of Keats, Shelley, and Byron's most influential writing. Now, nearly two centuries later, Hone's notoriety has faded, but he is still known for three major moments in his career: First, in December 1817, Hone successfully defended himself in court against ex officio charges of blasphemy and sedition brought by the Attorney General. At issue were three political pamphlets that took the form of parodies based on passages from the Book of Common Prayer. Hone's acquittals made him an instant celebrity and the records of *The Three Trials of William Hone* were frequently reprinted during the nineteenth century, becoming in fact a key legal precedent in the establishment of a free and politically critical press in England. Second, some months after his King's Court appearances Hone collaborated with the brilliant engraver George Cruikshank to produce a series of political squibs—*The Political House that Jack Built, The Man in the Moon, The Queen's Matrimonial Ladder,* and others. These works sold by the thousands, and quite literally defined public attitudes toward the Peterloo massacre of 1819 and the Queen Caroline Affair of 1820. Hone was likely the only writer and publisher in England who could have produced such works: the 1817 acquittals appear to have given him a kind of de facto immunity from further libel prosecution. In any event, the Tory government, probably leery of being twice humiliated in the courtroom, opted not to bring charges against this radical comic, despite their more aggressive pursuit of such fellow radicals as Richard Carlile, T. J. Wooler, and, later, John Hunt. Finally, in the late 1820s and early 1830s, Hone edited (and largely wrote) a series of descriptive volumes on folk customs and everyday life in England. *The Every-Day Book, The Table Book,* and *The Year Book* were quite popular in their day and are still useful as repositories of information on English street life and folk culture. It is these antiquarian works that Hone's young friend and admirer Charles Dickens found so appealing and that had no small influence on the good-natured attention to personal detail so characteristic of the novelist's work. Such are the high points of Hone's career in letters, and it seems clear, given this brief survey of his most productive moments, that Hone stands as a kind of transitional figure as the controversies of Romantic and Regency England are transmuted into the forms of Victorian literature.[3] What I would like to focus on here, however, are a few lesser-known examples of his parodic publications—examples, that is, of what I am calling Hone's hacker satire.

The first is the famous parody executed by George Cruikshank probably in late 1818 or early 1819 and published by Hone in January 1819—at the height of the paper money controversy. The circumstances that inspired the parody are perhaps already familiar.[4] Since the suspension of gold payments in 1797, the Bank of England had been circulating one-pound bank notes, which, of course, were explicitly "not to be duplicated." And yet, the notes were very easy for a reasonably good engraver to forge, and the forgeries were difficult to distinguish from the authentic bills; what is more, the temptation among the hard-pinched lower orders to pass forged notes was enormous, even though to do so was a capital offense. Dozens, perhaps hundreds of people were hanged as a consequence,[5] but, despite this disciplinary carnage, there seemed to be little effort on the part of the Bank of England to make the bills more difficult to duplicate, nor was there any serious effort on the part of the government to ease the economic plight of the lower orders and thus lessen the motivation to traffic in counterfeit bills. In Hone and Cruikshank's view, the Bank of England notes were essentially a vicious and cruel trap, and Cruikshank's engraving (see figure 9.1) illustrates the catastrophic effects of this cruelty—note, for instance, the £ sign drawn with a hangman's rope, the official seal made up of a grotesque figure of liberty eating her citizens, the design at the left side of the bill formed of images of interlocking shackles, and the official signature of "J. Ketch," the traditional name of the executioner. What is more, by its very existence, Cruikshank's bill demonstrates the ease with which one might duplicate the genuine objects.

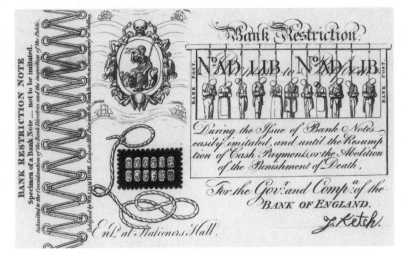

Figure 9.1. Specimen of a Bank Note, Hone and Cruikshank, 1819 (author's collection).

This familiar parody illustrates a simple point. The Hone/Cruikshank bank note is an effective counterdiscursive work—a satirical and parodic work—that doesn't really fit the traditional definitions of literary satire. Instead it is a creative, clever, and tactical response to the immediate historical moment. It takes advantage of a very local quirk—the ease with which one can duplicate notes that are specifically not to be duplicated—in order to make its point about the inherent cruelty of a paper-money economy in which written signs are all too easily mistaken, often with fatal results. And it was a demonstrably effective satire as well: when Hone put a copy of Cruikshank's banknote on display in his Ludgate Hill shop window, a large crowd gathered to see the exhibit, the event was covered in the press, and—just a few days later—the governors of the Bank of England met and decided no longer to circulate the one-pound notes. Later in his career, Cruikshank claimed that the engraving was "the most important design and etching I ever made in my life" because it actually saved a number of lives.[6]

The second exhibit here is Hone's 1819 publication, *Don Juan, Canto the Third!*[7] The work is a spurious continuation of Byron's *Don Juan,* which had been published anonymously by John Murray in July 1819. Hone detested Murray—not so much for what he published as for his refusal to own up to the publication of *Don Juan.* Hone makes his attitude very clear in a forty-page pamphlet called *"Don John," or, Don Juan Unmasked,* that was published just days after Byron's poem.[8] Predictably enough, Hone chides

Murray for a kind of cowardly hypocrisy. Here, after all, was the "Publisher to the Board of Longitude, and of the *Quarterly Review*—the Bookseller to the Admiralty, and a strenuous supporter of orthodoxy and the Bible Society" who was now anonymously publishing the politically and morally questionable *Don Juan*. For Hone's purposes, though, it is crucial that Murray did not attach his own name to the publication—as Hone puts it: "*Don Juan* appears without Mr. Murray's honest name to it. He publishes, but makes no sign." The poem was thus left as a kind of poetic orphan in the public sphere, with no author or publisher to claim it—no one, that is, but Hone, who soon produced his own third canto and thus moved quickly into the gap left open by Murray's cowardice. What is especially interesting about this work is the way Hone moves to claim not just parodic imitation but actual authenticity, as though he has now become Byron's publisher of choice. The opening stanza of the poem establishes Hone's claim:

> Miss Haidee and Don Juan pleaded well;
>   At least my publisher *of late* so tells me,
> Although the world he does not chuse to tell,
>   Yet every body knows 'tis he who sells me:
> To sing what furthermore the *pair* befel,
>   (As he declines my book and thus compels me,
> Because my "*guinea trash*" he will not own,)
> I send this Canto into Mr. Hone.
>
>   ("Don Juan Canto the Third")

Once again, Hone has exploited the momentary opportunity afforded by Murray's moral squeamishness to coopt the Byron name and press it into the service of radical politics. In this third canto, after all, Juan marries Haidee, the two have twelve children, and the whole family moves to London where Juan supports them as best he can by producing a political newspaper called *The Devilled Biscuit*. Juan's life, in fact, comes remarkably (though not surprisingly) to parallel Hone's own life, and the sympathetic portrait is presented as the authentic work of the popular author of the now infamous *Don Juan*.

The third exhibit is chronologically the earliest and probably the least familiar to literary and historical scholarship. In May of 1815 Hone wrote what may be his first parody, *Buonaparte-phobia, or Cursing Made Easy to the Meanest Capacity.*[9] The 3,000-word text of this single news sheet adopts the form and even the characters of Laurence Sterne's *Tristram Shandy,* using them to forward a satirical attack on John Stoddart, the outspoken lead-writer of the *Times* whom Hone casts as the incompetent obstetrician, Dr. Slop. The narrative commences with Dr. Slop, "My Father," and "My Uncle

Toby" sitting quietly in Dr. Slop's parlor. A Printer's Devil soon arrives with the still-wet proofs of Dr. Slop's lead article for the *Times*, which, as it happens, is preceded on that day by an engraving and a paragraph announcing the London display of David's celebrated portrait of Napoleon.[10] Dr. Slop, famed for his vehement anti-French rhetoric, immediately launches into a lengthy and energetic stream of epithets and curses:

> Doctor Slop vociferated:—"No sooner is a piece of successful villainy achieved by this *Monster,* than our print-shops exhibit the *iron countenance* of NAPOLEON THE GREAT!—the *portrait* of the execrable *Villain!* that *hypocritical* Villain! that *bare-faced* Villain! that *daring* Villain! that *perjured* Villain!—that *Disgrace of the Human Species!*—the *Corsican!* the *low-minded Corsican!* the *wily* Corsican! the *vile* Corsican! the *once-insolent* Corsican! the *beaten, disgraced, and perjured* Corsican! the *faithless, perjured, craft-loving* Corsican!." . . .

To the astonishment of Uncle Toby and the narrator's father, Dr. Slop's vituperations continue in this vein through most of the three-column sheet, only slightly rechanneled halfway through by Uncle Toby's plea for calm and his unwelcome reminder that only a few years earlier Dr. Slop had himself sympathized with the Jacobins.[11] Finally, after commenting briefly on the ineffectual nature of "small curses," Uncle Toby and the narrator's father withdraw "under cover of Doctor Slop's exclamations."

This minimal narrative reveals a good deal about Hone's satirical strategies. It is important, for instance, that Hone chooses Sterne's novel as the formal basis for the parody; it is also significant that the work was published as a single news-sheet made to look physically like the front page of the *Times.* But what is most germane to the discussion here is the language of the irrepressible Dr. Slop. Dr. Slop, of course, sees his language as distinguished by its "strength"—meaning, presumably, its emphatic vigor and what Dr. Slop assumes is his ability to define public attitudes toward Napoleon. Thus, in a boastful comparison of his own writing to that in an allied newspaper, Slop claims that "St—t [T. G. Street, editor of the *Courier*] is a capital hand at a *leader,* strong! strong! like myself—sometimes; but cannot *do* a column and a half, or two columns, every day, *strong* all the way through!" Given his pride over the supposed strength of his own rhetoric, Dr. Slop is naturally exasperated when Uncle Toby characterizes that rhetoric as intemperate and when the narrator's amiable Father suggests that Dr. Slop's "small curses" are "but so much waste of our strength and soul's health to 'no manner of purpose,'" a line quoted directly from Sterne. But the real genius of Hone's satire here lies in the source of Dr. Slop's language: the curses Dr. Slop levels at Napoleon (and printed in italics in Hone's parody) are quoted directly from Stoddart's columns in the *Times*. Stoddart's discourse, in other words, becomes not merely a stylistic characteristic so mechanical as to be easily imitated in parody but rather the actual source of the parody's language. This is not Stoddart imitated, this is Stoddart himself, and herein lies the ingenuity, power, and maybe even "strength" of Hone's pamphlet.

Parody, by definition, mimics some already existing and usually well-known text or discourse—in effect, a channel is opened between the model text(s) and the parody, with the effect of the latter depending upon the reader's recognition of its imitative relation to the former. The analytical emphasis in most literary studies of parody has tended to focus on the description and explanation of the parody itself as a secondary text, usually involving an elucidation of sources and immediate historical allusions. But viewed in a broader context, it becomes clear that the channel opened by the act of parodic imitation works both ways. Once a reader "gets" the parody—"gets" in the sense that one might "get" a joke—then a reversal can take place in which the parody becomes the background text when the reader once again encounters the original. Hone's use of Stoddart's own language instead of a more general imitation of his style serves to facilitate this kind of reversal since it establishes not so much an imitative link as a direct identification between the original and the parody, thereby collapsing the distinction that relegates parody to its familiar status as a distinctly secondary discourse.

In any case, a perceptive reader of *Buonaparte-phobia* could no longer view Stoddart's daily blasts against Napoleon in the *Times* and be naively or unequivocally swayed by their implicit claims of "strength." Hone has performed a successful maneuver in a kind of discursive jujitsu: he uses Stoddart's own language in a parodic Shandyan context that makes it look ridiculous at best. Then, thanks to the irony-generating reversal of parodic and model texts, Stoddart's extreme language continues to look ridiculous even when encountered once again in the columns of the *Times*.[12] After the appearance of Hone's broadsheet, Stoddart's "strength"—his signature cursing—became his liability, and his tenure as chief lead-writer for the *Times* lasted only a few more months, despite a six-year contract he had signed in April 1814. It is, of course, impossible to know to what degree Hone's parody was responsible for Stoddart's demise at the *Times,* but it is clear that the "Doctor Slop" nickname continued to embarrass the Tory ideologue for years to come. Henry Crabb Robinson's diaries and William Hazlitt's journalistic writing consistently refer to Stoddart as "The Doctor," and the Preface to Hone's 1820 reprint of *Buonapartephobia* rightly claims that the 1815 publication was the source of the epithet.[13]

So much for this general introduction to Hone and his parodic and satirical publications. The crucial point here in terms of the broader issues of Romanticism is that Romantic-era satire is easily misunderstood if it is viewed simply as a kind of fading echo of eighteenth-century neoclassical models, what Raymond Williams would likely call a "residual" cultural form. Hone's writing in this instance clearly diverges both from the modes of sincerity typically associated with canonical English Romanticism and from the modes of writing that usually fall under the rubric of satire—even if the definition of satire is expanded to include the composite, heterogeneous form that Dyer calls "radical satire." In Hone's hands, parodic satire becomes not so much a distinct, quasi-literary genre as a dialogizing counter-movement to the implicit truth-claims of *all* monological discourses, be they literary, political, philosophical, or theological. The cultural force of the satire is anchored not in some intrinsic formal quality of the work but in the two-way *dialogical* negotiation the work establishes between its source texts and its immediate historical circumstances. It is precisely this practice, this quickly produced verbal parrying in the public sphere, that is the early-nineteenth-century's contribution to the history of satire.

In my introductory remarks I gave this element of Hone's work an admittedly provocative label: "hacker satire." The historical analogy implicit in the name may at first seem preposterously anachronistic—founded on a strained etymological link between the so-called hack writers of the eighteenth century and the computer hackers of the twenty-first who find pleasure and power in navigating and sometimes manipulating the chartered circuits of the World Wide Web.[14] But on closer inspection, a number of legitimate historical parallels present themselves. First, in order to flourish, both Hone's hacker satire and the activities of computer hackers require an environment of relative freedom of expression. Hone's "freedom"—especially after the passage of the draconian Six Acts in late 1819—was a kind of historical anomaly; having embarrassed the government in his 1817 trials he could afford to be less fearful than most other radical publishers of a repeated libel prosecution in 1820. Similarly, much theorizing about the emergence of digital networks and the cyberculture(s) they make possible is founded on the mantra that "information wants to be free," and certainly, as the most cursory examination of the discourse in Internet chatrooms and bulletin boards will amply demonstrate, computer network hackers and Web aficionados certainly do not feel their discourse to be constrained by any recognizable civil or moral censors. Second, for hacker satire to be effective, it has to be produced and distributed very quickly, for only through the speed of production can the satire collapse the difference between original and secondary discourses that is crucial to the "jujitsu-effect" of works like *Buonaparte-phobia* and *Don Juan, Canto the Third!* In Hone's case, speed seems to have been a characteristic of his composing process, no doubt because Hone's compositions were often cut-and-paste efforts based on already familiar texts. (He wrote—"compiled" might be the better term—*The Polit-ical House that Jack Built* in a single night, for example.) And finally, as a corollary to the required speed of production, hacker satire demands that the satirist have immediate access to the technologies of production, be it Hone's Stanhope press, print shop, and bookselling establishment or the computer hacker's networked desktop machine that is now routinely more powerful than the bank of computers that sent Neil Armstrong to the moon in the 1960s. When these elements come together, as they did in Hone's work dur-ing the Regency period, the result is a leveling of discursive authority, or more accurately, a seizing of authority by those who had heretofore been ex-cluded from a place in English public discourse. And it is probably entirely predictable that a figure like Hone's Dr. Slop would so vehemently object to the rapidity with which "our print shops" should circulate what Slop sees as a noxious plebeian discourse.

It is a commonplace of Romantic-era literary and cultural history that the period witnessed the emergence of what might be called a multimedia cul-ture. For a number of cultural and technological reasons, access to print ex-panded dramatically during the early years of the nineteenth century, and "print culture" came to encompass a much broader cross-section of the Eng-lish population as a whole than had been the case during the previous cen-tury. While not universally celebrated (Wordsworth, for instance, famously lamented that pscyho-social condition in which people crave "gross and vio-lent stimulants" that are provided for them by the hourly communications of the press), what was at stake was little more than the democratization of pub-lic discourse. This historical context is inevitably hostile to the conservative tendencies of neoclassical satirical forms, and it is no surprise to see Dyer (among others) argue that the Romantic period saw the death of these tradi-tional modes as they became transformed into the more dialogical forms characteristic of Victorian fiction. The kind of cultural production I have called "hacker satire" here is, in effect, a transitional stage in this transforma-tion. It is significant, of course, that each of the examples from Hone and Cruikshank is marked by a kind of parodic seizing of cultural authority. Whether attacking the lead writer from the *Times,* capitalizing on the cachet of Byron and the John Murray publishing house, or even mocking the Bank of England itself, each of these publications seeks to exploit the contradic-tions it discovers in these pillars of print culture and then employs the tactics of satire to expose, disarm, and ridicule their pretensions to authority. It is ul-timately this process of verbal jujitsu, a process for which Hone is the most famous but by no means the sole practitioner, that opens the generic path for the rise of the more comprehensively social forms of the Victorian multi-plot novel, the more diverse and variegated print culture of the later nineteenth century, and the electronic culture of our own historical moment.

Notes

1. Marcus Wood, *Radical Satire and Print Culture, 1790–1822* (Oxford: Clarendon Press, 1994); Gary Dyer, *British Satire and the Politics of Style, 1789–1832* (New York and Cambridge: Cambridge University Press, 1997).

2. Steven E. Jones, *Satire and Romanticism* (New York: Palgrave, 2000); hereafter cited parenthetically in the text.

3. Joss Marsh, *Word Crimes: Blasphemy, Culture, and Literature in Nineteenth-Century England* (Chicago: University of Chicago Press, 1998), 56, has argued recently that Hone himself appears as an image in this literary-historical transformation: she identifies the old bookseller in *Oliver Twist* as a Dickensian caricature of Hone.

4. George Cruikshank and William Hone, *Bank Restriction Note; Specimen of a Bank Note—not to be Imitated* (London: William Hone, [1819]). The details of the *Bank Note*'s composition and publication can be found in Robert Patten, *George Cruikshank's Life, Times, and Art. Volume I: 1792–1835* (New Brunswick, NJ: Rutgers University Press, 1992), 144–49.

5. Patten (p. 145) claims that more than 300 persons had been hanged for forgery since the paper bank notes were introduced.

6. Cruikshank's claim came late in his life in a letter to the editor of *Whitaker's Journal,* December 12, 1875. A facsimile copy of the letter can be found online at <http://www.money.org/gcarticle.jpg>.

7. *Don Juan, Canto the Third!* (London: William Hone, 1819). A more detailed discussion of this parody can be found in my "William Hone, John Murray, and the Uses of Byron," in *Romanticism, Radicalism, and the Press,* edited by Stephen C. Behrendt (Detroit: Wayne State University Press, 1997), 192–202.

8. *'Don John,' or Don Juan Unmasked; being a Key to the Mystery, Attending that Remarkable Publication: with a Descriptive Review of the Poem, and Extracts* (London: William Hone, 1819).

9. *Buonaparte-phobia, or Cursing Made Easy to the Meanest Capacity:—A Dialogue between the Editor of "The Times,"—Doctor Slop, My Uncle Toby, & My Father* (London: William Hone, 1815).

10. Hone's parody is printed on one side of a single half-sheet with BUONA-PARTE-PHOBIA placed above the familiar *The Times* at the top, the text of the parody filling the three long columns in the body of the work, and the engraving of Napoleon at the top of the second column, squarely in the center of the broadside.

11. The narrative of Stoddart's relationship with the *Times* can be found in *"The Thunderer" in the Making,* in the series *The History of the Times* (London: The Times, 1935), 156–70.

12. This infectious power of parody was made explicit in 1817 during Hone's famous libel trials. The Attorney General Samuel Shepherd argued that, once having read Hone's parodies, it is difficult during the church service to listen innocently and reverently to the ritual language.

13. The claim also explains the two epigraphs that appear on the title page of the 1820 reprint: "I have conferred on him a glorious Immortality!" and "With

his name the mothers still their babes!," both from *Henry VI*. The motivation for Hone's republication of the *Buonapartephobia* satire in 1820 was no doubt that Stoddart had recently established a new Tory newspaper called *The New Times*. Hone would soon publish what may be his best comic work, a parody of this new daily called *A Slap at Slop and the Bridge Street Gang*.

14. *The New Hacker's Dictionary* claims that the contemporary term was "originally, someone who makes furniture with an axe" though the editor offers no documentation to support the claim (Eric S. Raymond, *The New Hacker's Dictionary*, third edn. [Cambridge, MA: MIT Press, 1996]). Now the term "hacker" indicates a person "who enjoys exploring the details of programmable systems and how to stretch their capabilities." For the historical context of the "hacker ethic," see Stephen Levy, *Hackers: Heroes of the Computer Revolution* (New York: Penguin, 1984), 40–49.

Chapter 10 ～

"Trimming the *Muse of Satire*": J. R. D. Huggins and the Poetry of Hair-Cutting

John Strachan

> The particularity of this man put me into a deep thought whence it
> should proceed that of all the lower order barbers should go further in
> hitting the ridiculous than any other set of men. Watermen brawl, cob-
> blers sing: but why must a barber be for ever a politician, a musician,
> an anatomist, a poet, and a physician?
>
> —Sir Richard Steele on "Don Saltero"

This chapter examines the work of the New York barber, satirist, and indefatigable self-publicist John Richard Desborus Huggins, the author of *Hugginiana; or, Huggins' Fantasy, being a Collection of the most esteemed modern Literary Productions* (1808), an extraordinary, though highly neglected, collection of advertisements that were first published in the East Coast public prints. Huggins was simultaneously a commercial advertiser, a gifted parodist, and an accomplished literary, social, and political satirist. His extraordinary advertisements, published in newspapers from Boston to Philadelphia and stuck up on the walls of his various premises in the metropolis from 40 Greenwich Street to 92 Broadway, granted him both commercial success and a reputation as a wit in early-nineteenth-century New York. Huggins was a former classical actor in Harper's Rhode Island

Company[1] who left the stage during the 1790s to establish himself as a barber. His businesses were enthusiastically promoted in an endless stream of comic advertisements. As Van Wyck Brooks writes—in a rare critical mention of Huggins—in *The World of Washington Irving* (1944), Huggins'

> fame as a wit had spread from Georgia to Maine when, having shaved Tom Moore and Joel Barlow, he began to write squibs and satires to emulate them. His epigrams on Jefferson, Randolph and others had long been the joy of the Federalist in the *Evening Post* and all the wits and fashionables had thronged his shop in order to be able to say they had been barbered by Huggins. The jokes and lampoons of all the wags had been stuck on this Pasquin of New York, and they had even been collected in a volume of *Hugginiana,* with woodcuts by Alexander Anderson and designs by Jarvis.[2]

Brooks's assertion that Huggins was inspired to the writing of satire by trimming the hair of Moore and Barlow is very likely apocryphal,[3] but whatever the truth of the matter, Huggins' advertisements demonstrate a wideranging use of literary satire and parody; as the New York *Evening Post* declared in 1805, "J. R. D. H. is scarcely better known by his skill as a frissure, than his humor as a writer. State-papers, tragedies, and ballads are rendered equally subservient to his purpose."[4] Huggins, seeing himself as fitted for "the delicious task of trimming the *Muse of Satire*" (*Hugginiana,* p. 118), employs a range of comic models in his work: parody, imitation, satire, burlesque, and pasquinade. His use of parody is wide-ranging, with formal models drawn from literary greats such as Shakespeare, Milton, and Pope through to his contemporaries Cowper, Sheridan, Darwin, Southey, and Wolcot. That said, Huggins' imitative genius is not confined to literary models alone: nursery rhymes, Jeffersonian rhetoric, playbills, business cards, phrenological pseudo-science, Napoleonic edicts; all are grist to his advertising mill. And Huggins' aims transcend the engendering of new business; I shall demonstrate that this barber was also an able political satirist whose work engages with both European geopolitical conflict and with contemporary American party politics.

I

J. R. D. Huggins was not the first literary barber to use ornate advertising copy, or indeed, the first advertising frisseur to use satirical and parodic literary models. Self-eulogizing hairdressers, combative figures who bombastically endorse their own artistic skills and downcry their pernicious and talentless rivals are not uncommon in the history of advertising. One of Thomas Hood's most particular favorites in his February

1825 *London Magazine* article, "The Art of Advertising made Easy," which surveys the contemporary advertising scene, is a puff for one C. Macalpine, "Hair Cutter and Peruquier" to George IV. Simultaneously aesthete and warrior, this Bobadil among barbers vigorously challenges all rivals to his supremacy:

> Hebe herself wears not a more youthful nor Venus a more lovely appearance than do the British Fair when adorned by the magical touch of Macalpine . . . Macalpine, on an average, operates personally upon three hundred heads of hair weekly, and pledges his professional reputation, which he values more than life, that others are paid for disfiguring that beautiful ornament which a skilful man can alone preserve in classic and luxuriant tresses. Macalpine being the only hair-cutter who obtained a prize, and that of 200*l.* challenges all Europe to a trial of skill for 100 guineas. Come the four corners of the Globe, with comb and scissars, and his great superiority has "stomach for them all"!!! He will hurl them to the tomb of the Capulits.[5]

Hood dryly suggests that Macalpine "really should give lectures on the poetry of hair-cutting."[6] His comment, though facetious, is not entirely fanciful, given that the history of laborer class poets features several examples of barber-poets. The most notable of all is, of course, Allan Ramsay, but there are other, less well-known figures, jobbing barbers who cultivated the muse. The Pontefract periwig-maker and barber John Lund produced several volumes of tales and satires in the mid-eighteenth century, and an even earlier example of a poetical barber is the famous James Salter, the self-styled "Don Saltero." Salter was an Irish barber and tooth-drawer who was patronized by Sir Hans Sloane and eventually set up a museum of curiosities at Cheyne Walk in Chelsea. Salter was adept at self-promotion, and produced ingenious advertising copy on behalf of both his gallery of ephemera and his tooth-drawing and barbering business for the public prints. For instance, a poetic advertisement published in the *Weekly Journal* in June 1723 described Salter's life journey, his progress from a barber-surgeon to the proprietor of the "Chelsea Knackatory":

> SIR,—Fifty years since to Chelsea great,
> From Rodnam on the Irish main,
> I stroll'd with maggots in my pate,
> Where much improved they still remain.
> Though various employs I've past,
> Toothdrawer, trimmer, and at last,
> I'm now a gimcrack whim-collector.
> Monsters of all sorts are here seen,
> Strange things in nature as they grew so;

> Some relics of the Sheba queen,
> And fragments of the famed Bob Cruso
>   . . .
> Now if you will the cause espouse,
> In journals pray direct your friends
> To my Museum-Coffee house:
> And in requital for the timely favour
> I'll gratis bleed, draw teeth, and be your shaver.[7]

The eccentricities of Salter, and indeed of barbers in general, were noted by Richard Steele, who writes that "The particularity of this man put me into a deep thought whence it should proceed that of all the lower order barbers should go further in hitting the ridiculous than any other set of men. Watermen brawl, cobblers sing: but why must a barber be for ever a politician, a musician, an anatomist, a poet, and a physician?"[8] By the mid-eighteenth century, the barber with pretensions to intellectual accomplishment becomes a stock figure in English comic writing, most notably in the two greatest novels in the English picaresque tradition, *Tom Jones* and *Roderick Random,* in the characters of Partridge and Strap.[9]

The direct artistic predecessor of J. R. D. Huggins is another former barber, the razor-strop entrepreneur George Packwood, a key figure in the development of late Georgian advertising. As *Harper's Magazine* noted in 1866, "Packwood, some fifty years ago, led the way in England of . . . systematic advertising, by impressing his razor-strop indelibly on the mind of every bearded member of the kingdom."[10] Packwood was an ingenious and witty self-publicist whose puffs, many of which use variants of literary parody, are collected in *Packwood's Whim, or, The Way to Get Money and be Happy* (1796), a remarkable collection of comic advertisements that has been brilliantly treated by the historian Neil McKendrick in his important essay "George Packwood and the Commercialisation of Shaving: The Art of Eighteenth-Century Advertising or 'The Way to Get Money and be Happy'" (1982).[11] However, even Packwood must give way to the resourceful Huggins. In the advertising techniques of this Broadway frizzer, we see the most sustained and perhaps the most inventive use of parody and satire in contemporary advertising literature. And in the case of Huggins, a politically committed partisan of the Federalist interest, the satire is as important as the advertising. Huggins aims to sell his services as a barber, and his combs, razor-strops, and wigs, but his work directly intervenes in the key political debates of the age, both local and global: the controversies between Jeffersonian Republicanism and Federalism, and the Napoleonic wars that were convulsing Europe in the first decade of the nineteenth century.

II

During the first ten years of the nineteenth century, John Richard Desborus Huggins poured out a series of striking comic advertisements in East Coast newspapers. In his earliest advertisements, published at the turn of the nineteenth century, he presents himself first as a "Knight of the Comb." However, Huggins eventually promotes himself to the "Emperor of Barbers," issuing Imperial Proclamations and signing himself "H. I. M.," "His Imperial Majesty." In 1808, the Emperor of Barber's puffs were collected in *Hugginiana; or, Huggins' Fantasy, being a Collection of the most esteemed modern Literary Productions. Exposing the art of making a noise in the world, without beating a drum, or crying oysters; and shewing how, like Whittington of old, who rose from nothing to be Lord Mayor of London, a mere Barber may become an Emperor, if he has spirit enough to assume, and talents enough to support the title.* This book, a remarkable but utterly neglected work, and one rare outside of statutory libraries, was published by H. C. Southwick of No. 2, Wall Street, "Most Excellent Printer to his most BARBER-OUS Majesty." The influence of that other entrepreneurial shaver and advertiser George Packwood is obvious in *Hugginiana,* and is openly acknowledged in the frontispiece, which shows the Emperor Desborus mounted on a charger and blowing a trumpet from which Packwood's name emerges. And like his master Packwood (whose products are enthusiastically eulogized throughout *Hugginiana*), Huggins is adept in the "blast of puffery."[12] In his imitation of Mark Antony's famous speech from *Julius Caesar,* Huggins declares himself to be the sole agent for Packwood in New York:

> By aid of PACKWOOD's Strop,
> The greatest, noblest, best of all inventions
> (Of which he here stands sole and only agent)
> He looks for greater gains.
>
> (*Hugginiana,* p. 251)

The link between the two men is reinforced by one of *Hugginiana*'s plates, in which "The Genius of Shaving is seen issuing from Packwood's Warehouse, 16 Grace Church Street, London and showering down razor strops into Huggins, 92 Broadway, New York." And that link, highly appropriately, is both commercial and literary. Huggins places himself in the tradition of Packwood, endorsing his shaving wares and demonstrating a similar ingenuity in his advertisements. Though I would argue that the pupil exceeded his master, the clear model for *Hugginiana* is *Packwood's Whim, or, The Way to Get Money and be Happy.* Huggins styles himself the "sole New York agent" for Packwood's razor strops, and the link between Packwood and Huggins is as much artistic as it is commercial; the "Genius of Shaving" metaphorically represents the Packwoodian muse entering the premises at 92 Broadway.

Hugginiana collects and republishes puffs published between 1801 and 1808 and sees Huggins achieving a marketer's dream: making consumers pay for the advertising as well as the product. The advertisements are strung together by a connecting narrative tissue that gives the text the air of a picaresque novel, portraying Huggins' rise in the world, his battles with a baneful host of rival barbers, and his elevation to undisputed imperial eminence. In the English picaresque manner, the text is loosely structured and episodic, with the presence of a central character (Huggins in this case) the sole uniting factor. And if Huggins' picaresque journey, from Greenwich Street to Pine Street to Broadway, is no great distance in geographical terms, in his own metaphorical terms it is a momentous one.

An array of self-promoting individuals populate the pages of *Hugginiana*. Huggins himself occupies the center, of course, but there is also an extensive cast of other characters, most notably the rival barbers Edward Quirk, H. J. Hassey, and Don Emanuel Antonio de Biscarolaza ("Ladies and Gentleman's Hair Dresser, No. 72, Wall-Street"). Biscarolaza and Quirk are former colleagues of Huggins who eventually set up businesses on their own and, in the epitome of capitalistic competition, start to produce exotic advertisements in the manner of Huggins. Biscarolaza, for instance, was, according to Huggins, "once my journeyman—a lad of dull parts—Finding I could make nothing of him, I taught him how to pen an advertisement, and then set him adrift to shift for himself." Huggins then offers samples of Biscarolaza's copywriting: "His proficiency in the art may be gathered from the specimens which follow; many of which are in no wise inferior to my own."[13] Despite disingenuously declaring that "There is nothing Don Emanuel holds in greater contempt than the ridiculous practice of puffing in the newspapers," Biscarolaza shows himself an able practitioner of the art of advertising. After several relatively restrained puffs, he eventually reinvents himself as "late Comb-Major, and Tonsor Generalissimo to his Most Catholic Majesty Carlos III, Dei Gratia Hispania et India Rex" and launches off in imitation of Huggins' wilder flights of fancy, boasting of his "scratches" (i.e., wigs) made from mammoth hair and describing expeditions to the moon in search of tonsorial product innovation. Biscarolaza declares that he "has received patterns of wigs, frizettes, &c. from the planet Venus, which have the most enchanting effect in heightening female beauty. Also, a few fierce whiskers from Mars, of the most courageous cut, suited for military gentlemen. These form a most pleasing addition to his former stock of Spanish, Roman, Grecian, and Mammoth scratches" (*Hugginiana*, p. 42).

Some of Biscarolaza's puffs, like those of many of the rival hairdressers featured in *Hugginiana,* feature knocking copy aimed at Huggins. These animadversions are then duly reprinted in *Hugginiana,* which, in the manner of *The Dunciad* and the *Anti-Jacobin* before it, reproduces the effusions of its enemies within its pages. Allied to this is Huggins' inclusion of verse tributes, press commentary on his work, and such writing on the subject of the dressing of the hair as catches his eye. It is also probable that at least some of Huggins' puffs were imitative tributes written for him by politically sympathetic literary customers such as Anthony Bleecker and Samuel Woodworth,[14] or the Connecticut wits Richard Alsop and Theodore Dwight, the acerbically anti-Jeffersonian satirists whose most notable work *The Echo* (1807) contains an extensive tribute to Huggins[15] and provided some of the cuts reproduced in *Hugginiana.* All of this means that the book, on occasions, has the appearance of riotous heteroglossia, full of competing voices all claiming to be in possession of the true secret of the care and maintenance of the hair.

"The Puff Candid," first published in the New York *Morning Chronicle* in February 1805, is a good example of Huggins' poetical copy:

To dress the hair with gentlest strokes of art,
To tangled locks graceful charm impart,
To wave them loose in many an airy fold,
Or clip them short in crispy curls unroll'd:
For this immortal HUGGINS wields the comb,
Within his "Academic Dressing Room";
Where Belles and Beaux with eager footsteps stray
To "School for Fashions," 92 Broadway.
Frizzers in vain their puffs and powder keep,
And staring shavers wonder while they weep.
HUGGINS disdains with vulgar jerks to twirl,
The martial whisker or bewitching curl—
Such vulgar jerks your stupid barbers show
Whose *heads* of block, nor taste, nor fashion know
He bids your hair with gentlest touches rise
(Not twigs—that fetch the water in your eyes)
Fashion confest on Fredish heads he shews
Like Paris Belles, or dashing London Beaux!
No common object to your sight displays,
But what the stylish throng with joy surveys
A lovely fair's loose locks, in graceful state,
Or close cropt buck, with rough and curly pate,
While HUGGINS' fingers move by fashions laws,
Who'll risk his head in *graceless* BARBER's *paws*?
Who sees him curl, but envies every wave?
Who views him lather, but must wish to shave.

(*Hugginiana,* pp. 94–95)

Such Popean effusions are the most common prosodological manner of contemporary poetic, or "jingle," advertising copy[16] and *Hugginiana* also offers much more ingenious literary imitation. For example, this spoof playbill, in imitation of Goldsmith, published in the *Commercial Advertiser* for June 27, 1808, shows Huggins offering a feast of theatrical entertainment:

THE STROPS DO CONQUER;
Or, The Razors Out-Whetted.
The principal parts to be sustained by *Packwood's Razor Strops,* and Gentlemen
of the Imperial Household.
Between the Play and farce, a new
MELO-COSMEOTIS.
In which DESBORUS THE FIRST will sing the ancient Ballad, "I'm Emperor of
Barbers here."
A dissertation on WIGS, by *Mr. Edwards,* formerly of the Dublin Theatre.
The Grand Shaving Duet; or, the Wounded Segar, by Messrs. Paris and Fennemore.
HUGGINS' ODE ON the Fashions, by Shanewolf, Prince of PULL-TUSK.
        . . .
The whole to conclude with a superb *transporting scene,* in which the Emperor is
pourtrayed in the act of receiving the dollars, half dollars, quarters, shillings, and
sixpences in his right hand, and graciously depositing them in the *till* with his left.

(*Hugginiana,* pp. 248–249)

The evening was "reviewed" in a follow-up notice by "Cocky Doodle," published in the *Advertiser* on July 8: "Mr. HUGGINS was in fine voice, and sung with extraordinary *spirit* and humor. . . . We cannot too highly extol the display of *Hair Work, Perfumery,* &c. in the second act, which for beauty of design, tasteful disposition, and superior finish, are certainly without parallel" (*Hugginiana,* pp. 252–253).

Huggins' puffs grow in invention from the early, relatively modest effusions of 1801 and 1802 to the baroque invention and ingenuity of the work published later in the decade. An example from 1808 is Huggins' print, "The House that Jack Built," which—eleven years before William Hone makes the same imitative gesture in *The Political House that Jack Built*—uses nursery rhyme parody to make its point. Huggins also imitates more elevated literature. An 1807 advertisement in verse begins by quoting verbatim the first four lines of Erasmus Darwin's "Apostrophe to Spring" and then launches into Darwinian parody:

> Born in yon blaze of orient sky
> Sweet May! thy radiant form unfold;
> Unclose thy voluptuous eye,
> And wave thy shadowy locks of gold
> The beauteous locks that from the head depend
> Beneath his care in gracious ringlets end;
> His style of dressing only now is priz'd,
> Huggins, by every beau is patroniz'd
> . . . No barber he whose rough plebeian steel
> Causes the chin those horrid pangs to feel
> . . . Such is his art that tender, timid, brave
> All come to HUGGINS when they want to shave

Thus sings the bard—but "the proof of the pudding is in the eating." Come then, all ye who doubt, to the DRESSING ACADEMY, No. 92 Broadway, and if ye are not convinced, it will not be from a lack of assiduity on the part of Your obedient, truly devoted and very humble servant, J. R. D. Huggins.

(*Hugginiana*, pp. 187–88)

On other occasions, Huggins offers his own critical readings of the classics of English poetry, which are interpreted, of course, in the light of their relevance to his tonsorial activities. For example, a November 1806 puff in the *Daily Advertiser* begins by quoting from Cowper's eulogy of winter in book IV of *The Task* :

> Oh Winter, ruler of th' inverted year,
> Thy scattered hair with sleet like ashes fill'd
> Thy breath congeal'd upon thy lips, thy cheeks
> Fring'd with a beard made white with other snows
> Than those of age, thy forehead wrapp'd in clouds

Huggins, who is of the opinion that his talents are more expansively expressed in winter than in the heat of a New York summer, feels that Cowper could not have captured his position better had the poet himself been a barber. He comments that had Cowper "been destined to regulate the ton; had he, like him too, felt the difference between a winter's harvest in the field of fashion, and the uncongenial and unprolific heat of a summer's sun, he could not more feelingly have painted in the preceding lines, the rapture, with which the IMPERIAL CHIEFTAIN, hails the approach of Winter. It is then that his talents are called into full exercise—it is then his genius soars to the upper regions, and plants on every eminence, the monument of his skill" (*Hugginiana*, pp. 201–202). In a spoof allegorical interpretation of the poem, Huggins goes on to offer close readings of sections of *The Task*, demonstrating their relevance to his work. Thus, for instance, lines 543–44 of Book IV ("Indebted to some smart wig-weaver's hand / For more than half the tresses it sustains") signify that each of the Emperor's customers is "Indebted to the mighty (*Huggins'*) hand / For more than half the tresses it sustains." Huggins' tendentious criticism musters its evidence well: what else but hairdressing does Cowper's "*Curling* tendrils gracefully dispos'd" depict? He ends with a salute to his shop and more gleeful citation from Cowper, this time of the famous passage in the *Task* where the poet lampoons contemporary advertising:[17]

> His shop, too! Behold his Shop!! at
> No. 92 BROADWAY,
> Where may be found all that taste and fashion can require, fancy conceive,
>   or
> art invent;
> "———A wilderness of strange,
> But gay confusion, *roses* for the cheeks,
> And lilies for the brows of faded age;
> ———*Ringlets* for the *bald*,
> Heaven, earth and ocean plunder'd of their sweets,
> Nectarious *essences,* Olympian dews."
>
> (*Hugginiana*, p. 202)

Here Cowper's parody of the advertising columns in his daily newspaper, with their puffs for wigs and cosmetics, forms part of a parodic critical essay that is itself an advertisement. Cowper's advertising parody is transformed into parodic advertising, leaving the poet to act as the mouthpiece for the very products, wigs and hairpieces, with which he had made sport in *The Task*.

III

Huggins' rise from a knight to an emperor is an elevation that echoed in his change of premises, each one more fashionably situated—from 40 Greenwich Street, thence to 41 Pine Street in 1802, and finally to No. 92 Broadway in the following year. Huggins eulogizes his new location in the *Evening Post* for June 10, 1803, in sprightly anapestic verse in the manner of Christopher Anstey:

> J. HUGGINS informs all the *heads* in the state,
> Of the wonderful change he has pass'd thro' of late:

Promoted from Pine-street's dull glimmering ray,
To the clear shining regions of *stylish* Broadway;
Where the Goddess of Fashion, he dares to presume,
Will soon fix her seat in his new Dressing-Room.

(*Hugginiana*, p. 43)

92 Broadway, the "*Razor*-voir of taste," becomes an Eldorado for those in search of hair care and hair care products.

The move to 92 Broadway follows the dissolution of the firm of Huggins and Quirk, and Edward Quirk swiftly becomes one of the anti-heroes of *Hugginiana*. Hostilities begin almost immediately after the severance of the partnership, with the puff quoted above, where Huggins contrasts "Pine-street's dull glimmering ray" with "the clear shining regions of *stylish* Broadway," infuriating Quirk (who was still trading in Pine Street) and prompting him to reply three days later in the *Morning Chronicle* by pointing out that the much-vaunted site in Broadway was actually uncomfortably close to a graveyard: "'tis really laughable when he talks of the . . . gloomy situation of Pine-street, [when] his Dressing Room [is] in Broadway, where he presents you with the elegant prospect of graves and tomb-stones."[18] Quirk also had his own line in puffing verse:

Where elegance with art is led,
T' adorn and ornament the head,
And curling tongs, and razors keen,
Put hair in curls, and smooth the chin,
The above and all such other work
Is now performed by
EDWARD QUIRK

(*Hugginiana*, p. 137).

Huggins, who "looks down with sovereign contempt on the quiblings and QUIRKINGS of his insignificant enemies" (*Hugginiana*, p. 146), replies to Quirk by reprinting the English satirist John Wolcot's ("Peter Pindar's") fable, "The Pig and the Magpie," in which a pig, enraged at a magpie's theft of a few hairs from his back, scalps himself by invading the magpie's nest in a bramble. Huggins adds "This is a pretty tale of Pindar's—aye and pat, / To folk like you, so clever *verbum sat.*"[19]

The epitome of self-improvement invoked in the full title of *Hugginiana*, Dick Whittington, was, of course, accompanied by a cat and so is Huggins, as an almost equally noteworthy resident of 92 Broadway is his famous "ski-agraphic Cat." Huggins declares in the *Commercial Advertiser* for April 23, 1804, that he is "the keeper of one of the most beautifulest animals in creation, together with a tame rat for the amusement of the Ladies." This prompted another of Huggins' rivals, one H. J. Hassey, to attempt to outdo the Skiagraphic cat by offering an entire menagerie for sale at his premises at No. 122 Front Street, which was barber shop, aviary, and kennel rolled into one. 122 Front Street, declares Hassey, contains a "numerous and choice collection of Birds, Pigs (that is, Guinea Pigs), Squirrels, Rabbits and Dogs of every sort, size and colour." And in March 1804, Hassey arrives in the New York *Evening Post* in the new guise of Miltonic imitator in a sprightly assault upon Huggins, who is compared to the figure of Sin in Book II of *Paradise Lost:*

> Thus when with boasted vaunt the Barber pours
> His epithets, of pride and envy mix'd,
> On more successful rival in his trade
> Crown'd with fair fame, well earn'd, and grac'd withal
> By modest manners, the foul Brood return
> To gnaw, in secret, his envenom'd sides,
> And prick, with self condemning stings, their Sire.
> With vast pretensions and high-sounding phrase,
> Phantasmagoric, Cat-like, mewing noise;
> A razor in his hand, and strutting forth
> In furiate in his heart, yet feigning fair,
> And offering to the crowd smooth words like soap.
>
> (*Hugginiana,* p. 199)

Hassey, or possibly in this case his paid poetical copywriter, writes a most able Miltonic burlesque in the manner of John Philips's "The Splendid Shilling." Huggins next becomes Satan himself and is described in council with a host of servile lackeys:

> Amid his Block-Heads and the gaping throng
> Of menial hirelings crowding to the stall
> Where he presides, like Satan midst his friends.
>
> (*Hugginiana,* p. 69)

Against the mendacious boasts of this demonic throng, the figure of Truth personified appears, introducing a new hero, a Christ-like redeemer who will triumph over the forces of evil. This is none other than H. J. Hassey of 122 Front Street:

> Yet when radiant TRUTH
> Angelic led forth HASSEY to his view,
> Her Hassey—and recited half a page
> Of his unrivall'd worth, the charm was broke.

Apall'd the shaver shrunk; nor dar'd awhile
T'assail the ear of beauty, as of old
The ear of Eve by Satan was beguil'd
With false assurance and fair promise won
To her destruction:—Silence clos'd the mouths
Of the Grim Monster and the Knight of Soap.

(Hugginiana, p. 69)

The poem continues with a vision of Hassey's "Feather'd choir" of birds triumphing over Huggins' Skiagraphic cat and ends by describing Hassey surrounded by his aviary, a picture of contentment that is contrasted with the dire fate awaiting Huggins:

Protected by his worth, while one retires
To useful labour, 'midst his warbling throng,
The other struts and puffs in empty boast,
Finds all his bluster vain—then dies forgot!

(Hugginiana, p. 70)

Four days later, also in the *Post,* Huggins notes that Hassey, the "bird-catcher," "seems anxious to be on a par with the Skiagraphic cat, which is an enemy to the feathered tribe." Huggins warns Hassey that he is in danger of having the Skiagraphic cat set upon him: "this infuriated animal . . . will be let loose, and the consequences will be truly *barberous*" (*Hugginiana,* p. 71)

On July 11, 1808, the readers of the New York *Commercial Advertiser* were presented with "A Modern Rape of the Lock." This is the full text of the puff:

A MODERN RAPE OF THE LOCK.

"HAPPY the FRISSEUR, who in *Delia's* HAIR,
    With licens'd fingers uncontroul'd may rove;
And happy in his death, the DANCING BEAR,
    Who died to make *Pomatum* for my LOVE.

Last night, as o'er the page of Love's despair
    My *Delia* bent, deliciously to grieve,
I stood, a treacherous loiterer, by her chair,
    And drew the FATAL SCISSORS from my sleeve.

And would not at that instant oe'r my thread
    The SHEARS OF ATROPOS had open'd then,
And when I rent the Lock from Delia's head
    Had cut me sudden from the sons of men.

> She heard the *scissors* that fair lock divide,
>   And while my heart with transport panted big.
> She cast a fury frown on me, and cried
>   You stupid puppy, you have spoil'd my WIG."
>
> *Instanter* go—bid HUGGINS quickly fly,
>   "Tis he alone, the mischief can repair—
> He gave the touch, that thus deceiv'd thy eye,
>   And made the Wig to look like natural *Hair.*

Very few of the *Advertiser's* readers will have known of the source of this poem, and Huggins offers no hints to guide them. The poem sees him pressing recent British parodic writing into the service of his wigs, or "Fac Similes of the Human Head of Hair." The first four stanzas derive from Robert Southey's *The Amatory Poems of Abel Shufflebottom.* The opening quatrain is the third stanza of Southey's "Elegy III" (in which "The Poet Expatiates on the Beauty of Delia's Hair") and stanzas two to four are borrowed almost verbatim from his "Elegy IV." Here Huggins gestures toward contemporary English parody, aligning himself with that currently vibrant tradition and exploiting its comic energy. Yet Huggins also offers an interesting and suggestive refinement of his formal model. Southey's parody of the florid and rococo extravagances of Della Cruscan sensibility was prompted by William Gifford's glancing reference in *The Mæviad* (1796) to the callow superficiality of poets who have "learn'd by rote, to rave of Delia's charms."[20] Gifford had previously offered, in his *The Baviad* (1791), a fearsome and vitriolic assault upon the bejeweled and overwrought nature of Della Cruscan verse. Though Southey does not endorse Gifford's polemic against the Jacobin politics of Robert Merry and his school, he follows the stylistic criticism leveled in the *Baviad* in the *Amatory Poems.* One of the key charges against the Della Cruscans in the satirical writing of both Gifford and Southey was that it paid undue attention to mundanities: "the death of a bug, the flight of an earwig, the miscarriage of a cock-chaffer, or some other event of equal importance."[21] Huggins, however, is in the business of the rhetorical elevation of the mundane. The artifice implicit in a lady's wig, a signifier of misplaced poetic priorities in Southey, and a signifier of misplaced moral priorities in the poem of Pope's echoed in Huggins' title, is here celebrated. "A Modern Rape of the Lock" borrows a parodic attack upon poetic over-elaboration and the bejeweled celebration of triviality and co-opts it to sell hair-pieces.

IV

The relationship of Huggins' work to the "muse of satire" is not limited to acts of parodic imitation of satirical models borrowed from the likes of Cowper, Southey, and Wolcot. *Hugginiana* contains much explicit political satire. As well as fighting battles with rival hairdressers, Huggins also has an eye on rather more deadly strife. Huggins' puffing rodomontade has clear political overtones, and I shall now offer an analysis of the sociopolitical context of *Hugginiana* and its relationship both to European politics and the more provincial, but related, concerns of American partisan conflict. As the East Coast newspaper the *Troy Gazette* notes in 1806, "John R. D. Huggins, a hair dresser in New York, proverbial for his . . . humorous advertisements, frequently turns the greatest events in the political and military world to his own account, and makes them subjects for his wit and raillery."[22] Thus, for example, shortly before the Battle of Trafalgar, Huggins comments that "Lord Nelson is doubtless yet in pursuit of the French fleet; but were he and his officers to land at New-York, there is a strong presumption they would repair to the Dressing Academy of John R. D. Huggins, No. 92, Broadway" (*Hugginiana,* pp. 98–99). The Anglophilia evident in Huggins' constant parodic borrowings from British poetry is echoed in the pro-English bias of his political satire. After Trafalgar, Huggins' sympathies are made even more explicit in his announcement that he has for sale two new kinds of combs, "the Collingwood cable and the much admired TRAFALGAR LAURELS for ladies heads" (*Hugginiana,* p. 110), named after the English triumph and one of its heroes, Cuthbert Collingwood (who commanded the British fleet after Nelson was mortally wounded). Unlike Nelson's navy, the French fleet would be less than welcome at the Dressing Academy, as Huggins manifests a clear anti-Gallicanism in his work. His oft-repeated refusal to stock Parisian hairdressing accessories and ceaseless celebration of British goods such as Packwood's strops are charged with Anglophile political resonance. This antipathy to France is perhaps best understood in terms of contemporary American politics. Many of Huggins' advertisements were originally published in the pro-Federalist New York *Evening Post,* and in this period anti-Gallicanism was one of the defining characteristics of the Federalist party, as opposed to the studied neutrality or residual pro-Revolutionary sympathy still evident in Jeffersonian Republican circles. Underpinning *Hugginiana*'s "wit and raillery" is pro-Federalist political satire. Indeed, Jefferson receives some fairly rough satirical handling in *Hugginiana* In June 1805, Huggins describes his caricature of PRAIRIE DOG:

> Although of the canine species, it represents a certain *Great Personage,* of whom the head of the animal preserves an exact likeness. Bonaparte is represented as a *Hornet* stinging him behind; which severe discipline, acts as a violent *emetic* on the terror-struck Spaniel—While under the dreadful operation of this new medicine, well known in Holland, Spain, Italy, and most parts of the Continent of Europe, by the name of *Napoleon Physic,* he

reluctantly disgorges TWO MILLIONS OF DOLLARS at the feet of a certain Marquis. The cruel and unfeeling Don exultingly capers and sings all this while before poor Tray, who is represented to be in the most convulsive agonies.

(Hugginiana, p. 128)

The great personage referred to is doubtless President Jefferson and the money flushed out of him by "Napoleon Physic" refers to the Louisiana Purchase. Huggins' political satire is best understood as part of the Federalist satirical tradition established by the Hartford, or Connecticut, Wits during the 1780s and 1790s in the work of Huggins' customers and eulogists Dwight and Alsop, and in that of Lemuel Hopkins, John Trumbull, and Joel Barlow before his conversion to Jeffersonianism. The Hartford group's vigorous political satire attacked Jeffersonian democracy and French infidelity in all its forms. Federalist polemic such as that of Dwight attacked the pernicious influence of French thought in the new republic: "The outlaws of Europe, the fugitives from the pillory and the gallows, have undertaken to assist our abandoned citizens, in the pleasing work of destroying Connecticut. . . . Can imagination paint anything more dreadful on this side of hell!"[23] Huggins shared his friend's antipathy to France, and his anti-Gallicanism extends beyond his unwillingness to sell French hair care products. Writing in the midst of the Napoleonic wars, his self-appointment as "Empereur du Friseurs" is underpinned by a preoccupation with another notable contemporary emperor, Napoleon. *Hugginiana* is dedicated to George III and Gustav Adolphus (who had joined the anti-French alliance in 1805), a choice explicitly made because of their status as bulwarks of the anti-Napoleonic cause: "To George the Third, King of Great Britain, and Gustavus Adolphus the Fourth, King of Sweden, the only reigning Monarchs, myself excepted, who have made an effectual stand against the arms of influence of the *TYRANT OF THE WORLD,* This Work is most graciously dedicated, by their Imperial, Royal and BARBER-OUS Brother, DESBORUS THE FIRST" (*Hugginiana*, p. 5). In the *Evening Post* of January 13, 1806, Huggins writes that Napoleon is "now Emperor of the French" while "J. R. D. HUGGINS maintains his empire in the circle of brilliant fashion and elegant taste." However, he goes on, "mark the difference! Bonaparte acquired his supremacy by usurpation, whereas the *Imperial Leader* of the *Frizzing tribe,* and principal of the Fashionable Seminary, by hair cutting" (*Hugginiana*, p. 110). In the same month, Huggins adopts the tone of Napoleon himself in a bulletin from "The Emperor of the Frisures, to the Citizens of the Metropolis":

CITIZENS!—Victory has every where rested on our razors. The enemy has been defeated in all directions. I hasten to communicate the detail. On the

25th Thermidor, a courier arrived, bringing intelligence, that the enemy were in the vicinity of Rue de Broadway, and endeavouring by forced marches to turn our left. I immediately sent a strong detachment, composed of the fifth regiment of *Puffs,* who are the *flower* of my forces, the 4th Brigade of the division of Pomade; and a *corps de reserve* of the Pioneering *Curlers;* under the command of Generals Dawsonet, Hearte, and Paris, with orders to *beat the enemy.* The rencounter took place at the fort of *Rue de Greenwich*—it was severe indeed—the enemy gave way in all directions, and before the *combing* up of the main body, they were completely routed—not a man of them escaped. 531,000,000 were found dead in the field. We took 675,000,000 stand of arms and all their Artillery, &c. . . . The EMPEROR will feel himself flattered by the congratulations of the citizens, on this splendid victory over his inveterate rivals, at his Head Quarters, No. 92, Broadway—where he executes all kinds of ornamental Hair-work, &c. in a style of *Imperial* perfection.

J. R. D. HUGGINS
Emperor de les modes, et Roi de Barbiers.
(*Hugginiana,* pp. 114–15)

The *Troy Gazette* sees this parody as "severely satirizing the 'enlightened' Corsican, . . . a shrewd and enlightened burlesque on the style of modern European bullies and braggadocios."[24] "Bulletin the Fourth" of March 28 is reproduced alongside a cartoon that makes Huggins' pro-English sympathies even more explicit. Huggins, mounted on a charging bull wearing a collar marked with the words "John Bull" and wielding one of Packwood's razors, upends the tiny figure of Napoleon. The heroic figure of the strop-wielder is saying "I'll pack you to the Devil," while Bonaparte, his sword falling lamely to the ground, laments that "I rose like a rocket/ And I fall like the stick." The message of the fruitlessness of war is evident in the title of the cartoon, "The Unprofitable Contest of trying to do each other the most harm." The same advertisement contains a short blank verse poem, "Peace Proclaimed," which reinforces this sentiment:

Secure in foes defeated; battle won,
And Fashion's Empire subject to his sway;
Victorious Huggins smiles—not lavish he
Of Orphan's anguish, and of widow's tears; . . .
His razor oft in battle-blood embrued
He sheathes; and deck'd with many a Laurel, sleeps
The harmless Curler; or at Beauty's call
Down her fair neck in conscious mazes guides
The straying Ringlet; and delights to weave,
The graceful Frizette for the brow of youth.

(*Hugginiana,* p. 116)

Unlike Napoleon's, the victories of Desborus the First are "harmless" and are not achieved at the cost of great human suffering; children are not orphaned nor women widowed in his triumph over "Fashion's Empire." Huggins is "BARBER-OUS," while Napoleon is simply barbarous. Bonaparte and Huggins are both phlebotomists, but when the barber lets blood, it is in the cause of life and beauty rather than for the tyrant's lust for power.

The prefatory material to *Hugginiana* contains a tribute verse from *The Mirror* ("A small Poetical Volume by a Friend to the Fair"), which also lends credence to the reading of Huggins' puffs as anti-Napoleonic satire. "Flaxen Love Locks" salutes "the *Emperor* of the tongs and comb" and envisages the flower of American womanhood wearing tresses dressed by Huggins alone and burning French-produced wigs:

> Through nature's garb, we will our lilies show
> Soon let her ringlets o'er our bosoms flow,
> And burn our wigs to let proud Gallia know,
> With Huggins' tasteful art we'll kill each beau,
> Nor with false locks, from guillotine, make show.
>
> (*Hugginiana*, p. 12)

The author recognizes and sympathizes with Huggins' anti-Gallicanism, and shares his repudiation of "proud Gallia," whose superficially fashionable beauty is underpinned by violence and terror. In this context, Huggins' boast that he "has for sale at his School for fashions, an elegant and extensive assortment of hair work, executed by the first artists of his profession in London" (*Hugginiana*, p. 110) seems charged with Anglophile political resonance.

V

I shall conclude with a discussion of the implications of Huggins' use of imitation and parody, which is complex and suggestive. First of all, his work consciously exploits the techniques of English burlesque, notably of mock-heroic burlesque. Such poetry, after the manner of Philips' "The Splendid Shilling," often exploits a humorous discrepancy between elevated form and mundane content. Thus the comic impact of Isaac Hawkins Browne's *A Pipe of Tobacco* derives from the application of the idioms of the likes of Pope, Thomson, and Swift to the subject of smoking. Huggins' parody relies upon the same incongruity, but, at the same time, offers an interesting variant upon burlesque. Applying an inappropriately grandiose manner to announce his qualities as a barber is amusing—and wit to this day is a key technique of advertising—but in the end Huggins' ironic and knowing exploitation of the dislocation between his register and his theme actually serves to dignify his subject. The cumulative effect of Huggins' parodic method is subtly to associate his advertising copy with decidedly more elevated cultural forms. Because of its verve and engaging comic brio, *Hugginiana*'s parody, while it exploits the cultural remove between its form and its content, does not involve the diminution of Huggins' products, which are subtly celebrated and, in the final analysis, elevated. Huggins' mercantile burlesque has its comic cake and eats it, too.

Huggins' comic, almost encyclopedic mixing of cultural forms is close to Northrop Frye's notion of the Menippean satire, the heterogeneous satire that mixes literary genre. Gary Dyer's description of Peacock's novels might as easily be applied to *Hugginiana:* "Menippean satires often employ multiple narrative voices, reproduce poems or songs, contain dialogues or symposia . . . or vary their media to draw attention to their materiality."[25] Also of relevance here is Gary Kelly's notion of the "quasi-novel," a term he uses to describe various Romantic-period Menippean works: Egan's *Life in London,* Southey's *The Doctor,* and Wilson's *Noctes Ambrosianae.* Kelly's description of the quasi-novel as "disconnected and desultory, to accommodate . . . diverse materials, . . . [and] loosely held together by a narrative frame of recurring characters"[26] is highly pertinent to Huggins' method. Furthermore, his argument that the quasi-novel "incorporated elements of other, accepted literary discourses . . . in order to dignify the subliterary form of the novel" is absolutely central to *Hugginiana,* a work in a cultural form, advertising copy, that is a step or two lower down the "subliterary" ladder than the novel, and, indeed, one that marks its cultural aspirations by incorporating novelistic techniques themselves, as well as gesturing toward the *belle-lettrist* forms employed by more orthodox quasinovelists. If the quasi-novel works through assimilative incorporation, then in *Hugginiana* this elevation is achieved through the work's governing parodic and imitative methodology.

I shall conclude with a brief discussion of a related aspect of *Hugginiana,* in which its crossing of generic boundaries is taken to its logical conclusion, given that the text seems in places to seek to erase its own generic status as advertising copy. Early in *Hugginiana,* Huggins offers a disquisition upon what one might label tonsorial linguistics, arguing that there is a clear difference between the activities of the everyday barber (which he describes as an "ignoble trade") and his own profession: "superficial observers will not readily discover the distinction between A KNIGHT OF THE COMB and a *barber;* [but] to correct minds that distinction will be obvious. The one is a proficient not only in embellishing the *head* and beautifying the countenance divine, but in all the accomplishments of a finished gentleman: the other is a mere *Jaw scavenger*" (*Hugginiana,* p. 21). Thus "Knight of the Comb" is not a circumlocutory method of saying "barber"; the two signifiers mark an actual and tangible distinction between different things. Similarly,

Huggins does not work in a shop, but in his "dressing rooms," and calling them such is not the dignifying periphrasis common in advertising copy, but a reflection of their real difference from a "barber's shop": "in short, there is as manifest a difference between a Knight of the Comb and a Barber, as there is between HUGGINS' DRESSING ROOMS and a barber's shop" (*Hugginiana,* p. 21). Here his copy seeks to disguise and deny its reliance upon rhetorical artifice. Huggins attempts to convince us that his self-presentations as the Emperor, the Knight, the proud possessor of the Dressing Rooms and later the "Academy of Fashions, 92, Broadway" are not shameless exaggerations, but the actual facts of the matter. Similarly, the full title of *Hugginiana,* while it draws attention to its self-reflective preoccupation with the art of advertising ("the art of making a noise in the world"), simultaneously emphasizes that it is not rhetoric alone that has elevated Huggins to his current preeminence as an Emperor, given that he has "talents enough to support the title." Indeed, on occasions Huggins offers mock disdain for the very activity of advertisement: "Modest merit is content with the approbation evinced by the unexampled liberality of a discerning community: else may J. R. D. H. as is the fashion among the subordinate ranks of his community, claim extraordinary notice by the aid of newspaper PUFFS.—But this he disdains" (*Hugginiana,* p. 98). Other barbers puff, Huggins reflects reality: "John R. D. Huggins is never flattered in being extolled as the best shaver in New-York or the known world" (*Hugginiana,* p. 103). In an advertisement placed in the *Evening Post* on December 21, 1805, Huggins condemns empty puffing: his rivals in the "*Ignoranti*" have fancied, that [they had] only to scribble off an advertisement, and they would at once be exalted to [a] high state of public patronage. . . . But dull as their own razors must they be, if they cannot discriminate between the support of *genius, worth* and *talents,* and that short lived patronage, the effect of *curiosity, pity* or *ignorance*" (*Hugginiana,* p. 108). Huggins "obtained his title" by merit, having "*genius, worth* and *talents*" enough; it is his rivals who rely upon specious puffing and who are unable to substantiate their rhetoric, making a noise that is ultimately empty, relying upon self-promotion rather than actual talent. Huggins has been "called" the "best barber" rather than idly claiming that role for himself. Huggins attempts to convince us that his self-presentation as an Emperor is not dependent upon extreme forms of advertising rodomontade, but simply presents the truth. If the quasi-novel gestures toward generic forms above and beyond those of the novel, then *Hugginiana* attempts an even more ambitious escape from its genre. Huggins' final, paradoxical manoeuvre, in these puffs that deny their status as puffery, is to claim that his work is not advertising at all.

Notes

1. See Arthur Hornblow's discussion of the early New York stage in *A History of the Theatre in America,* 2 vols (Philadelphia and London: J. B. Lippincott, 1919), I, 41–65.

2. Van Wyck Brooks, *The World of Washington Irving* (New York: Dutton, 1944), 201–202.

3. Moore's visit to the United States in 1803–1804 took place after Huggins began his work, and before the poet of the *Thomas Little* lyrics began his satirical career, and the diehard Federalist Huggins would have found the Jeffersonian politics evident in the apostate Barlow's later work hard to stomach.

4. Quoted in John Richard Desborus Huggins, *Hugginiana; or, Huggins' Fantasy, being a Collection of the most esteemed modern Literary Productions. Exposing the art of making a noise in the world, without beating a drum, or crying oysters; and shewing how, like Whittington of old, who rose from nothing to be Lord Mayor of London, a mere Barber may become an Emperor, if he has spirit enough to assume, and talents enough to support the title* (hereafter *Hugginiana*) (New York: H. C. Southwick, 1808), 10–11; hereafter cited parenthetically in the text.

5. Quoted in Thomas Hood, "The Art of Advertising," *London Magazine and Review,* N.S. (February 1825), I, 251.

6. Ibid.

7. Quoted in Jacob Larwood and John Camden Hotton, *The History of Signboards* (1866), new edition (London: Chatto and Windus, 1914), 95–96.

8. *The Tatter,* ed. Donald F. Bond, 3 vols. (Oxford: Clarendon Press, 1987), III, 253.

9. The original of Strap was the barber Hugh Hewson, who died as late as 1809, and who festooned his premises in St. Martin-in-the Fields with Latin quotations. See *Notes and Queries,* 3.68 (February 15, 1851), 123.

10. *Harper's Magazine,* November 1866, 788.

11. Neil McKendrick, "George Packwood and the Commercialisation of Shaving: The Art of Eighteenth-Century Advertising or 'The Way to Get Money and be Happy'," in Neil McKendrick, John Brewer, and J. H. Plumb, *The Birth of a Consumer Society: The Commercialization of Eighteenth-Century England* (London: Europa Publications, 1982), 146–94.

12. The phrase is Thomas Carlyle's. Thomas Carlyle, *Past and Present,* ed. A. M. D. Hughes (Oxford: Clarendon Press, 1918), 128.

13. Biscarolaza replies that "Don Emanuel amused himself for a short time after his arrival from the Spanish court, in the shop of *the knight of the comb* merely to keep his hand in: but was careful to avoid contracting any bad habits, of which he will be happy to convince any person who will do him the honor of calling at his dressing office No. 72, Wall-street" (*Hugginiana,* 43).

14. Woodworth's *Poems, odes, songs, and other metrical effusions* (1818) contains a poetic eulogy to Huggins, "Cupid's Lamentation, or the Puff Allegorical."

15.   From Barber's shops what benefits we trace?
       How great their 'vantage to the human race?
       That source of civil culture unpossess'd,

What wonder reason slowly fills the breast?
Thou knight renown'd! possess'd of equal skill
The comb to flourish, or to ply the quill,
Whose bright effusions, wond'ring, oft I see,
And own myself in message beat by thee,

Richard Alsop and Theodore Dwight, *The Echo* (New York, 1807), 173.

16. For the extensive use of poetic copy in late Georgian advertising, see my "'The Praise of Blacking': W. F. Deacon and Early Nineteenth-Century Advertising-Related Parody," *Romanticism on the Net* (August 1999), <http:// users.ox.ac.uk/~scat0385/warren.html>.

17. The best discussion of this passage is Marcus Wood's *Radical Satire and Print Culture 1790–1822* (Oxford: Clarendon Press, 1992), 188–91.

18. Quirk published the following squib in July 1806:

Reader! didst ever hear of little Jack,
The *puffer Barber* frizeur *quack?*
Who holds out sign, come in who may
At number ninety-two Broadway;
And strives by every art to lug in
All who've heard of Jacky Hug-in?

Huggins republished this lampoon in the *Commercial Advertiser* for July 28, 1806, with the following parodic lines added:

"This right hand, rudest, doggrel club in
Shall give the knave a dreadful drubbing:
Ere long I'll write some lines sonorous,
And *quack, quack, quack,* shall be my chorus."

(*Hugginiana,* 135)

19. *Hugginiana,* 141–42.

20. William Gifford, *The Baviad and The Maeviad* (London: S. Tipper, 1810), 89.

21. Ibid., 48.

22. Quoted in *Hugginiana,* 11.

23. Attributed to Theodore Dwight in Vernon Louis Parrington, *The Colonial Mind* 1620-1800 (New York: Harcourt, Brace and Co., 1927), 360.

24. Quoted in *Hugginiana,* 12.

25. Gary Dyer, *British Satire and the Politics of Style, 1789–1832* (Cambridge: Cambridge University Press, 1997), 18.

26. Gary Kelly, *English Fiction of the Romantic Period, 1789–1830* (London: Longman, 1989), 253. Kelly's concept is something of a catch-all, designed as it is to categorize a number of Romantic-period works that defy categorization as "novels."

Chapter 11 ∿

Pantomime as Satire: Mocking a Broken Charm

Marilyn Gaull

> Perhaps 'tis pretty to force together
> Thoughts so all unlike each other;
> To mutter and mock a broken charm,
> To dally with wrong that does no harm
>
> —S. T. Coleridge, *Christabel,* lines 666–69

The most popular British theatrical form in the early decades of the nineteenth century, pantomime not only reflected and shaped the audience, the dramatic tradition, and such contemporary poets and novelists as Wordsworth, Keats, Byron, Jane Austen, and Dickens, but also it reflected and shaped the intellectual life of Great Britain during its tumultuous passage from the Enlightenment to the Modern period.[1] With its topical jokes and transgressive behavior, it clearly was not the frivolous entertainment that traditional drama historians considered it to be, nor, as Allardyce Nicoll claims, did it "retard the development of more serious drama." (IV, 153). Rather, among certain contemporaries such as Hazlitt and Thackeray, whether they liked pantomime or not, it was, at the very least, as Leigh Hunt claimed, "the best medium of dramatic satire" (*Examiner,* January 26, 1817). Specifically, between 1806 and 1823, when Joseph Grimaldi played the part of Clown at Covent Garden, pantomime, according to David Mayer in *Harlequin in His Element,* evolved from "a cheerful and somewhat mindless entertainment" to "the only effective means of satire to hold the stage" (p. 6). And in her sweeping and original study, *Illegitimate Theater in London, 1770–1840,* Jane Moody, points out that while still at Sadler's Wells, Charles Dibdin as the arranger, Grimaldi, "transformed" the pastoral pantomime of John Rich "into a satirical, whimsical entertainment which took as its subject the entrepreneurial and illusory character of the early nineteenth-century city" (p. 210), and, more, "seemed to capture the desires and nightmares of a modern metropolis" (p. 225). Before Steven Jones, however, in *Satire and Romanticism,* no one to my knowledge had suggested the range and complexity of its satiric role or suggested any other role.[2]

Whatever its reputation—as popular, frivolous, powerful, satirical—with no surviving authentic examples, pantomime is something of a mystery. Arranged rather than written, improvisational in many ways, there are no complete scripts although the songs and scene sequences survive in the souvenir booklets sold at the theaters (Mayer 365–68). In the context of other performances, however, and in an extended historical and contemporary context, pantomime appears to be the consummate expression of both Romanticism and of satire, which, as Steven Jones observed, mutually define each other (p. 1). Among the many Romanticisms, the one that is most suited to satire and to pantomime is, like most of the writing during the period, primarily urban, social, and terrestrial, as committed to human experience as even that reputed isolationist and nature poet, William Wordsworth, was committed to "the world / Of all of us,—the place where, in the end, / We find our happiness, or not at all" (*The Prelude,* 1805, XI, 143–45). Pantomime recorded and offered a critique of "the world / Of all of us," of contemporary culture, however it was conceived, the taste, style, manners, fashions, commerce, technology, laws, literature, politics, the theater itself. Indeed, although new ones only appeared at best four times a year, and as an afterpiece in a long theatrical evening, pantomime was so encompassing, allusive, and eclectic that it serves, again to cite David Mayer, as "an unofficial and informal chronicle of the age" (p. 7).

But it also expressed the historical preoccupations of the age: its energies were derived from the past, both ancient and cumulative, reaching back to the ritual prehistory of drama, back to the same British folk festivals that influenced Shakespeare, back to the intellectualized satire of the Enlightenment, and out to the popular entertainments in contemporary London markets and street fairs, which themselves reenact festivals beyond memory. However complex its ceremonial, aesthetic, historic, and political referents, in the opening decades of the nineteenth century, pantomime animated and explored those perennial human forces and appetites that are the subject of all drama and just as often the object of all satire in that hybrid form that is characteristic of Romantic writing. In brief, like *The Intimations Ode,* or *Ode to the West Wind, Childe Harold, Don Juan,* even *The Marriage of Heaven and Hell,* the pantomime is a mighty summing up, a raucous assimilation of competing, even irreconcilable ancient and contemporary styles, periods, ideas, ontologies (as Anne Mellor calls them in *English Romantic Irony*), creating in the end a totally new but familiar form—the generation of such forms being itself a defining characteristic of Romantic literature.[3]

The pantomime that I am interested in, the Covent Garden pantomime from 1806 to 1830, extended the potential of a stage that already, in spite of legal restrictions, held unprecedented power. Six to eight thousand people a night could and did attend the theaters in London, while many thousands more attended performances by both touring companies and local talent in provincial capitals such as Bristol, Edinburgh, and Manchester all over the kingdom. Perhaps the stress of the long war against Napoleon, the threat of invasion, the economic deprivations, social unrest, inadequate educations, the failure of religious institutions, the whole litany of what made urban life in England so ripe for reform also created a hunger for theater, for the familiar and communal experience it offered, the repetitive, ritualistic, and symbolic behavior. Still, the theater was an unpromising if not hostile place for any art except satire. With spoken drama restricted and censored since 1737, plays that did reach performance had been sanitized, both religion and politics, the two great subjects of tragedy, set aside as too dangerous for the volatile crowds that attended the theater and too sacred for such a profane setting.[4]

In the unlicensed houses, where pantomime developed in the eighteenth century, restrictions against speech on stage became creative opportunities for all kinds of performance: dramatists approached the forbidden obliquely, elevated domestic life into an analogy for the nation, used the common man in his common life with common miseries as analogies for an impoverished, overworked, and displaced population, and substituted popular superstition and supernatural effects for divine interventions. Limited in language, all illegitimate drama—though none as extravagantly as pantomime—developed stunning visual effects in settings, stage manners, technological tricks, and music, which, although legally required to accompany dialogue, became essential to drama, as it still is, and stimulated another art form. Experiments with melodrama, historical spectacles, burlettas, animal and nautical dramas, and pantomime tested the limits of the law, while developing that broad gestural and mostly mimed style of acting and signage that recalled and parodied both Greek drama and Shakespeare and became the comic codes of the music halls and silent films.

The licensed theaters adopted similar techniques, styles, and subjects to attract larger audiences that were, in turn, and ironically, too noisy for the subtleties of speech they were actually allowed to offer. Competing for audiences, the licensed theaters appropriated from the unlicensed the creative techniques for their Otways and Sheridans, for the high tragedies and sentimental dramas, and, consequently, without question, trivializing high drama, in effect parodied, and even satirized it. Implicitly, such appropriations became not only an artistic critique of legitimate drama, but also of legitimacy itself, its insufficiency, its failure to represent itself in the public domain, its dependence on the techniques of popularity and illegitimacy.

Reacting against, circumventing, or overtly playing out the implications of the licensing acts, all dramatic performance was not only a satire of the authorities that enforced the laws but also a satire of the dramatic tradition from which most theaters, actors, and dramatists had been excluded. This principle is nowhere better illustrated than in the most restricted of theaters, the true popular theater, the "penny gaffs," where the satirical overtakes even the sentimental to which, along with anything lurid and bloody, these audiences were addicted. For these performances, a hundred to a thousand people, all of whom could have been arrested merely for attending, gathered in warehouses, storefronts, even pits dug in the ground, where undernourished children, prostitutes, or actors who had failed on all other stages offered burlesques, bawdy songs, reenactments of local crimes, and twenty-minute versions of *Hamlet* or *Macbeth*.[5] Always on the run, setting up shop in a different place every day, sometimes several times a day, no one was better than these criminal-actors at impersonating kings and courtiers, at the simplification, the discrepancies, the critical juxtaposition, the trivialization, and the critique of royalty, of authority on which satire depends.

For the actors, however, and the audiences, the "penny gaffs" were satirical in both the contemporary and traditional sense. In contemporary terms the performances were satirical in the exaggerations, simplifications, and literalizations of familiar public or literary figures, their language, manners, and ideas, the trivialization of power and of grand passion in the rags and patches of popular theater, revealing or ridiculing the pretensions and arrogance of the classes from which the actors and many in the audience were excluded and defending the social values of their community. In the traditional sense, the "penny gaffs" perhaps more than any other performance other than pantomime, reverted to the prehistory of the theater, acting out the human necessity for illusion, for a dramatic tradition that had been denied to them, for mastering power by imitating and trivializing it, a ritual behavior as ancient and unaccountable as courtship and religious ceremony. Pantomime, insofar as it uses many of the techniques of the penny gaffs, partakes of this subterranean energy, ritual necessity, as well as the sophistication of the licensed stage.[6]

Given the conventions and conditions of all theater during the Romantic period, any drama in performance, especially in the licensed houses, appeared satiric: an ironic displacement of reality, noble ideals and grand emotions simplified, exaggerated, trivialized, translated into irrelevant gestures, inaudible rhetoric, inappropriately juxtaposed, in massive spaces with small stages, bad air, grotesque lighting, to a noisy, inattentive and indifferent audience—who themselves were often satirized on the stage. Consider the usual comic or even tragic actor, isolated from common experience in a two-dimensional setting, his desperate, heroic, idealistic, or merely inflated goals and self-conceptions expressed to musical accompaniment in an artificial language, to another character or to no one in particular, in a bounded space, entangled in contrived conflicts, pretending to ignore the larger world from which it is being observed, an audience that intrudes with comments, insults, even animals sounds, or worse, totally disregards him even while they comprise the social reality against which the character's behavior is implicitly measured.

Moreover, each actor's performance is in the shadow of all the other actors who have played the part before him, with constant comparisons being raised by the new form of theater reviews. Or, because actors are under contract to playhouses, and may play many different parts, his or her career may appear to be a crazy collage of characters, an accumulation of irreconcilable roles that a popular actor or actress such as a Kean, Garrick, or Siddons has played before—today Macbeth, tomorrow a clown. And, because actors owned their own costumes, they often wore the same robes and crowns, however anachronistic, shabby, ill-fitting, or unsuitable, in wildly different performances. Expose this character to spectators who have paid money, not a lot of money, to be distracted or amused or even enlightened by its discomforts, to judge its reactions, repeatedly abused and applauded, and this grotesque and inhumane activity that we call drama becomes satire. At some point, the dislocation, simplification, juxtaposition, exaggeration, trivialization, and artifice of drama become the familiar techniques of Gulliver in Brobdingnag.

The most elegant and sophisticated dramas become satirical merely from the discrepancies between the play and the theater, between the action on the stage and the auditorium in which it is played, between characters being played and the larger context that includes an audience of dandies and shopkeepers, observers who cannot hear or understand the script, who have financially invested in imaginary ordeals, judging them more on how moving or authentic the suffering rather than the outcome, which was often altered to suit the public's preference for happy endings. Just as it was common in ancient Greece to conclude a series of tragedies with a "satyr" play, a comedy such as Euripides' *Cyclops,* which ridiculed the gods and parodied the heroes, in Romantic theater, a six- or seven-hour evening of melodrama and interludes would end with a pantomime. Even *King Lear,* the quintessential tragedy, looks quite different when, as on June 1, 1807, the program on which it appears concludes with the eighty-fourth performance of *Mother Goose,* in which the supernatural agent is played by the aging cross-dressing Samuel Simmons, who might be Lear himself in some warped afterlife.[7]

If the very size of the theaters, the conventions of acting, and the behavior of the audience created the conditions for satire, so did the new aesthetic. Conventionally, fantasy, artifice, and illusion were the dramatic realities, the only dimensions that worked on these stages. The new realism, however, scenic verisimilitude and naturalistic acting, which Gillen Wood traces so insightfully in *The Shock of the Real* (pp. 17–46), "mimic sights that ape / The absolute presence of reality," as Wordsworth observes, become satirical, a "life-like mockery" (*The Prelude,* VII, 248–49, 263).[8] Ideally, theater was an escape, an alternative reality that succeeded best when it offered illusion: "How willingly we travel, and how far!" (*The Prelude* 1805, *VII,* 300), Wordsworth observes of a scene in *Jack and the Beanstalk,* at Sadler's Wells, in which Jack dressed in black and wearing a sign on his chest declaring him "*Invisible*" sneaks up on the sleeping giant. The realism that panorama and diorama introduced into pantomime also contributed to the satiric effects, the allusions to contemporary events and the juxtaposition of familiar settings against which fantasy characters acted out their bizarre and lawless parts.

While the new "naturalistic" aesthetic appeared in both the performing and fine arts, London life itself had acquired a curious theatrical quality, as if artifice and performance had been displaced in part by the regulation of the stage. Dramas, novels, poetry, newspapers, engravings and cartoons, even letters, all depict street scenes, politics, industry, courtship, war, as a theatrical experience, everyone preoccupied with appearance and disguise, with uniforms that convey roles and fashion that disguises them, with manners that mislead, mirrors that enhance, window displays, parades, exhibitions, with being seen as much as seeing and controlling one's public image. Certainly, as Mary Jacobus writes, "Wordsworth's London is above all a city of performance and play-acting, viewed with the 'quick and curious eye' of the half-seduced satire" (p. 33), citing the amazing passage in book VII of *The Prelude* in which he offers the best contemporary impression, satirical in tone, of those who attended the theater: politicians, preachers, merchants, of everyone "in hall, / Court, theatre, conventicle or shop, / In public room or private, park or street, / Each fondly reared on his own pedestal, / Looked out for admiration. Folly, vice, / Extravagance in gesture, mien, and dress, / And all the strife of singularity" (1850, 575–12).[9]

London life itself was the source for historical spectacle, a curious and popular dramatic form that anticipates docudrama, a staging of public and contemporary events, commemorative, celebratory, patriotic, indeed, often the only source of information about great public events such as battles or royal ceremonies, or the only means of disseminating it among the illiterate working and upper classes. *Tableaux vivants,* pageants, and spectacles depicting recent events and contemporary history, "things yet warm with life" (*The Prelude* VII, 313) as Wordsworth observes, encouraged even more authentic scenery, costumes, the "naturalistic" style of acting, which he, among others, believed were "too serious theme for that light place" (*The Prelude* VII, 295). Because exalted or serious subjects enacted in a trivial setting are inevitably satirical, the more accurate the production, the more authentic the details, the more satirical the effect. With the wounds still fresh, the terror of invasion and of loss still pervading London, the storming of the Bastille, or the death of Nelson were translated to the stage in miniature boats, murderous mobs represented by ten people pretending to shout in French, harmless canons, children acting as sailors, all forced to mime or sing by the licensing acts, even the ocean diverted from a nearby stream, the heroic, the epic, the brutality of war, the dignity of death, rehearsed, confined, observed, and repeated—all were, Wordsworth says, "too holy theme for such a place, / And doubtless treated with irreverence" (*The Prelude* VII, 317–318).

Similarly, *Gallic Freedom,* a pageant presented at Sadler's Wells on August 31, 1789, depicting the fall of the Bastille to musical accompaniment, was a spectacle that was produced in an unlicensed, illegitimate, restricted theater, where even the actors were not allowed to speak, as far from free as any place in England. Moreover, as a prison scene it was not only self-referential but also called up the nearly ubiquitous metaphor of the prison-house with which everyone from Bentham to Blake were preoccupied, and evoked the Newgate street festivals where criminals were still publicly executed often for minor crimes, the profound injustice that still marked the lives of the British laboring classes, the very ones who were attending such unlicensed theaters as Sadler's. While it may have been intended to condemn the riots across the channel, it offered instead a vicarious release to the acquiescent citizens of London.

On the other hand, in the *Coronation,* produced at the Drury Lane in August 1820, Robert Elliston mounted a ninety-minute replica of the coronation of George IV, playing the King himself: he included a facsimile of the interior of Westminster Abbey and a procession of 400 authentically costumed actors, an opulent and patriotic celebration of a decadent aristocracy and its ceremonial privileges in an age of popular unrest and democratic revolution, which the populace paid to attend. Surely the production of such an event in such a place for 104 performances was the most devastating royal satire imaginable.[10] Inadvertently, then, confined by the censored script, the stage, and the stylized conventions of acting, these precursors of what we now call docudrama, while educating the public, disseminating contemporary history, and awakening patriotism, satirized the aristocracy of England, the warped legal system which governed the theater, and the people who attended it. As satire, they offered a potent if subversive critique of war, of the arrogance of power, of the wasteful pursuit of money and land, and of the worship of all false gods that were the perennial enemies of art. Since all satire requires at least an implicit defense of values, it is the power of drama itself, of representation, illusion, that is defended even in the historical reenactments, a power that overcomes the reality on which it is based.

Pantomime, however, denies the power of the stage, the power of everything, for while it takes place on the stage, it is as much ritual or even festival as drama. While most theatrical historians trace the pantomime to the commedia dell 'arte, from which it evolved in the eighteenth century, in *The Prelude* Wordsworth astutely identifies the prototype in "ancient comedy," "Thespian times," (1805: 311–312), "When Art was young" (1850, 290). And, after 1806, when Grimaldi appears and the emphasis shifts from Harlequin to Clown, from the lover to the rogue, the obstacle, the fool, it reconnects with its roots in the performances that predated theater. According to Aristotle, tragedy, indeed all drama, originated in such rituals: in satyrs, dithyrambs, or phallic songs, processions of masked and dancing men dressed in goat skins with phallic appendages, playing on improvised musical instruments, chanting insults or "invective" to dispel evil spirits and defend themselves from the dark side of this powerful god while invoking his creative and fertile powers (Elliot, pp. 49–99).

Given the history of Hellenism as an erotic principle in eighteenth-century England, the frequent invocation of the ancient Hellenic tradition in the theaters in everything from the architecture, the ornaments, the names, fashions, and themes in the pantomimes themselves, many of which, at least in the eighteenth century, were adapted from Ovid's *Metamorphoses,* the spirit of ancient Greece suffused the pantomime. To some degree it is an ironic subtext for the forbidden overtly religious satire: banishing the clergy and institutional religion from the stage protected their dignity while inadvertently creating a major public revival of pagan themes, practices, and beliefs.

But the religious satire is both richer and more complicated: since the Middle Ages, institutionalized religion, especially the Catholic church, allowed if not encouraged popular and vulgar rituals, which, like drama, were regulated, celebrating religious occasions by combining folk customs with church rituals. These are the bases for what Bakhtin refers to as carnival. In the annual Feast of Fools, for example, celebrated all over France, masked figures, grotesques, disguised as women or wild animals, danced through the villages, invaded the church during mass, sang obscene verses in the choir, fouled the altar with their greasy food, gambled, fornicated, and burned foul-smelling incense of excrement or old shoe leather. However transgressive, they are, according to Lewis Hyde in *Trickster Makes This World* (1998), "profoundly conservative," "officially sanctioned and clearly contained," like Mardi Gras, their space allotted and their timing carefully controlled: "Mocking but not changing the order of things, ritual dirt-work operates as a kind of safety valve, allowing internal conflicts and nagging anomalies to be expressed without serious consequences" (p. 187).[11]

Secularized, commercialized, by the middle of the eighteenth century, in both England and France, these festivals became the urban street fairs commemorating historic occasions or merely themselves, and providing an opportunity for marketing, exchange, exhibition, competition, mating, and feasting. While some features are traditional and familiar, the street fairs and the processionals that initiated them were disruptive, spontaneous, and closer in spirit and character to the pagan festivals that preceded the European carnival. By the early decades of the nineteenth century, therefore, they are not the conservative safety valves, the "psychic and social drainage system," as Hyde calls them (p. 187), in the end containing subversion and affirming the status quo. Rather, the street fairs are agents for change, rebellions against the social, political, and religious order. They also began with processions, often along the streets where a royal progress might have taken place, led by some nominal and rather comic figure, perhaps a municipal officer, sometimes impersonating generic royalty and sometimes a historic king. Unlike contemporary masquerades, the costumes were grotesque, men often dressed as women, with frightening masks, wild dancing, homemade musical instruments, and outspoken abuse of everyone, spectators shouting obscenities and participants shouting them back. The procession included all the animals being led to slaughter, all the laborers and showmen, the puppets and monsters, the learned pigs and shaven monkeys, and led to an orgy of eating, drinking, petty crime, and sexual encounter.[12]

Wordsworth's description of St. Bartholomew's Fair in September 1802 conveys the energy, vulgarity, bestiality, disorder, and rage, the visual truths that no artist to my knowledge captured: starting with the boxing and wrestling matches, "buffoons against buffoons / Grimacing, writhing, screaming," the music from a hurdy-gurdy, trumpet, salt-box, fiddle, kettle drum and timbrel, the equestrians and tumblers, the cross-dressers, "the women, girls, and boys, / Blue breeched, pink vested, and with towering plumes"

All movables of wonder, from all parts
Are here: albinos, painted Indians, dwarfs,

The horse of knowledge and the learned pig,
The stone-eater, the man that swallows fire,
Giants, ventriloquists, the invisible girl,
The bust that speaks and moves its goggling eyes,
The wax-work, clock-work, all the marvelous craft
Of modern Merlins, wild beasts, puppet-shows,
All out-o'-the-way, far-fetched, perverted things,
All freaks of nature, all Promethean thoughts
Of man—his dullness, madness, and their feats—
All jumbled up together to make up
This parliament of monsters

(VII, 671–691)

Although the government tried to control them as they did the theater, because local officials found them profitable, fairs such as St. Bartholomew's sprang up at every square and crossroads in London, and in Paris as well. While they were ostensibly about making money and finding a mate, they also encouraged theft, fraud, drunkenness, and physical brutality. Politically, as a "parliament of monsters," they expressed the latent and disruptive power of the urban lower classes—often outside the very doors of the theaters. To the audience, the actors, and the arrangers who had conceded some of their raw freedom in exchange for artistic power, the street fairs were as familiar as the comic or satiric tradition on which many thought that pantomime had been based. And while the action on the stage was highly regulated as much by convention as by law, the audience was, like Clown himself, anarchic, riotous, gluttonous, including prostitutes and pickpockets, all without boundaries.

The pantomime derives its distinctive character from the lawless contemporary street culture it brings to the licensed stages of Drury Lane and Covent Garden, along with the dramatic conventions it satirizes. For while there is magic, transformation, and tricks to inspire wonder, the rest is as much a formula as a contemporary Harlequin romance novel, the lovers fleeing, the parent pursuing, the street scenes, the monuments and countryside, the faux-Oriental trimmings, the pushcarts and peddlers, tailors, storefronts, soldiers, beggars, chimney sweeps, and constables, all of them going about their predictable daily business—until they encounter the single disruptive force: Clown, the Trickster. Primarily, as Moody writes, the pantomime is urban, metropolitan, "an unstable, contingent spectacular world . . . a place of metamorphosis, innovation and relentless self-fashioning" (p. 218). The urbanization of these ancient rites, from which the street fairs are descended, their displacement and restoration to the stage where they began, their juxtaposition to the elitist dramatic tradition with which they once shared a stage, offer a complicated critique of the theater itself, its loss of relevance to the population it initially served and to those gods, of fertility and creativity, the human forces they represent, in whose honor they were initially conducted.

Pantomime offers two versions of satire, which I have previously introduced according to their surface features.[13] They are distinct and possibly contradictory: the historical, ritualistic, and festive, on the one hand, and the rhetorical and intellectual on the other. Historically, satire was descended from the satyr as either a processional, as Aristotle claims, that evolved into drama, or, as Horace says, developed later as a comic inversion of the tragedies that preceded it on the program. In either case, the satyr was performed in honor of Dionysus, in part to cleanse and heal, to appease his spirit, or to dispel a god who could harm as much as help the community. Like the satyrs, drawing on the processionals of street fairs, pantomime also uses the stage as sacred space, dedicated to amoral folk-gods and goddesses whose arbitrary use of power can transform themselves, the world around them, and those who believe, or worse, disbelieve in them. As a performance, either an ancient satyr or a pantomime, it is both familiar and terrifying, through loud music, dance, and fetish objects creating a communal identity by engaging a large and heterogeneous anonymous audience in the performance itself.[14]

Produced on Christmas and Easter, with a strong secular and entrepreneurial theme, the pantomime enacts a transition between the pagan and the Christian, the ancient and the contemporary. It joins the mystery and power of Dionysus-Satan with Hermes, the Trickster, the partly terrestrial figure, the shape-shifter, the presiding spirit of commerce, of invention and mathematics, of thieves, pleasure, and of the road, doorways and other boundaries, the one whose powers and spaces are the subjects of so many Romantic poets. The goat-footed Dionysus, appearing in Christian popular myth as the goat-footed Satan, has mostly become a god of biological transgression, of carnal sins and physical excess, of vampires and those who foolishly wish for eternal life. Hermes, however, the Trickster-god, as universally admired and feared, as thief or as merchant, is the god of transition between nature and civilization, between the savage and the sacred. Hermes is the god of emerging culture and Clown, the ultimate and true Trickster, his incarnation. Clown not only invents the tricks that drive the pantomime along, performs all the shape-shifting visual illusions, a thief, a glutton, a liar, sexual predator, with no loyalties, as much victim as villain, like pantomime itself, always testing the boundaries of what is legal, socially and morally acceptable, always escaping, another scene, another landscape. "Once a witless buffoon," Moody observes, "Clown was changing into a morally ambivalent character, neither entirely civilized nor wholly savage" (p. 213).

On the other hand, pantomime expresses the values and functions of more familiar rhetorical satire, artistic, literary, religious, political, and social by implication and public. The object of this satire is always explicit, topical, familiar and the techniques obvious: such contemporary excesses as fashion, patriotism, dandies, travel, antiquarianism, technology are ridiculed, deflated, exposed, parodied by simplifying, exaggerating, or literalizing them, representing them in their excess in the confined space of the stage. Theatrical history and practice is satirized by invoking specific dramas, such as "Faust" or "Don Giovanni," in the unlikely context of the pantomime. The pomposity and arrogance of parental and political power are satirized by undermining them, noble and heroic aspirations by trivializing them, and passion by exaggerating it. Like Clown, the pantomime itself is a surrogate voice affirming the values of the community, expressing the norm against which the subjects of satire are being judged, or providing the artful means—the scenery, the tricks, the bizarre characters—by which the judgment is accomplished. The form of pantomime follows the ritualistic satiric tradition, while the content depends on the rhetorical.[15]

As both ritual and as rhetorical satire, pantomime offers primarily a critique of theatrical practice, the exaggerated sentimentality, the rigid acting, the musical intrusions, the sense of risk and escape, the misplaced patriotism, whatever appeared on the program before it—and by extension the culture and social behavior that it claims to represent. But it is also a critique of theatrical forms, especially melodrama, the degraded romance tradition that it reflects, and in turn, the degraded form of religious quest—the implicit assumption that there are no great gods anymore to live for or to die for. By applying an ancient form to a contemporary experience, and trivializing tragic literary figures such as Faust or Don Giovanni, or overtly alluding to familiar scenes in contemporary productions of Shakespeare, the pantomime points out the impossibility of heroism, grandeur, or redemptive love in contemporary England, which, no matter the title, is always the setting.

As romance, the plot offers the usual two young lovers, a tyrannical figure who plans to imprison or murder the young suitor, often played by a woman, so that his daughter can marry an older, richer, and usually less appealing figure—wealth, riches, and ugliness precluding romance except in such animal-groom stories as "Beauty and the Beast" or "Psyche and Cupid," which were often adapted to the Harlequinade. As the theme is presented in the opening, the characters are disguised in enlarged paste-board heads and loose garments so that they resemble the ancient Greek actors from whom they are ritually descended, contemporary clergy, royalty, scholars, or judges. But they also resemble the cartoon figures to whom, in the satirical tradition, they are similarly related. Probably, however, to this audience, the figures most closely resembled the hand puppets from the street fairs, market-places, and pleasure gardens around London, which began appearing in the 1790s, and, like the pantomime, enacting subjects from folk and fairy tales. While puppets have a distinguished history going back to Plato and before, "Punch and Judy," a brutal anti-domestic satire, was the most popular in London for several decades. It featured an abusive and enraged but very clever Punch, who in an Oedipal fit murders his baby, beats his wife to death, kills a police officer, hangs the hangman, even kills the devil himself, to the great delight of the shrieking audience. In spite of his delinquencies, his disregard for the most common and popular human virtues of benevolence, generosity, and kindness, the audience cheers Punch on, a figure who, like them, is afflicted with frustrations, rages, impotence, with whom they identify as the helpless instrument of a faceless and anonymous puppeteer's hand.[16] Punch and Pantaloon are cousins. Similarly, when in the pantomime the enlarged heads and long robes fall away, when Mother Goose or another "friendly agent," some common figure from folklore or Greek myth, magically transforms the characters from puppet figures into Harlequin, Columbine, Pantaloon, and Clown, the contemporary social clichés become perennial symbols of human appetites, and in the mayhem that follows are reduced to instincts and opportunities.

The plot consists of an extended chase in which Clown and Pantaloon pursue Harlequin and Columbine through twenty or thirty scenes and a procession of contemporary characters—soldiers, cooks, shop girls, constables, and dandies—the very people likely to be in the audience, and familiar street scenes, authentic shop signs and commercial establishments. In a mock quest to prove himself worthy of Columbine, Harlequin is assisted by a magic bat, or slapstick, or sword, which the friendly agent has given him, and which he in turn uses to transform objects into obstacles to deter Clown and Pantaloon. When, toward the end, they fall asleep in a grotto, the "dark scene," Clown briefly gains control of the bat, but the friendly agent intervenes, rescues Harlequin and Columbine, and the whole thing ends in an "apotheosis scene" in a temple or a palace, where they are all reconciled and the young lovers married.

Taking its fantastic and unlikely characters through a primitive ritual enacted in a contemporary and materialistic setting, pantomime requires the most advanced technical skill to produce. Yet, it took place during a strange long transitional period when many of the devices for technical tricks existed but no one knew how to use them. So, for example, while electricity had been around for about fifty years, it had no application as a source of power or light. Using it was a game: the famous test to see what happens if one electrifies a line of monks holding hands across a stream, or electrifying corpses. Technical skill largely involved optical illusions, trap doors mostly, diorama, wind or steam machines, disappearing acts, high-wire acrobatics, and transformations. Still, this "material performance of illusion," as Jones calls it (p. 173), is a triumph of pantomime, the ironical gesture that captures the poles of Romanticism, of satire, and anticipates the achievements of twentieth-century media. The enactment of fantasy made possible by technology, like Wordsworth's Skylark, true to the kindred points of heaven and home, assimilates the fantastic into the evolving utilitarian, positivistic, and industrialized world.

The obvious irony involves Harlequin: given the magic bat and its great traditional power to transform, he lacks the imagination or the courage to use it well, and like those folktale fools who exchange the cow for beans, merely turns old ladies into furniture, buckets into boots, creates obstacles and food, and then, loses it by falling asleep. The bat, like the phallic appendage of ancient ritual, is both a source and sign of procreative power, the ultimate transformation. However, because Harlequin is played by a woman, the "principle boy," the power is presumably wasted on him/her, and by implication the power of transformation is withheld from human beings.

The concept of transformation is both performed and satirized in pantomime, the satire being in the display of machinery that allows it to happen, the "foregrounding of formal artifice," as Jones calls it (p. 176). But its appearance is more broadly significant than the pantomime itself: like many major ideas, concepts, styles of thought, on which great cultural shifts depend, transformation appeared in diverse, subtle, and unlikely places before it was so commonplace that only intellectual historians could remember a time when transformation was confined to magic, alchemy, theology, pagan myths, and the folk and fairy tales derived from them. In natural history, transformation was literally unthinkable, both in its illicit prehistory and its delayed recognition during the Romantic period; it was among the great and lasting mysteries of the Western world. Yet it represents a shift of thought about reality upon which most of the scientific and technological advances of the nineteenth century depended, a shift that also marks Romanticism, not merely the literature, philosophy, and religion (where it was conventionally called organicism) but also in the material and physical culture, which the contemporary study of Romanticism includes.

In the eighteenth century, philosophy, science, history, all of intellectual and political life were engaged in classification, taxonomy, definition, protocol. Transformation was associated with ancient satyr rituals, with Ovid, with Christian belief and even mysticism, or with the fantasy in those recently published collections from which pantomime themes were drawn: the Arabian Nights, Perrault's fairy tales, the Brothers Grimm's cottage tales. Along with the romance novels and narrative poems of the period, they offered imaginative experience with transformation, from humans to animals, animals to humans, humans into trees, gods to men, dross to gold, transforming angels into demons, demons who changed identities, good people into bad, and bad into good, poor into rich, pumpkins into carriages, toads into princes, body parts into people, serpents into lovers. The transformative power was the master spirit of Erasmus Darwin's *Temple of Nature,* of Thomas Beddoes' *Death's Jest-Book,* James Hogg's *Confessions of a Justified Sinner,* Mary Shelley's *Frankenstein.* The concept of transformation was the most fascinating attribute of the imagination, for Blake, Wordsworth, Coleridge, and for Keats, whose *Lamia* dramatizes the challenges and confusion it inflicts on human beings who do not understand it. For Keats, the transformations of pantomime, Steven Jones proposes, and I believe, lay behind his thoughts on negative capability, which he formulated after seeing the pantomime (p. 196)

And transformation is the master trope of all carnivals, street fairs, puppet shows, and theater, not only of drama turning people into actors, words into actions, settings into scenes, but also in such nondramatic performances that were conducted on stages of one sort or another, the public demonstrations of magic, chemistry, electricity, astronomy, performed by an array of quacks such as Dr. James Graham whose Celestial Bed, demonstrated at street fairs, was supposed to restore virility, and by legitimate natural philosophers such as Priestley, Beddoes, and Davy. It was their demonstrations of gasses and electricity in the lecture halls that helped create the well-mannered and attentive audience of the future who would disseminate their radical ideas, all of which depended on transformation.[17] These performing scientists disseminated ideas about photosynthesis and metabolism that made human bodies analogous to animals, both transforming and subject to transformations.

Applied to humans, transformation was a disagreeable idea: if one accepted photosynthesis, then merely breathing and eating made them participants in the same ecological system as goats and pigs, living not by some divine inspiration but by air produced in green and growing things, exhaling gasses that are essentially poisonous—analogous to the gas lights that would soon illuminate the theaters. Collectively, over several decades, these sciences turned human bodies into great food-processors, like cattle or house-pets, like Grimaldi the Clown devouring immense amounts of sausages and fish. Whenever Grimaldi-Clown performed his most popular trick, losing a body part, he replaced it with a vegetable—his nose with a potato, an arm with a carrot—enacting the terrible biological drama of transmutation. Or when he made a creature out of stolen vegetables, or soldiers out of barrels, which Harlequin in turn animated with his bat and chased him around the stage, here was the Faustian retribution for dabbling in those sacred arts that left Dr. Frankenstein dead on a polar ice-cap and an immortal but lonely monster, another version of Clown, of Hermes, free in the world.

Since there is no reason to believe that Grimaldi, Dibdin, or any of the arrangers and actors in pantomime were students of contemporary science, that they were even conscious, for example, of the Abernethy and Lawrence debates on the nature and origins of life, or that they knew or cared about photosynthesis or evolution, there is no explanation for the common threads that run through them, for a synchronicity that is as puzzling as transformation itself. [18] I do know that they encountered the idea of transformation in the same ancient myth, folk tales, and fairy tales from which they drew their themes. In performance, they applied it to the contemporary technology that would depend on such a concept in order to harness the energies that would ultimately propel the machines, or to understand the functioning of the human body and the importance of environment, or any of the other now familiar but basic and to so many in the nineteenth century inconceivable ideas about how things and people work. Thus, while pantomime satirically deflated the conventional static views of nature, it helped to disseminate the concept of transformation into the culture. Those tricks focusing on transportation offered a double transformation: from stationary objects to mobile ones, balloons, steam carriages, steam boats, each one illustrating the imaginative transformation of some kind of force into power.

By invoking and then violating the rules and conventions of the stage, by crossing boundaries of laws and behavior, by mocking authority and eluding punishment, by assimilating the irrational and magical into the rigid decorum of social representation, by recovering the roots of human behavior in the primitive rituals from which it was descended and then judging contemporary life by those standards, pantomime, consciously or not, I believe, challenged, developed, and extended the imagination and expectations of a public that was in itself, on all levels, undergoing transformation. Like the rest of the theater during the period, in ridiculing the laws and the authorities that controlled it, the pantomime participated in a great transfer of power from the Christian religion that was banished from the stage to a pagan art that was revived, from an irrelevant royalty who could not be depicted on the stage to the ordinary citizens who thereby found their voice. Yoking "thoughts so all unlike each other," mocking "a broken charm," drawing on both the contemporary practice of satire as it appeared in the periodicals and cartoons as well as on the ancient pagan satyr, pantomime helped to secularize and democratize the once sacred and elite theatrical arts and by extension the people who participated in them.

Notes

1. To Americans, British pantomime is an exotic experience. My first encounter with pantomime was in London, Boxing Day, 1969, when I saw Richard Wordsworth appearing in *Peter Pan,* in a role he called "Captain Hooks" after

a performance when, forgetting he was wearing a hook on one hand, he grabbed an auxiliary hook in his free hand as he rushed on the stage, the audience of children shrieking with delight at his artful confusion and discomfort. Capturing the improvisational spirit of pantomime, the self-satire of the villain, the double-hook became part of his performance. I included a section on pantomime in *English Romanticism: The Human Context* (New York: W.W. Norton, 1988; hereafter cited in the text), which I began writing shortly thereafter, and suggested that during the Romantic period, pantomime compensated for the imaginative austerity of British childhood in the eighteenth century, before the folk-tale and fairy-tale tradition on which pantomime depends had become a regular feature of the nursery. My debts then remain: Richard Altick, *The Shows of London* (Cambridge, MA: Harvard University Press, 1978); David Mayer III, *Harlequin in His Element: The English Pantomime* 1806–1836 (Cambridge, MA: Harvard University Press, 1969), hereafter cited in the text; Allardyce Nicoll, *A History of English Drama 1660–1900* 6 vols. (Cambridge, UK: Cambridge University Press, 1952–59), hereafter cited in the text; Michael R. Booth, *The Revels History of Drama in English,* Vol. VI: 1750–1880 (London: Methuen, 1975); Maurice Disher, *Clowns and Pantomime* (New York: Blom, 1968); Edwin Eigner, *The Dickens Pantomime* (Berkeley: University of California Press, 1989).

2. Jane Moody, *Illegitimate Theatre in London, 1770–1840* (Cambridge, UK; Cambridge University Press, 2000); and Steven Jones, *Satire and Romanticism* (New York: Palgrave, 2000), both cited hereafter in the text.

3. Anne K. Mellor, *English Romantic Irony* (Cambridge, MA: Harvard University Press, 1980); David Simpson, *Irony and Authority in Romantic Poetry* (Chicago: University of Chicago Press, 1993); Stuart Curran, *Poetic Form and British Romanticism* (Oxford, UK: Oxford University Press, 1986).

4. Moody, chapter II; Leonard Conolly, *The Censorship of British Drama 1737–1824* (San Marino, CA: The Huntington Library, 1976).

5. James Grant, *Penny Theatres* (London, 1838), The Society of Theatre Research, no. 1 (1950–51).

6. Dustin Griffin, *Satire: A Critical Reintroduction* (Louisville: University Press of Kentucky, 1994); Robert C. Elliott, *The Power of Satire: Magic, Ritual, Art* (Princeton, NJ: Princeton University Press, 1960).

7. The playbill featuring this juxtaposition was exhibited at the Grolier Club, New York City, March 2002, on loan from the Harvard University Theater Collection.

8. Jonas Barish, *The Antitheatrical Prejudice* (Berkeley, CA: University of California Press, 1981); Martin Meisel, *Realizations: Narrative, Pictorial, and Theatrical Arts in Nineteenth-Century England* (Princeton, NJ: Princeton University Press, 1983); Gillen D'Arcy Wood, *The Shock of the Real: Romanticism and Visual Culture, 1760–1860* (New York: Palgrave, 2001), chapter 1; George Taylor, *The French Revolution and the London Stage 1789–1805* (Cambridge, UK: Cambridge University Press, 2000), chapters 4 and 5.

9. Mary Jacobus, "'The Great Stage Where Senators Perform': *Macbeth* and the Politics of Romantic Theatre," *Romanticism, Writing and Sexual Difference:*

Essays on The Prelude (Oxford, UK: Oxford University Press, 1989, 1994), 33–69.

10. Christopher Murray, "Elliston's Coronation Spectacle, 1821," *Theatre Notebook* (1971), 57–64.

11. Mikhail Bakhtin, *Rabelais and His World,* trans. Helene Iswolsky (Bloomington, IN: Indiana University Press, 1984); C. L. Barber, *Shakespeare's Festive Comedy: A Study of Dramatic Form in its Relation to Social Custom* (Princeton, NJ: Princeton University Press, 1959); Lewis Hyde, *Trickster Makes this World: Mischief, Myth, and Art* (New York: North Point Press, 1999); Norman O. Brown, *Hermes the Thief* (New York: Vintage, 1969).

12. Joseph Strutt, *Sports and Pastimes of the People of England* (London, 1801); Sybil Rosenfeld, *The Theater of London Fairs in the Eighteenth Century* (Cambridge, UK: Cambridge University Press, 1960); Mona Ozouf, *Festivals and the French Revolution,* tr. Alan Sheridan (Cambridge, MA: Harvard University Press, 1988).

13. Mayer describes the satire as dividing into "normative" and "retributive"; I have taken a longer historical view of the stage, and a wider one of cultural performance (pp. 50–58). George Taylor in *The French Revolution and the London Stage, 1789–1805,* offers the intriguing idea, one among many, that pantomime may, on the one hand, provide "archetypal metaphors for confronting parental authority with either childlike omnipotence or comical subversion" while, as an "annually repeated ritual, " it was also therapeutic (pp. 195–196).

14. Victor Turner, *Dramas, Fields, and Metaphors: Symbolic Action in Human Society* (Ithaca, NY: Cornell University Press, 1974); Richard Schechner, *Between Theater and Anthropology* (Philadelphia: University of Pennsylvania Press, 1985).

15. I believe that Northrop Frye's conception of "ironic myth" might also be useful, an "application of romantic mythical forms to a more realistic content which fits them in unexpected ways," *Anatomy of Criticism: Four Essays* (New York: Atheneum, 1968), 223.

16. Scott Cutler Shershow, *Puppets and 'Popular Culture'* (Ithaca, NY: Cornell University Press, 1995).

17. Jan Golinski, *Science as Public Culture: Chemistry and Enlightenment in Britain, 1760–1820* (Cambridge: Cambridge University Press, 1992) and *Making Natural Knowledge: Constructivism and the History of Science* (Cambridge, UK: Cambridge University Press, 1998).

18. In a popular and often public debate on the nature of life, John Abernethy believed that life was a force analogous to electricity, which was added to the body, while Lawrence believed that, if the origin of life could be known at all, it would come along with form (Gaull, 359–60). For an excellent recent study and bibliography, see Alan Richardson, *British Romanticism and the Science of the Mind* (Cambridge, UK: Cambridge University Press, 2001).

Contributors

STUART CURRAN is Vartan Gregorian Professor of English at the University of Pennsylvania. Author of two critical studies of Shelley and editor of the *Cambridge Companion to British Romanticism* (1992), and of the comprehensive study of genre and literary history, *Poetic Form and British Romanticism* (1986). He is preparing a CD-ROM edition of Mary Shelley's *Frankenstein* for the University of Pennsylvania Press; and is writing a study of women poets during the Romantic period.

GARY DYER is Associate Professor of English at Cleveland State University. He is author of *British Satire and the Politics of Style, 1789–1832* (Cambridge University Press, 1997), and articles on Scott, Wordsworth, Coleridge, Peacock, and representations of women's charity bazaars in nineteenth-century Britain. He is currently working on a book provisionally titled *The Sexual Economy of Chivalry in the Romantic Period.*

TIM FULFORD is Professor of English at Nottingham Trent University. Among his books are *Landscape, Liberty and Authority* (1996), *Romanticism and Colonialism* (1998, co-edited with Peter J. Kitson), and *Romanticism and Masculinity* (1999).

MICHAEL GAMER is Associate Professor of English, the University of Pennsylvania, author of *Romanticism and the Gothic: Genre, Reception, and Canon Formation* (Cambridge University Press, 2000) and editor of editions of Horace Walpole's *Castle of Otranto* (Penguin) and, with Jeff Cox, *Romantic Drama: An Anthology* (Broadview Press).

MARILYN GAULL is Professor of English at Temple University and Adjunct Professor of English at New York University. She is editor of *The Wordsworth Circle* and author of numerous articles on Romantic literature as well as the book *English Romanticism: The Human Context* (W. W. Norton, 1988).

KYLE GRIMES is Associate Professor of English, the University of Alabama at Birmingham; his research focuses on Regency-period radicalism and he is author of articles on authors such as Hone, Cobbett, and Shelley, as well as editor of an online hypertext edition of Hone and Cruikshank's *Political House that Jack Built* (Romantic Circles).

Steven E. Jones is Professor of English, Loyola University Chicago. Editor of the *Keats-Shelley Journal* and co-editor of the Romantic Circles Website, he is author of a number of articles on Romantic-period literature, and of *Shelley's Satire: Violence, Exhortation, and Authority* (Northern Illinois University Press, 1994) and *Satire and Romanticism* (Palgrave/St. Martin's, 2000).

Karl Kroeber is Mellon Professor of Humanities at Columbia University. He is author of a great number of important books and articles on the Romantic poets and their period, including, recently, *Ecological Literary Criticism: Romantic Imagining and the Biology of Mind* (Columbia University Press, 1994).

Donelle Ruwe is Assistant Professor of English at Eastern Illinois University. She is the author of a number of critical articles and chapters on the Romantic period, including treatments of canonization, women authors, and children's literature.

John Strachan is Principal Lecturer in English Studies, University of Sunderland, UK. He is co-editor with Graeme Stones of the five-volume *Parodies of the Romantic Age* (Pickering & Chatto, 1998) and is currently editing a complementary collection, *Satires of the Romantic Age*.

Nicola Trott is a Lecturer in English Literature at the University of Glasgow. She is author of numerous articles on British Romantic authors, including Wollstonecraft, Wordsworth, Coleridge, and Keats, and on Victorian women novelists; she is also editor of *The Blackwell Annotated Anthology of the Gothic Novel*.

Marcus Wood is lecturer in English at the University of Sussex. Among other works, he is author of *Radical Satire and Print Culture, 1790–1822* (Clarendon Press, 1994) and *Blind Memory: Visual Representations of Slavery in England and America, 1780–1865* (Manchester and Routledge, 2000).

Index